GOD
Real or Imagined?

CHRIS PARK

Published by Zaccmedia
www.zaccmedia.com
info@zaccmedia.com

Published October 2013

ISBN: 978-1-909824-01-0

British Library Cataloguing-in-Publication Data
A catalogue record for this book is available from the British Library

Contents

ACKNOWLEDGEMENTS VII

FOREWORD IX

CHAPTER 1. THE GOD DEBATE 1

CHAPTER 2. WAYS OF SEEING 12

CHAPTER 3. RELIGION AND THE IDEA OF GOD 26

CHAPTER 4. GOD IN THE DOCK 53

CHAPTER 5. DOUBT AND DENIAL 71

CHAPTER 6. SCIENCE AND THE CHALLENGE TO GOD 86

CHAPTER 7. ARGUMENTS FOR GOD 120

CHAPTER 8. PERSONAL EXPERIENCE OF GOD 158

CHAPTER 9. THE NATURE OF BELIEF 181

CHAPTER 10. RE-FRAMING GOD 217

REFERENCES 232

NOTES 246

INDEX 268

For my nearest and dearest - Penny (who I know has read it),
and Emma, Andrew, Sam and Elizabeth (who I hope
will read it one day) - with love.

ACKNOWLEDGEMENTS

To quote Isaac Newton, "If I have seen further it is by standing on the shoulders of giants." In this case, the giants are the many theologians, atheists, scientists, philosophers, psychologists, religious studies experts and others whose books (listed in the Bibliography) helped to challenge, inform and shape my thinking on the wide range of themes I have tried to bring together into a coherent narrative in this book. I apologise to any whose work I have misunderstood or misrepresented, and I take full responsibility for any errors that have crept into the text.

I am particularly grateful to three local giants for carefully reading the manuscript and pointing out typos, grammatical slips, and places where my intended meaning was unclear - Penny Park, Cyril Ashton and Pete Hope. My good friend Cyril Ashton, who has helped me and many others much more in their journey through life than he will ever realise, very kindly agreed to write the foreword.

FOREWORD

In this book Chris Park issues an invitation to anyone who wants to engage intelligently with the God Question. He is not out to persuade people but to provide a forum for thoughtful, sensitive debate. In Shakespeare's play *The Tempest*, the dialogue between Prospero and Miranda throws out the question, "what seest thou else?" In other words, having seen and heard all that is immediately obvious, what deeper truths are there to be discerned? This book is an attempt to get behind the rhetoric that often swamps conversations about God and find a way to listen with respect to those who have a different view. In doing this Chris cheerfully steers a course between religious and atheistic fundamentalism.

This is a thoughtful book which challenges the unthinking fundamentalism of some religious groups on the one hand, and the aggressive fundamentalism of atheistic secularists on the other. It offers a direction which takes Christians and atheists seriously and provides a market place in which different views and voices can be heard.

Chris Park inhabits a dimension which invites calm and fresh thinking. He wants us to leave behind insecure rhetoric and create a space in which dialogue can be encouraged. He moves us away from cheap put downs and sarcasm and into a much more nuanced debate. He makes it clear where he stands and at the same time initiates a broad ranging conversation free from doctrinaire prejudice.

In an article criticising Faith Schools, A.C. Grayling a prominent atheist who makes common cause with Richard Dawkins, makes the very good point that, "young minds...are to be treated with the utmost respect, not twisted into shapes that conform to antique dogmas." Chris Park's book thoroughly endorses this, and at the same time holds up a mirror to secularists inviting them to recognise this predisposition in themselves.

This book would make an excellent study guide for groups who want to take the subject matter seriously, and it offers a rich menu of themes and sources to enable discussion. It seeks to lift up the level of debate without diminishing the importance of opposing views or rubbishing the people who hold them. Neither ignorance nor prejudice should play any part in keeping open the God Question.

The Rt Rev'd C.G. Ashton (formerly Bishop of Doncaster)

CHAPTER 1

THE GOD DEBATE

"Despite the secular tenor of much Western society, the idea
of God still affects the lives of millions of people."

Karen Armstrong (1993)

M any people would argue that, like sex and politics, religion is not an appropriate topic of conversation in polite company. Robert Wright goes further, in arguing that "in modern intellectual circles, speculating seriously about God's existence isn't a path to widespread esteem. Indeed, the first decade of the twenty-first century made god-talk an even graver breach of highbrow etiquette than it had been at the end of the twentieth."[1] As a result today, particularly in the West, God is often viewed as the "elephant in the room", something that may well be important but whose very existence is generally either not acknowledged or deliberately ignored.

Curiosity and the religious instinct

As humans we are natural curious creatures; we are hard-wired to want or need to know, to ask questions and seek answers. As far as we know, we are the only species endowed with this sense of wonder and curiosity. This inbuilt inquisitiveness is often keenest when we are young, when "Because it is" is not a sufficiently persuasive answer. I can well remember my own childhood, when my dad took me for a walk along our street and (he tells me) I constantly pestered him with questions like "why is the sky blue?" or "why is the grass green?" Whatever answers he gave me failed to silence me, or to put my mind at rest.

As we grow up, our questions change. As life gets serious, our responsibilities grow, the years fly by, and we are confronted by multiple challenges. As adults we often ask ourselves "What is it all about?" and "Is this it, all there is to life?" We wonder "Why do bad things happen, particularly to good people?" Question after question, not all of them answerable we now know. But it doesn't stop us wondering, thinking, searching.

This incessant curiosity about things beyond our everyday experience is one of the unique qualities of being human. It is the product of a dissatisfied mind in search of some kind of peace. Natural curiosity is deep-rooted, and it lies at the heart of the question of God. Although it is expressed in many different ways, this need to know is found in all cultures, places and times. Kathleen Jones argues that "the religious instinct is innate."[2]

We can look back through history and beyond and find that most societies and cultures have some belief in one or more gods. Charles Darwin noted in *The Descent of Man* (1871) that "a belief in all-pervading spiritual agencies seems to be universal."[3] Richard Carlyon suggests that "there has never been a culture that did not express an awareness of the divine, and these expressions have been as varied and colourful as the cultures themselves."[4] According to anthropologists, religions in most cultures and at most times have had certain supernatural features in common, including belief in a non-physical God or gods, belief in some form of afterlife, and belief in the ability of rituals or prayers to change the course of human events.[5]

US scientist E.O. Wilson pointed out that "the predisposition to religious belief is the most complex and powerful force in the human mind and in all probability an ineradicable part of human nature."[6] Despite the apparent ubiquity of 'the religious instinct', Richard Dawkins remains stubbornly dismissive of it. In *The God Delusion* he writes that "no known culture lacks some version of the time-consuming, wealth-consuming, hostility-provoking rituals, the anti-factual, counter-productive fantasies of religion."[7]

So, we seem to have an inbuilt tendency to wonder if there is something above and beyond the everyday world we encounter directly through our five senses. Something pervasive yet elusive; something beyond our reach or full understanding. That something is the idea of God, or as Robert Winston calls it, the "Divine Idea".[8]

God-talk

God often pops up in everyday conversation these days, even when people don't attach any particular religious meaning to the word. Sometimes God gets the blame for things over which humans have little influence or control. For example, people often describe something that might or might not happen as being "in the lap of the gods", or something really useful but perhaps unexpected as a "God-send." Insurance companies claim exemption in their policies from being liable for "acts of God" (often meaning acts of nature) which cannot be avoided. Few English football fans can forget the "the hand of God" which helped Diego Maradona to score the goal which allowed Argentina to beat England 2-1 in the 1986 World Cup final.

Nonetheless, the word 'God' is woven into the fabric of everyday life. Think how often you hear people say things like God bless (meaning "Sleep sound" or "Look after yourself", or after someone has sneezed), God help us ("I hope we cope or manage OK"), God speed ("Hope you have a safe journey"), God willing ("all being well"), For God's sake or For the love of God ("Please do as I ask"), So help me God ("I promise"), There but for the grace of God ("that could easily be me"), Honest to God ("I know you don't believe me but I'm telling the truth"), and God only knows ("Don't ask me, I haven't got a clue!")? The latter expression, used as the title of a song by the Beach Boys, is believed to have been the first popular record to include the word God in the title.[9] Writer Brian Wilson and his partners apparently had some concerns over whether that might harm record sales, but they proved groundless because the track became one of their most popular and iconic numbers.

The media often take a particular interest in God stories; after all, it sells copy. There was great interest, for example, when Alistair Campbell (his Press Secretary) was repeatedly asked about British Prime Minister Tony Blair's faith and about whether he had prayed with US President George W. Bush before taking military action in the Middle East, famously said "we don't do God."[10] Barack Obama told an interviewer a few years before he succeeded Bush as President "I have a deep faith. I'm rooted in the Christian tradition. … [but] I think there is an enormous danger on the part of public figures to rationalise or justify their actions by claiming God's mandate."[11] There was also widespread coverage in the British press when

Pope Benedict XVI visited the UK in September 2010 and commented that Britain was the home of a lively debate about "the big questions of God and faith;"[12] he spoke of "the need to re-evangelise a cynical society that has lost its way amid the vain enticements of this world and celebrity culture."[13]

Media coverage of God is often light-hearted and sometimes quite funny. For example, a joke did the rounds of the internet a few years ago – "What's the difference between God and Bono (front-man of the Irish rock group U2)? God doesn't go around Dublin pretending to be Bono!"[14] Similarly, José Mourinho (the football manager who describes himself as The Special One[15]) told a journalist who asked him what he believed God thought about him "He must think I'm a really great guy. He must think that, because otherwise He would not have given me so much ... He must have a high opinion of me."[16] As a long-time fan of legendary guitarist Eric Clapton, I admire the nerve of the admirer who in 1967 painted "Clapton is God" on a wall at Islington station on the London Underground.[17] I smiled when I read that in 2005 one fan wrote on an online blog that "contrary to what was/is popular belief, Clapton is NOT God! But damn if the Boy cannot play some *mean* guitar."[18]

Whilst God himself may not be as popular as he once was, there's no denying the high level of interest amongst the general public in questions about ultimate meaning and purpose. This was clearly borne out in a 2010 survey of 1.1 billion queries made on the website *Ask Jeeves* (*Ask* in most countries)[19] since it was launched in 2000, to find the Top 10 "unanswerable" questions.[20] The top two, based on the number of times asked, were 'What is the meaning of life?' and 'Is there a God?'. 'Is there anybody out there?' came in at number 5, ahead of 'Who is the most famous person in the world?' (number 6) and 'What is love?' (number 7).

Defining God

Our discussion so far has taken it for granted that we all mean the same thing when we use the word God. But of course that isn't the case; the term God means different things to different people.

Karen Armstrong points out that "all talk about God staggers under impossible difficulties. ... We have to decide whether the word 'God' has any meaning for us today."[21] A good place to start is by trying to define the word itself, although that apparently simple task is not without its challenges - type "define God" into Google and you are offered over 30 million pages on the internet!

The word (of) God

The *Oxford English Dictionary* defines 'god' as "a superhuman being or spirit worshipped as having power over nature or human fortunes; a deity", and it adds "(in Christianity and other monotheistic religions) the creator and ruler of the universe and source of all moral authority; the supreme being."[22] The Merriam-Webster dictionary defines 'God' as "the Being perfect in power, wisdom, and goodness who is worshipped as creator and ruler of the universe" and 'god' as "a being or object believed to have more than natural attributes and powers and to require human worship."[23]

A quick note on spellings and meanings. Some people talk about the 'gods' (plural) while others talk about 'god' in the singular; this book is mainly about the idea of a singular 'god'. Some start the word with a lower case 'g' (god) while others start it with a capital (God). The lower case 'god' is usually used when referring to the general idea of a supernatural being, which can take many different forms. The upper case 'God' is almost always used when referring specifically to the God of Judaism, Christianity and Islam, or as biblical scholars often put it, the God of Abraham. Throughout this book I follow these normal conventions when using the terms 'god' and 'God.'

Muslims use the word Allah rather than God, but the two words mean the same thing. In the Jewish tradition it is not regarded as proper to even say the word God because God is so holy, so Jews use the name Yahweh (YHVH, Jehovah) or Lord, again to mean the same thing. When I use the word 'God' in this book I am using the word in its inclusive sense, to mean the God of Judaism and Islam as well as of Christianity.

What do we mean by the word God?

Nobel Prize-winning physicist and atheist Steven Weinberg cautions that "some people have views of God that are so broad and flexible that it is inevitable that they will find God wherever they look for him. ... Of course, like any other word, the word 'God' can be given any meaning we like."[24]

Even arch-atheist Richard Dawkins agrees that "if the word God is not to become completely useless, it should be used in the way people have generally understood it: to denote a supernatural creator that is 'appropriate for us to worship'."[25]

Atheist Mortimer Adler emphasises that "we cannot think of God as a physical object. Consequently, we must think of God not only as inherently imperceptible, but also as inherently undetectable in the ways that elementary particles or black holes are detectable."[26] Not being able to think of God as a physical object goes some way towards explaining why people who have a naturalistic outlook on everything (which we will explore in Chapter 2) either cannot visualise or struggle to allow for the possibility of God. It also helps explain some of the tensions which underlie many of the controversies between science and religion, which we shall explore further in Chapter 6.

Beyond being a "supernatural creator" and not a physical object, what do people have in mind when they think or talk about God? The two most common images of God are as a spirit or as a being.

Many people feel comfortable thinking of God as a spirit of some form, rather than a being. Singer Annie Lennox admits that the word God "always troubles me. ... if you say God is a word to describe the life-force that has created all, and creates and maintains the energy, the source of all living things, I'll go with that."[27] Interviewer Cathleen Falsani describes Lennox's spirituality as "Confused. Complicated, searching. Unanswered and unfinished."[28] This type of New Age spirituality borrows from pre-modern world-views (see Chapter 2) such as that of some Native American and First Nations cultures in the New World, who view the world and everything in it as being created and governed by the Great Spirit or Great Mystery.[29]

Others think of God as a disembodied being - a being without a body - of some form. Denis Baly argues that the idea of "a Supreme Being is so firmly established in Western minds that the use of the word 'God' almost automatically conveys the idea of 'somebody up there'."[30] This anthropomorphic perspective visualises God as like a person, with qualities like a human, informed by the Biblical statement that God "created man in his own image."[31] It is coloured by Michelangelo's famous painting on the ceiling of the Sistine Chapel in Rome, which portrays God as like a wise, old, white-haired, white-skinned man, wearing a long, white, flowing robe.

The 'somebody' God can take many different forms. Views vary along three particular dimensions:

[i] Absent or present: many people think of God (sometimes jokingly referred to as "him upstairs") as like a remote absentee landlord who originally made the universe but has long since kept out of it. Others visualise a more active God who continues not only to watch over the universe but to take an active part in it.

[ii] Unknowable or knowable: many people suspect that, even if God is present rather than absent, he mysteriously lurks somewhere out of sight and out of reach, while others regard that God as personally knowable.

[iii] Bossy or loving: some think of God as a critical judge or benevolent dictator who must be obeyed at all cost. John Betjeman referred to God as "The Management"[32] and Terry Eagleton describes how some people see God as "a kind of cosmic version of the CIA, keeping us under constant surveillance."[33] Others have a much more positive image of God. For example, C.S. Lewis referred to God as 'Joy'[34] and British journalist and agnostic John Humphreys wrote of God who "seemed to be exactly the sort of person you'd want your daughter to marry if he were human: kind, merciful, immensely loving; all-powerful and just."[35]

A quick note on gender. Whilst through the ages most people in the West have pictured God as male, in recent decades some have argued that it is equally valid to think of God as female. There are sound reasons for both views, but throughout this book I shall follow the Christian tradition and refer to God as male. Because it is generally accepted that unlike humans God has no physical body, so in many ways the question of male/female is something of a red-herring ... except that the assumption of a male God is often used to justify patriarchal attitudes and behaviour, and it is politically correct these days to write of God either as s/he or interchangeably as he and she.

Whether or not they actually believe in God as a being, and an active and knowable one at that, many people are intrigued by the idea of actually meeting him and having a chat with him, just like meeting a friend down at the pub. Joan Osborne's 1995 song *One of Us* was a surprise hit, particularly given that it was about God. The song invites the listener to consider how they might relate to God, asking "If God had a name, what would it be? And would you call it to his face, if you were faced with him in all his glory? What would you ask if you had just one question? If God had a face what would it look like? And would you want to see if seeing meant that you would have to believe in things like heaven and in Jesus and the saints and all the prophets?"[36]

A 2006 survey on the Yahoo web site took this idea of meeting God in person a step further. It asked respondents to imagine they are standing face-to-face in front of God, then report what they think they would say to him. People gave many different answers, from the flippant to the ultra-serious. The one voted best by viewers was "Forgive me because of my sins. Am I going to go to heaven?" Other answers included "I would say, "Hey God... what's up!"; "I would treat him just like I do all my friends!"; "Show me some of your moves, I heard you move in mysterious ways."; "Where you been all my life, not that it matters coz I did good without you."; "What took you so long?"; and "if you love everyone, why is that you treat some people better than others?"[37]

The God Delusion

The God debate has become very lively over the past decade or so, partly as the result of the emergence of so-called New Atheism, which we will look at more closely in Chapter 5.

Richard Dawkins' 2006 book *The God Delusion*[38] quickly became the set text of New Atheism, and continues to serve as its best-quoted manifesto. Although the book's title is punchy and memorable, it is not entirely original: British theologian David Jenkins (later to become Bishop of Durham) opened his 1969 book *Living with Questions* with the sentence "God is either a gift or a delusion."[39] Dawkins fails to credit Jenkins, probably unaware of the book's existence.

Dawkins declared that his intention in writing *The God Delusion* was to "raise consciousness to the fact that to be an atheist is a realistic aspiration, and brave and splendid one. You can be an atheist who is happy, balanced, moral, and intellectually fulfilled."[40]

The God Delusion quickly became an international best-seller, and it will have done no harm to its author's pension fund. The book also raised his global profile as the voice of New Atheism, and not by accident. It sold in vast numbers and continues to be widely talked about, but one wonders how many of those who bought the book actually read it from cover to cover. As John Humphreys put it, *The God Delusion* was "one of the most unlikely best-sellers of the past few years. It might not have threatened *Harry Potter* in the charts, but for a serious book on a serious subject it justified the overused description 'a publishing sensation'."[41]

One might ask why *The God Delusion* sold as well as it did, given that religious books have notoriously limited appeal in the market-place. Several factors came together at the same time, to create something of a publishing perfect storm. No doubt the book's deliberately provocative but very eye-catching title helped a great deal; his publishers clearly knew a good thing when they saw it. A second factor was Richard Dawkins' credibility as an academic scientist, a former Professor of the Public Understanding of Science at Oxford University. He has a well-earned reputation as a writer of good popular science books; even amongst his critics he is described as "one of the most exciting and informative writers on science, especially on evolutionary biology."[42] Added spice came through his well-known antipathy to religion, which had been aired in some of his earlier books. Dawkins the self-proclaimed "*Devil's Chaplain*"[43] was already known for his strong views on religion. As what British author A.N. Wilson describes as "Darwin's most ardent representative on earth (since the death of Thomas Huxley)"[44], Dawkins believes religion to be a by-product of human evolution, not a product of divine inspiration or creation. Dawkins was also tapping into the popular vein of humanism and secularism which ran through late twentieth century Western society, so there was a broad and receptive audience to appeal to. Dawkins also has apparently unlimited energy and enthusiasm in the area of self-promotion, and he was interviewed widely across the media as a spokesperson for the new zeitgeist, the spirit of the age which reflected popular disinterest in if not outright hostility to organised religion.

It's not all good news for Dawkins and his particular brand of atheism, however. Scientist and theologian Alister McGrath dismisses *The God Delusion* as "a work of theatre rather than scholarship – a fierce, rhetorical assault on religion, and a passionate plea for it to be banished to the lunatic fringes of society, where it can do no harm."[45] Physicist and theologian John Polkinghorne dismisses the book as "simply an atheistic rant – a disappointing book full of assertions but devoid of real engagement with theological arguments."[46]

Irish philosopher Michael Dunne believes that *The God Delusion* is a book that "the author will regret writing. ... [not only because] there is a terrible tendency in the book towards rhetoric and point-scoring rather than argument. ... he blunders into many areas where angels would fear to tread. ... the erratic nature of his arguments, the lack of fair-mindedness in the people he targets, make him a floating mine, a threat to friend and foe alike."[47] Even atheist James McBain is not convinced that *The God Delusion* has achieved its goal, because "many ... parts of the book are either cheap shots, the resting (or better yet piggy-backing) on the shoulders of others ..., raging bluster, and bad arguments that the book simply does not motivate the closet-atheist off the couch ... and this atheist is mad as hell that he failed."[48]

The God Question

American philosopher Andrew Pessin wrote a book called *The God Question*[49], in which he looked at how thinkers through the ages have sought to clarify the idea of a Supreme Being. It's a simple but effective title, which captures something of the allure and mystery of God, and why ideas about God have run through people's thoughts and hopes since the earliest of days.

Put simply, the "God Question" is - Does God exist? Behind that overarching question are a series of important questions which lie at the heart of the debate about God. These include -

[i]   If God exists, what is God like?

[ii] What does God do, or what did God do?

[iii[Does the idea of God have any relevance today, even if God doesn't actually exist?

[iv] If God exists, is it possible to *know* God, not just know *about* God?

[v] Given the available evidence, which is the most sensible approach - to believe in God, or not believe in God?

[vi] Is it possible to change from belief to non-belief in God, and vice versa? If it is possible, how does that process work?

[vii] How and why do believers and non-believers often find it
        difficult if not impossible to understand and appreciate the views
        of the other camp?

Each of these questions is addressed in the chapters that follow, either
directly or indirectly.

Chapter 2

Ways of Seeing

"Five senses; an incurably abstract intellect; a haphazardly selective memory; a
set of preconceptions and assumptions so numerous that I can never examine
more than a minority of them - never become even conscious of them all.
How much of total reality can such an apparatus let through?"

C.S. Lewis (1961)

Many people today have a sense that "there must be more than this";
there must be more than just the physical world we see all around
us, and we must be more than just a collection of atoms and a cocktail
of chemicals. Radio presenter John Humphreys, a confirmed sceptic on
matters of God, has admitted "It has always seemed to me that the default
position for the human condition is that there is 'something out there'.
Dunno what, we shrug, but this can't all be one big accident, can it? It is
usually said in an almost wistful way, more an expression of hope than of
belief. We want to feel there's a purpose to our lives, that we've been put
on earth as part of some divine plan, and if not divine then at least pre-
ordained for some reason beyond our understanding. We want to believe
that there's more to life than this brief passage and, with a bit of luck, that
there might even be something nice waiting for us when we finally turn
up our toes."[50]

Despite the natural curiosity we all have and the religious instinct that
many people are aware of, it is a matter of fact that some people believe
in God and some don't. But believers and non-believers share the same
physical world and have access to the same evidence about that world,
yet they view, interpret and understand the evidence in different ways. A

central thread running through this book is the question of why that is the case. A key part of the answer to that question is the world-view that each of us has, which informs how we 'see' reality and make sense of everything going on around us.

Layers of reality

We can't begin to understand the debate about God without acknowledging the importance of different ways of 'seeing' reality. US theologian Marcus Borg points out that before the late seventeenth century "the vast majority of humankind took it for granted that there were minimally two kinds or layers of reality: a spiritual kind and a material kind."[51] Material reality is the natural world we see around us; spiritual reality is the supernatural world which remains hidden from sight but nonetheless affects our everyday existence in multiple ways.

Today many people including atheists and scientists are convinced there is *only* material reality. Many others, including believers, accept material reality but are also comfortable with the idea of spiritual reality, on intellectual grounds (it makes sense to them) and/or on experiential grounds (they have direct or indirect experience of it).

World-views

A world-view is a lens through which we view the world around us and understand our experiences with it. Each of us has a world-view, whether we are aware of it or not. Most of us are unable to give our world-view a name or articulate it to other people; it's so familiar to us that we take it for granted. Differences in world-views help to explain why we sometimes can't make sense of someone else's take on reality, and why other people can think of us as odd, different or plain stupid.

A world-view is a comprehensive framework of our basic beliefs about things. It allows us to make sense of all we see and experience. It is far from arbitrary; it is cohesive and every part of it fits together comfortably. A world-view ties together our basic beliefs about things, including our sense of what is real, matters of general principle, and how we should live our lives. It is based on a set of assumptions and presuppositions which we hold, sometime unknowingly, and which cannot be verified or disproven by the procedures of natural science. We don't consciously choose our world-view, it is a largely subconscious thing shaped by factors such as culture, education, family background and friendship groups. Whether or not a particular world-view is 'true' is not the issue; what matters is that we hold that view, it makes sense to us, and it informs how we see things, explain them, and deal with them. It helps define who we are, how we think, and in turn how we behave.

Whilst each of us has a world-view, and they can and do differ between individuals, particular world-views dominate a given culture at any point in time. Thus, for example, the dominant world-views held by people in traditionally Christian countries like Britain and the United States today differ from those held by many people in Islamic countries. Within a given culture people of different faiths have different world-views, and scientists often have different world-views from religious believers.

Given that they are so deeply rooted within both our conscious and subconscious minds, can we as individuals change our world-view? It would be hard to do so simply by deciding to, but we can change when forced to by the emergence of new evidence and/or when our experience challenges the integrity of our existing world-view. This is particularly the case with whether or not we accept that there is such a thing as 'spiritual reality'. It can work both ways - experience causes some people who previously rejected the idea to accept it, which allows them to 'come to faith' by having a religious conversion; conversely, for a variety of reasons some people who previously accepted it can later reject it, which causes them to lose their faith. We will explore this whole area further in Chapter 9.

Dominant world-views also change through time, swept along by waves of cultural change. Sometimes the change in world-view is caused by broader cultural change, at other times it causes it. In Western cultures it is possible to distinguish between pre-modern, modern, and postmodern world-views.

Pre-modern world-views

Archaeological and anthropological evidence shows that many traditional cultures around the world held a dual view of reality as consisting of both material and spiritual 'layers'. Many so-called primitive cultures continue to do so today. In these world-views there are no tensions or incompatibilities between 'rational' thinking and spiritual or religious thinking; each has its role in explaining the order of things.

We find such beliefs central to the thinking of the ancient Greek philosophers. For example, Plato (427-347 BC) believed that God took pre-existing unordered matter and ordered it to create the world we see today. As Andrew Pessin puts it, Plato believed that God "made humans and horses and stones, and everything else, by imposing Humanity, Horsehood, and Stoniness, respectively, on the matter of the world."[52] Aristotle (384-322 BC) believed in a hierarchy of existences, with God - an eternal, spiritual, thinker that he called The Unmoved Mover - at the top and causing all the motion and activity in the universe.[53]

The medieval philosopher Augustine (354-430) also had no problem explaining everything as having been created by an eternal God *ex nihilo* (out of nothing). As English theologian Keith Ward explains, Augustine "conceived all the Forms or Essences, headed by the Form of the Good, as ideas in the mind of God. Then he made God the creator of matter, so that it had no independent existence. And finally he demoted all the ancient gods to angels or demons, servants of the one creator God. Thus he gave the whole cosmos one simple and elegant explanation in the will of a creator God, who was the sole proper object of human worship and devotion."[54]

Few people in the Western world challenged the idea or existence of God before the latter part of the seventeenth century, because most thinking was influenced and informed by the Christian faith. Whilst they are referred to as 'pre-modern', these world-views are not confined to ancient history - key elements of them survive in contemporary religions and ideas about God, which accept spiritual reality as a given. Atheists seize on this link with the past, and use it to dismiss a religious perspective as outmoded and outdated, having been replaced by the more rational perspective of modern science.

Modern world-views

Pre-modern world-views were to be challenged and progressively replaced by the modern world-view that emerged during the Enlightenment, which began in Europe at the end of the seventeenth century and we are still living in today in many ways.

The Enlightenment was a wide-ranging period of intellectual, cultural and social change which seriously challenged prevailing orthodoxies and influenced if not shaped most of the views most of us hold today about most things. It was perhaps the greatest and most significant period of intellectual ferment since the days of ancient Greece, and it gave rise to what is generally referred to as the Modern Period or Modernity, or is sometimes called the Age of Reason. Particularly from about 1750 onwards it spawned profound changes including major breakthroughs in technical mastery, the accumulation of capital, industrialisation, an intellectual awakening, political and social revolutions (most visibly the American and French Revolutions), increasing specialisation within a technical society, and the rise and development of modern science.[55]

Caroline Ogden describes the modern period as "an age of optimism and idealism, but without religion's emphasis on a non-material spirituality."[56] Alister McGrath describes modernity as "a confident, ebullient movement, convinced of the supreme ability of human reason to understand the world and hence to master and control it. There was no longer any need for God to confirm or underwrite a settled and stable order of moral values, social relations, or rules of thought."[57]

Modern world-views, founded on the assumption that the autonomous individual is the sole source of meaning and truth and on a linear view of history as never-ending progress, reject tradition in favour of reason and natural science. They are based on belief in the power of reason over ignorance and science over superstition. Two key hallmarks of the new way of thinking that the Enlightenment brought were humanism and materialism.

Humanism is a world-view (some call it a secular ideology) which focuses on human values and matters, with a particular emphasis on reason, ethics and justice. It also emphasises the power of human reason over divine revelation, and rejects the supernatural and religious dogma as a basis for moral judgements. Thus humanism unashamedly relegates the idea of God to the margins of popular thinking.

Materialism

Marcus Borg points out that "scientific ways of knowing were beginning to replace sacred tradition and divine authority as the basis of knowledge"[58] and "with its emphasis on scientific ways of knowing, [the Enlightenment] gave birth to the modern world-view with its image of reality as essentially 'onefold' - that is, material. What is real is the world of matter and energy within the framework of the space-time continuum, self-contained and operating in accord with 'natural laws' of cause and effect."[59]

The materialist world-view is based on the belief that nothing exists beyond physical 'things', ie matter and energy. It has no place, space or need for anything spiritual or supernatural. It sees everything (including human consciousness) in terms of physical matter and material interactions. As Borg points out, this material understanding of reality has several elements.[60] These include three key 'facts':

[i] Everything is made up of molecules and atoms (and even smaller parts);

[ii] Reality follows natural laws; and

[iii] Reality is like a huge, complex machine.

The 'facts', verified by science, are that the universe is almost unimaginably large (it may even be infinite), it is exceedingly old (certainly compared with what a literal reading of the Bible would suggest), and it contains a vast number of galaxies (our universe is only one of many; it is insignificant in cosmic terms).

Most people in the West today have modern world-views that are firmly rooted in materialism, which they see as the most objective way of looking at and making sense of the world around them. But popularity is no substitute for truth. Like all world-views, materialism has its blind spots and its limitations. Keith Ward highlights seven what he calls "discontents" of materialism:[61]

[i] The ultimate basis of matter now seems to be unknown;

[ii] Consciousness – thoughts, feelings, sensations, images, and intentions – remains almost wholly inexplicable in purely physical terms;

[iii] Morality seems very difficult to account for in physical terms;

[iv] We would have to renounce any sense of an objective purpose in life;

[v] Our commitment to rational thinking and to the postulate
     that our universe has an intelligible and rational structure …
     our commitment to reason points to the rationality of
     being itself;

[vi] For a materialist, there is no possibility of a final explanation of
      the universe; and

[vii] The thoughts of some of the greatest philosophers and the
      experiences of thousands of the wisest and most morally heroic
      mystics and religious teachers, will have to be set aside as
      delusions.

Gradually the development of humanism and materialism, which initially
appealed only to the educated elite in society, were adopted and embraced by
the general population. Through time they became the taken-for-granted
assumptions about what is real, what life is about, and how it should be
lived. The modern world-view is so deeply embedded in contemporary
thinking and taken for granted as "how we do things round here" that it is
the default world-view in western society. The fact that it rejects any idea of
spiritual reality helps explain the decline in mainstream religion and spread
of secularisation over the past century or so, and fuels the atheist argument
that God is just something that humans invented.

One reaction against the dominance of the modern world-view has been
to seek a way of integrating material and spiritual 'realities', adding to the
modern world-view "a notion of God as a supernatural being who created
the whole but who is essentially outside the process, except for the rather
extraordinary interventions recorded in the biblical tradition."[62] Marcus
Borg adds that this notion of God and God's relationship to the universe
makes God distant; "most of the time, God is uninvolved and not here."
This composite approach gave rise to deism which we will consider further
in Chapter 3.

Naturalism

Materialism - also known as physicalism - is also closely related to
naturalism, the belief that nature acts according to fixed laws, "excluding
origination or direction by a will."[63] Through that way of viewing things
nature is seen as an open book which, through rational, objective scientific

study, can provide answers to all of life's questions. We will explore the relevance of this further in Chapter 6.

John Haught outlines the seven tenets or pillars of 'scientific naturalism', the world-view that the New Atheists "share with many scientists, philosophers, and other contemporary intellectuals:

[i] "Apart from nature, which includes human beings and our cultural creations, there is nothing. There is no God, no soul, and no life beyond death;

[ii] Nature is self-originating, not the creation of God;

[iii] The universe has no overall point or purpose, although individual human lives can be lived purposefully;

[iv] Since God does not exist, all explanations and all causes are purely natural and can be understood only by science;

[v] All the various features of living beings, including human intelligence and behaviour, can be explained ultimately in purely natural terms, and today this usually means in evolutionary, specifically Darwinian, terms;

[vi] Faith in God is the cause of innumerable evils and should be rejected on moral grounds; and

[vii] Morality does not require belief in God, and people behave better without faith than with it."[64]

Postmodern world-views

Postmodernism emerged during the twentieth century as a reaction against modernist ideas of absolute truth and faith in the autonomy of human reason. It became popular in the 1950s, initially in art and literature, and since the late 1970s has been adopted by many of the social science and humanities academic disciplines, and in areas like architecture.

Karen Armstrong sees the emergence of postmodernism as a natural reaction to growing frustration with the inherent limitations of the Enlightenment project, when "truths hitherto regarded as self-evident were called into question: the teachings of Christianity, the subordination of women and the structures of social and moral authority. There was a new scepticism about the role of science, and modern expectation of continuous progress and the Enlightenment ideal of rationality. The modern dualities of mind/body, spirit/matter and reason/emotion were challenged."[65] Alister McGrath describes postmodernism as a "cultural mood that celebrates diversity and seeks to undermine those who offer rigid, restrictive, and oppressive views of the world."[66]

The rise of postmodernism was particularly a reaction against the general consensus that 'objective' science can explain reality, and what it can't currently explain it will be able to in the future as it develops further and gets closer and closer to the 'truth'. It is based on the belief that there is no single objective reality 'out there' in the world around us, as science assumes and insists, and it denies human thought the ability to arrive at any objective account of reality. Instead it is a question of what sense we make of our experiences and how we describe and interpret them.

A postmodern approach denies the notion of absolute truth. From this perspective reality shapes how we see and think of the world around us, but it is not directly mirrored in our understanding of it. The belief is that each of us builds our own personal view of 'reality' in our mind, making 'truth' a social construct rather than something absolute. From this perspective, each of us frames reality on our own terms; my notion of reality may be very different to yours, but it is just as important and counts just as much as yours does.

Key to this process of constructing our own 'reality' is how we interpret all that we see and experience. This depends on many things such as language (we can only think in ways for which we have words, and this varies between individuals and cultures), power relations (we see things differently depending on whether we "have a voice" or are marginalised, for example), and our reasons for engaging with particular things (is it by free will or coercion, for example). Thus my interpretation of 'reality' and 'truth' does not have to be the same as yours, even when we are presented with the same information. 'Reality' is my interpretation of what the world means to me personally, and 'truth' is what I define it to be. Apparent realities are thus social constructs, and liable to change.

In this way of looking at things, personal experience becomes more important than abstract principles. Yet everybody's experience will inevitably be relative and their interpretation of it will be fallible and open to error. As a result, each person constructs their own relative truths, and nothing is certain or universal. This is why postmodernism is sceptical of any explanations that claim to be valid for all groups, cultures, and traditions.

According to the postmodern world-view, knowledge and understanding and the way they are constructed and used, are products of how humans conceptualise the world around them. They share three important properties; they are:

[i] Relative (they are comparative not absolute; it all depends on who you are, what your experiences have been, and how reliable your interpretations are and construction of 'reality' is);

[ii] Contingent (likely but not inevitable); and

[iii] Contested (in competition with others; why should your 'reality' be more truthful than mine?).

A key implication of all this to our discussion about the idea of God is the denial of what postmodern writers call metanarratives (grand narratives), such as Marxism, liberalism, or Christianity. These are comprehensive explanations that bring everything together into a cohesive and consistent story. Narratives are designed to convey meaning, they are not works of fiction. Postmodernists dismiss metanarratives as illusions, nothing more than constructs of the human mind.

Historian of ideas James Sire writes that "with postmodernism no story can have any more credibility than any other. All stories are equally valid. ... We can have meaning, for all these stories are more or less meaningful, but we cannot have truth."[67] A postmodern perspective does not allow for any scientific, philosophical or religious 'truth' which will explain everything for everybody. This kicks the idea of God firmly into the long grass!

The advent of postmodernism poses major challenges to religious belief in God, given that – as Alister McGrath explains – "the world in which we live is now seen as a place in which nothing is certain, nothing is guaranteed, and nothing is unquestionably given. ... The Enlightenment stereotype of the all-knowing mind has been replaced by the image of the searcher, questing for truth and she journeys through an ambivalent and complex world, where simple answers are likely to be wrong answers."[68] Viewed this way, as Karen Armstrong reminds us, "truth is inherently ambiguous."[69]

From a postmodern perspective the personal is privileged over the collective. Thus, for example, personal development and self-realisation become important goals for the individual; personal spirituality and existential experience becomes more important than preserving or engaging with religious traditions; and personal ethics and one's own sense of morality become primary drivers of human behaviour. Such a view promotes a consumerist attitude to religion, in which the individual expects to be able to shop around and choose whatever form of religion suits them best. Taken to the extreme this can encourage people to engage in religious tourism by regularly moving between churches, denominations and even religions, avoiding allegiance to any particular one, moving on if and when they think there might be a better one (however defined) around the corner or over the hill.

The writer's tale

This quick overview sketches out the main characteristics and challenges of the three main types of world-view in Western cultures, but it is probably very abstract for many readers. One way of bringing it to life is to trace how my own world-view has evolved, having taken many twists and turns to reach the state it is in today.

I write as a participant observer in this never-ending debate about the idea of God. I write also as a journeyman Christian not a theologian. My story is my journey through life: for better or worse, these are my credentials for writing this book.

Like the proverbial football match, my life so far has been a game of two halves. During the first half (my first three decades) God was irrelevant to me, or so I thought. I was born into a non-religious family which only went to church for christenings, weddings and funerals - the 'hatched, matched and dispatched' beloved of most families. God was never mentioned at home, in any context. Exposure to the question of God during my school years was minimal, amounting to little more than religious studies lessons at secondary school which were in reality philosophy lessons. I went to university in Northern Ireland the year "The Troubles" started (1969) and was astonished at the tribalism and intolerance of people on both sides of the Catholic-Protestant divide; that gave me a dim view of church and religion. My degree course was in Environmental Science, and my view of the world was that of the clear-thinking scientist, convinced that everything has a rational explanation and there is no need for anything supernatural. That world-view served me well as a doctoral student back in England, and during the first phase of my career as an academic. I was intrigued by Lyall Watson's book *Supernature*,[70] which explores things that science can observe but not explain; it opened my eyes to the possibility that there are 'things out there', real tangible things, that science has no way of explaining … yet.

I would never have gone so far as to declare myself an atheist, but I most certainly was not a believer. To me, then, God was the stuff of myth, on a par with the tooth fairy, Loch Ness monster, and Father Christmas, believed only by people who could not see through it. If Richard Dawkins had written *The God Delusion* thirty years earlier, I would have read it out of curiosity, and would have agreed with most of what he wrote; I was already familiar with his books on evolution, which to me made good sense. Had I come across his term "brights" for atheists at that point in my life, I would probably have adopted it for myself.

All this was to change dramatically in my early thirties. My mid-life crisis came early, and it led me to start going to church. Initially I was drawn by the friendly and non-judgmental welcome, the clear joy of others during the services, and the engaging talks by the charismatic vicar. But I struggled to reconcile what I was being told in church with the rationalist scientific world-view that by then was so ingrained within me that I accepted it without question.

I did what academics usually do, and read as widely as I could. I read books by scientists, books by theologians, and most importantly some books by scientists who were also believers. Two particular books had a great impact on my thinking. The first was Brian Walsh and Richard Middleton's *The Transforming Vision*,[71] about world-views, which I had never heard of before. That book opened my mind to the possibility that the same things can be seen in different ways when viewed from different vantage points, either by one person through time or by different people. The second book was *Bent World*,[72] written by Ron Elsdon, an academic geologist but also a convinced believer; his arguments in favour of the idea of God were clear and persuasive. It was all slowly starting to make sense, and I caught glimpses of ways in which the idea of God might be reconciled with my Enlightenment world-view.

Further progress was inhibited by my overtly intellectual approach, but a major breakthrough came when I had a number of experiences of what German religious philosopher Rudolf Otto called 'the numinous, by which he meant "the non-rational feelings, the sense of the tremendous, the awful, the mysterious,"[73] in other words, direct experiences of or encounters with God.

We will look in more detail at direct experiences of God in Chapters 8 and 9, but I can't express it better than in the words of Marcus Borg who had similar experiences which "fundamentally changed [his] understanding of God, religion, and Christianity. ... They involved a rediscovery of mystery - not an intellectual paradox, but an experience of sacred mystery. These experiences, besides being ecstatic, were for me *aha!* moments. They gave me a new understanding of the meaning of the word *God*. I realised that God does not refer to a supernatural being 'out there' ... Rather, I began to see, the word God refers to the sacred at the centre of existence, the holy mystery that is all around us and within us. God is the non-material ground and source and presence in which, to cite words attributed to Paul by the author of Acts, 'we live and move and have our being.'"[74]

For me, God was now no longer an intellectual conundrum but an experiential reality. Moving from knowing *about* God to *knowing* God was a profound, life-changing experience, most definitely a life-enhancing experience. Danish philosopher Søren Kierkegaard said that "life can only be understood backwards, but it must be lived forwards."[75] I could never have anticipated such a radical shift in my world-view, but looking back I can get glimpses of how "the hound of heaven"[76] was pursuing me over a long period of time.

As Judy Collins sang in the 1970s, "I've looked at life from both sides now." Through personal experience I understand the perspectives of both the believer and the non-believer. Like a great many other people, I can appreciate both camps' take on 'the God Question', even though I now sit squarely in one camp, the opposite one from before. Both perspectives were sincerely held, informed by experience and understanding. The switch from one side to the other was the result of direct encounters with God, which radically and permanently changed my world-view from pure modern to a mixture of modern and pre-modern. The critical thing was a new understanding and experience of both the material and the spiritual 'layers' of reality working together to create the world I see around me and shape all of my thoughts, understandings and experiences..

This is who I am and what I believe.

CHAPTER 3

RELIGION AND THE IDEA OF GOD

"There is a case for arguing that Homo sapiens is also Homo religiosus. Men and women started to worship gods as soon as they became recognisably human; they created religions at the same time as they created works of art."

Karen Armstrong (1993)

U p to now we have thought about God as though it is simply the *idea* of God that matters, as if it is purely a matter for the intellect to deal with. But of course that's far from being the case, as both believers and non-believers know full well. Belief generally shapes attitudes and behaviour, and the outworking of the idea of God usually takes place through spirituality and religion.

As we shall see in Chapter 5, the New Atheists argue strongly against the very idea of God, but they direct their fiercest attacks against the behaviour of believers, both as individuals and collectively. They accuse organised religion of many crimes against humanity, but single out for particularly strong criticism Christianity and Islam. Richard Dawkins' central argument in *The God Delusion* is that people are conned into believing in the God of the Old Testament, which in turn makes them behave in ways that cause division, exploitation and conflict with other people and with nature.

Defining terms

It is important to consider how the idea of God affects people, and how what they believe about God shapes their attitudes and behaviour. In particular, it is useful to distinguish between spirituality and religion.

Spirituality

The *Oxford English Dictionary* defines spirituality as "The quality or condition of being spiritual; attachment to or regard for things of the spirit as opposed to material or worldly interests."[77] Alister Hardy, former Professor of Zoology at Oxford University, describes spirituality as "a feeling that 'Something Other' than the self can actually be sensed; a desire to personalise this presence into a deity and to have a private I-Thou [person-to-person] relationship with it, communicating through prayer."[78]

Religion

The *Oxford English Dictionary* defines religion as "Action or conduct indicating belief in, obedience to, and reverence for a god, gods, or similar superhuman power; the performance of religious rites or observances."[79] Oxford philosopher Tim Mawson describes religion as "those systems of thought that view physicalism as false, that claim then that there is something outside the physical world that accounts for it: there is something beyond the world that natural science describes and that something explains why there is a world for us to describe and why there is an us to do the describing."[80] John Cornwell points out that religion "is much more than a set of 'beliefs', although it may at points be inseparable from them."[81]

Spirituality and religion overlap but they are not the same thing. They differ in several important ways, including:

[i]   Personal vs communal: spirituality is based on personal belief, usually dealt with in private by the individual, whereas religion is a collective activity, usually dealt with corporately and in both the private and public domains;

[ii] Intellectual vs practical: spirituality may be a largely intellectual pursuit, though it may also be pursued through rituals or practices (such as meditation, prayer and contemplation), whereas religion always involves a combination of belief, dogma, traditions and practices (such as worship);

[iii] Informal vs formal: spirituality is generally loosely structured and personal to the individual, whereas religion by definition has formal expression and is organised to a greater or lesser degree; and

[iv] Conscience vs accountability: spirituality usually shapes an

individual's attitudes and behaviour, but usually by following their own conscience rather than appealing to external judgment, whereas religion shapes attitudes and behaviour in ways that are accountable to religious authority (either loosely or tightly defined).

The nature of religion

New Atheist Daniel Dennett concedes that "for many people, probably a majority of the people on Earth, nothing matters more than religion."[82] Whilst not all religions point to God or assume a belief in God, given the ubiquity and importance of religion it is essential that we understand how God and religion are inter-related, but at the same time appreciate that they are not the same thing. The idea of God is one thing, and the practice of religion is another, although they often converge and overlap.

Common ingredients of religion

Given the diversity of religions across the world today, what do they have in common? What ties them together? French sociologist Emile Durkheim identified five what he called "elementary forms of the religious life" which can be found in all religions.[83] These are the habit of seeing the world as composed of both sacred and profane (secular, with no spiritual basis) elements; belief in spirits; belief in God or gods; the practice of self-denial; and religious rites and traditions.

Historian of religion Ninian Smart deconstructs religion differently, and sees it as made up of six particularly important 'dimensions':[84]

[i]   Ritual (ceremony);
[ii] Myth (story, what has been said, whether true or false);
[iii] Doctrine (what is stated in theology);
[iv] Ethics (behaviour);
[v]   Social significance; and
[vi] Human experience.

Variations on a theme

Many non-believers (including me formerly) think of all religions as variations on a theme, different ways of dealing with the idea of God. From this perspective most religions look inter-changeable, allowing people to pick and choose to suit their tastes and personal preferences. Believers (including me now) naturally see things very differently.

The Baha'i faith is unique in believing that all religions are pathways to God. Howard Jones spells out the Baha'i view that "as there are many fundamental contradictions between one set of religious beliefs and another, it is logically untenable that any one of these accounts should be regarded as expressing unequivocal and unilateral divine truth, as this condemns the remaining religious beliefs to falsehood. The various bodies of scriptures should therefore be regarded as presenting accounts of different paths to the divine, created for different peoples at different times and different places in different social situations."[85]

With so many religions competing for people's attention, it is little wonder that many of them insist that theirs is the only 'true' one and all the other ones are flawed. The notion of truth in religion is hotly contested, and the claim is readily seized upon by critics (including atheists) as evidence of the delusional nature of religion. Through history it has also been the cause of a great deal of inter-religious rivalry and hostility, evidenced for example in the medieval Crusades, and more recently in Islamic jihad (a holy war against unbelievers).

Durkheim insisted that "in reality there are no religions which are false. All are true in their own fashion: all answer, albeit in different ways, to the given conditions of human existence."[86]

Literalism and fundamentalism

All believers can be located somewhere along a spectrum between moderate (liberals) and extremist (fundamentalists), reflecting the strength of their religious conviction and the extent to which it informs and is acted out through behaviour. Where an individual sits along that spectrum depends mainly on how they read and understand religious texts (such as the Bible for Christians and the Koran for Muslims). Fundamentalists are literalists, who accept the core texts of their religion as divinely dictated and read them literally, believing every word and expression; liberals typically view core texts as divinely inspired, and they read meaning into them without expecting every single word to be literally true.

Michael Novak comments that the New Atheists "are almost as literal in their readings of the Bible as the least educated, most literal-minded fundamentalist."[87] However, as theologian John Cornwell points out, they overlook the fact that modern Bible scholarship shows that "the collection of texts known as the Bible contains a variety of different literary forms, including homily, allegory, meditation, parable, chronicle, poetry, legend, folk memory, ironic aphorisms, prophecy, prayer."[88]

Fundamentalism emerged in most world religions during the twentieth century, as a resistance to and reaction against the modern world-view and modern notions of knowledge. In Christianity it emerged through conscious and deliberate insistence on "the Bible [read literally] as a source of divinely guaranteed factual knowledge," as Marcus Borg puts it.[89]

Fundamentalists have a reputation for being intolerant of the views of others. John Cornwell points out that they reject "pluralism of view points, values, creeds, religions, and indeed shades of doubt, scepticism, agnosticism, and atheism."[90] As Symon Hill reminds us, they are convinced "that only their religion or world-view has the truth. Other religions are regarded as false and often as evil."[91] Krista Tippett thinks of a fundamentalist as "anyone who not only has the answers for himself, but has them for all the rest of us too."[92] Cornwell adds that they are "determined, aggressive dogmatists, insisting that they, and they alone, are right: you are either with them or against them."[93]

New Atheist Sam Harris sees moderates as "fully committed to tolerance and diversity" but is critical of extremists who "would burn the earth to cinders if it would put an end to heresy."[94] Curiously, he blames the rise of fundamentalism on the tolerance of moderates, arguing that "religious moderation appears to be nothing more than an unwillingness to fully submit to God's laws … the religious moderate is nothing more than a failed fundamentalist."[95] Richard Dawkins echoes the sentiment, writing that "the teachings of 'moderate' religion, though not extremist in themselves, are an open invitation to extremism."[96]

Atheists point to two particularly damaging impacts of religious fundamentalism in the world today. First they claim that it is anti-science. Dawkins insists that it "actively debauches the scientific enterprise. It teaches us not to change our minds, and not to want to know exciting things that are available to be known. It subverts science and saps the intellect."[97] Secondly, they claim that it fuels religious and sectarian conflict. Dawkins regards religious fundamentalism - which he dismisses as dangerous "absolutism" which "rules the minds of a great number of people in the world today" - as "a major reason for suggesting that religion can be a force for evil in the world."[98] Sam Harris is particularly critical of Muslim extremists and "the degree to which they believe that modernity and secular culture are incompatible with moral and spiritual health."[99] In many ways the emergence of New Atheism signalled a backlash against the atrocity of the Islamic terrorist attacks on New York on the 11th of September 2001.

Mysticism

Another hallmark of some religions is mysticism, through which some people claim direct experience of God, even communion with God. It inevitably requires belief in spiritual reality as well as material reality (see Chapter 2), and it involves a sense, knowledge or experience of "states of consciousness, or levels of being, or aspects of reality, beyond normal human perception."[100]

Psychologist William James studied many examples and reports of mystical experiences for his book *The Varieties of Religious Experience*, and he found that whilst they might appear unusual to most people they are not as uncommon as many imagine. He identified four particular characteristics of mystical experiences:[101]

[i] Ineffability; they cannot be described in words. "It follows from this that its quality must be directly experienced; it cannot be imparted or transferred to others.";

[ii] Noetic quality; they involve use of the mind. "They are states of insight into depths of truth unplumbed by the discursive intellect. They are illuminations, revelations, full of significance and importance, all inarticulate though they remain ...";

[iii] Transiency; they are short-lasting. "Mystical states cannot be sustained for long. Except in rare instances, half an hour, or at most an hour or two, seems to be the limit beyond which they fade into the light of common day. Often, when faded, their quality can but imperfectly be reproduced in memory; but when they recur it is recognised."; and

[iv] Passivity; they happen to us. "Although the oncoming of mystical

states may be facilitated by preliminary voluntary operations,
as by fixing the attention, or going through certain bodily
performances ... yet when the characteristic sort of consciousness
once has set in, the mystic feels as if his own will were in
abeyance, and indeed sometimes as if he were grasped and held
by a superior power."

James emphasises that "Mystical states, when well developed, usually are, and have the right to be, absolutely authoritative over the individuals to whom they come. ... They break down the authority of the non-mystical or rationalistic consciousness, based upon the understanding and the senses alone. They show it to be only one kind of consciousness. They open out the possibility of other orders of truth, in which, so far as anything in us vitally responds to them, we may freely continue to have faith."[102]

The whole area of mysticism and direct experience of God is a hotly contested theme within the God debate, and we will explore it further in Chapter 8. Many people dismiss it as "obscure or irrational thought"[103], whereas others see it as one outcome or fruit of spiritual discipline (particularly contemplation, meditation and self-surrender). It is part of my own personal experience, and that of many other people I know who are intelligent, rational and well-grounded. Richard Dawkins would dismiss us all as seriously deluded.

Ritual and symbol

The French sociologist Émile Durkheim believed that the central characteristic of religion is the difference between the sacred and the profane or secular. He defined religion as "a unified system of beliefs and practices relative to *sacred things* [his emphasis], that is to say, things set apart and forbidden."[104] The profane, he argued, involves mundane individual concerns, whereas the sacred involves group interests, particularly belonging and unity. Key to achieving that unity is sacred group symbols or emblems (totems) which a group identifies with and which ties them together.

John Cornwell explains how religion "is as much a product of the imagination as art, poetry, and music. Religion's activities, its rituals, its mythologies, hymns, meditations, prayers, chants, poetry, images, parables, legends, taboos, and sacramentals (... holy objects, such as candles, incense, oils, vestments, holy water) are principally symbolic, often appealing to deep levels of folk memory. ... Religious rituals and symbols, from the dawning of human history, marked and celebrated birth, growth, age, death and burial, the making of families and communities, the coming together for feasts, husbandry, hunting, journeys, the life cycles of plants and animals, and human beings, the changing seasons, the diurnal, lunar, and annual rounds, the mystery of existence. The great world religions ... continue to enact and celebrate those cyclical experiences and underlying mysteries."[105]

The scale of religion

How many religions are there?

Religions are communal, practical, and generally formally organised activities, with a focus on God or gods, but they can take many different forms. Even counting how many religions there are in the world today is not without its challenges, because they can be situated along a spectrum which has few obvious thresholds along it. When, for example, does a spiritual interest shared by a few people become a cult? And when does a cult become a fully-fledged religion?

Daniel Dennett acknowledges that "what we usually call religions are composed of a variety of quite different phenomena, arising from different circumstances and having different implications, forming a loose family of phenomena, not a 'natural kind' like a chemical element or a species."[106]

According to the *World Christian Encyclopedia* there are 19 major world religions today, which can be sub-divided into 270 large religious groups and many smaller ones.[107] More than 34,000 separate Christian groups have been identified.

How many religious believers are there?

It is notoriously difficult to count exactly how many people belong to particular religions because data has to be pulled together from many different sources. But figures for 2001 show that Christians are the largest group world-wide, in the USA and in the UK. Worldwide, out of a total population of nearly 6 billion, there were 2.1 billion Christians, 1.5 billion Muslims and 1.1 billion non-religious people.[108] In the USA, there were 159 million Christians, 29.4 million non-religious, and 2.8 million Jews.[109]

In the UK there were 42 million Christians, 9.1 million non-religious, and 1.6 million Muslims.[110] Christians outnumber non-religious people roughly two-to-one globally and broadly five-to-one in the USA and the UK. At the world scale Islam gives Christianity a good run for its money and is fast catching up, but in the USA and the UK it currently lags some way behind, at least in terms of numbers of followers.

Whilst size does matter, the numbers don't tell the whole story. For many people 'religion' is a census category or cultural label rather than a personal belief or a way of life. People also vary greatly in the degree to which, in terms of religion, they are active (engaged and committed) or passive (nominal). Moreover, measures such as counts of church membership or even attendance are not good proxies for such things as strength of personal belief or degree to which belief shapes or determines behaviour.[111]

Surveys show that religious faith and belonging are much stronger in the USA than in Britain. Data for 2008 shows that three in five (61 per cent) Americans have 'no doubt' that God exists, compared with fewer than one in five (1 per cent) people in Britain.[112]

Religion is also a dynamic phenomena - it can change through time, both in terms of number of followers (which can rise or fall) and diversity of religions (which can also rise and fall). We shall see examples of this shortly, when we look at secularisation.

God in religion

Religions have many different views about God. Although most believe in existence of God, and point to God, not all do. Peter Lundstrom refers to belief systems which do not search for God, such as Hinduism and atheism, as "non-theistic."[113]

Different religions look upon God in different ways, and without an appreciation of these differences we run the risk of assuming that all religions see the same God the same way. This is one of many traps the New Atheists fall into, which diminishes the credibility of many of their arguments against religion.

One simple way of grouping religions into types is on the basis of what form of God they believe in (pantheism, polytheism and monotheism).

Pantheism

Pantheism is based on the belief that God and the universe are one and the same thing. The word is derived from the Greek *pan* (all) and *theos* (god) and it literally means "all is God."[114] From this perspective the whole universe and everything in it are seen as a manifestation of God, so it is "the only thing deserving the deepest kind of reverence."[115]

Richard Dawkins points out that "pantheists don't believe in a supernatural God at all, but use the word God [in a metaphoric or poetic way] as a non-supernatural synonym for Nature, or for the Universe, or for the lawfulness that governs its workings."[116] Peter Lundstrom elaborates a bit further: "pantheistic religions believe that God consists of the whole of nature. God is within all of nature and nature is God."[117]

Many of the so-called 'primitive religions', based on worshipping spirits in the natural world, are or were pantheistic. So too is the New Age movement which Terry Eagleton dismisses as "a reaction to a heartless world which stays confined to the sphere of feelings and values."[118] It is an avant-garde 'hippy' movement with roots in animism and pagan religions, based on ideas borrowed from Eastern mysticism and an interest in psychic phenomena. It is driven by the search for a new cosmic consciousness which denies the existence of a transcendent god and places great value on the individual person, centering on self-realisation through "a mystical experience in which time, space and morality are transcended"[119] giving the sense of becoming one with the cosmos, sometimes with the assistance of psychedelic drugs.

Polytheism

Polytheism is based on belief in and the worship of multiple gods. The word is derived from the Greek *polys* (many) and *theos* (god), and it literally means "of many gods."[120] As Peter Lundstrom puts it, "polytheistic religions believe in a vast host of gods who vary widely in character, purpose and influence."[121] Many primitive religions were polytheistic.

Hinduism is probably the best-known polytheistic religion today. Although Hinduism "is a conglomeration of distinct intellectual or philosophical points of view, rather than a rigid common set of beliefs"[122], Hindus worship hundreds of different gods and goddesses, each purported to represent a particular aspect of the one supreme being or ultimate deity.

There are three main deities in Hinduism - Brahma (the Creator), Vishnu/ Krishna (the Preserver) and Shiva (the Destroyer) - and some followers regard Vishnu as the ultimate deity while others insist it is Shiva.

Monotheism

Monotheism is based on belief in and the worship of a single God (capital G). The word is derived from the Greek *monos* (single, alone) and *theos* (god) and it literally means "one God."[123] The three monotheistic religions - Judaism, Christianity, and Islam - believe in a single God who is unique in every way. That God is also known as the 'God of Abraham', after the Old Testament character from whom Jesus is believed to be descended.

Each of the three monotheistic religions has its own take on the relevance of God and the purpose of life. In Judaism the core responsibility of believers is to obey Yahweh's (God's) commandments and live ethically; the focus is more on this life than the next. In Christianity the core belief is that the sins people commit separate them from God, to whom they can only be reconciled ('saved') through faith in God's son Christ. In Islam believers are expected to submit (*islam*) to the will of Allah (God) in order to gain Paradise after they die.

Monotheism - particularly Christianity - has long been the default belief system in western cultures, and it remains so today. Self-confessed agnostic Michael Shermer points out that "studies show that the vast majority of people in the Industrial West who believe in God associate themselves with some form of monotheism, in which God is understood to be all powerful, all knowing, and all good; who created out of nothing the universe and everything in it with the exception of Himself; who is uncreated and eternal, a non-corporeal spirit who created, loves, and can grant eternal life to humans."[124] This is the type of religion that offends Richard Dawkins so much and is the primary target of his barbed attacks in *The God Delusion*.

Monotheism can be sub-divided into two groups, based on beliefs about whether God is present and active in the universe he is alleged to have created (theism), or absent from it and passive about it (deism).

Deism

The word deism is derived from the Latin *deus* (god) and it simply means belief in God. But the term is widely used today to refer specifically to belief in the existence of a God who created the universe and the laws that govern it at the beginning of time (whenever that was) then abandoned it and left it to take care of itself. Oxford philosopher Tim Mawson describes how, in this view, God created the world "in the sense of starting it off, as someone might create a firework display by lighting the blue touch-paper and retiring."[125] This is the idea of a creator God who - like some *deus emeritus*, or retired God - has stopped interacting with the universe he created, taking no active role or moral interest in human affairs, and "assuming no control over life, exerting no influence on natural phenomena, and giving no supernatural revelation."[126] It denies that miracles can actually happen and seeks rational (usually scientific) explanations for apparent miracles. It sees God as effectively 'living in exile' out of reach and out of sight from humans on earth, or indeed anywhere else in the universe. This God is thus by definition impersonal and unknowable.

This way of visualising God is a form of theological rationalism based only on reason, without reference to divine revelation. It became popular in the eighteenth century because it allows some accommodation between the idea of God and the material modern world-view which emerged through the Enlightenment, as we saw in Chapter 2. Karen Armstrong explains how at that time "a somewhat paradoxical theology was developing. In the supernatural realm, God remained a mysterious and loving Father, active in the lives of his worshippers. But in the natural world, God had been forced to retreat: he had created it, sustained it and established its laws, but after that the mechanism worked by itself and God made no further direct interventions."[127]

Deism remains popular among many people today, although many people are effectively deists without knowing it. Some writers have argued that by excluding God from being actively involved in the world today deism represents a halfway house towards atheism. Richard Dawkins writes cryptically that "deists differ from theists in that their God does not answer prayers, is not interested in sins or confessions, does not read our thoughts and does not intervene with capricious miracles. ... Deism is watered-down theism."[128]

Theism

The word theism is derived from the Greek *theos* (god), so like deism it means belief in God. But unlike the absent God of deism, theism refers to belief in the existence of a God who created the universe and remains present, continuing to run it and govern it. As Tim Mawson describes, this is a view in which "God creates the world in the sense of keeping it in being from moment to moment ... The world ultimately depends on God's will for its existence and its character as expressed in the natural laws that govern the behaviour of its constituents."[129]

As well as continuing to sustain the universe, the God that theists believe in is a personal God who is actively involved in the world today. This God "knows about and cares about each individual human being,"[130] makes himself knowable to them (for example, through personal experience and by revelation, as we shall see in Chapter 8), and makes it possible for them to not only *know about* him but actually know *him*. This is the God who changed my life (as he has done for a great many people through the ages), as I described in the Introduction.

Like deism, theism remains popular today, although (again like deism) most people are effectively theists without knowing it and wouldn't call themselves one. US theologian John Haught points out that this is the idea of God that most people in the West associate with the term 'religion', by which they mean "belief in a distinct, personal, transcendent, divine being, endowed with intelligence, will, feelings, intentions, and responsiveness."[131]

It is also the idea of God that most of the New Atheists' attacks against God are targeted at and that Richard Dawkins insists otherwise sensible people are deluded or tricked into believing. He writes of the God who "answers prayers; forgives or punishes sins; intervenes in the world by performing miracles; frets about good and bad deeds, and knows when we do them (or even *think* of doing them)."[132] It is the God that most atheists claim not to believe in and dismiss as a product of the human imagination.

Einstein's God

Noble Prize-winning scientist Albert Einstein sometimes included the word God in his explanations of the nature and development of the universe, but as a confirmed atheist he was not using the idea of God in the same way that believers do. He thought and wrote of God in a metaphorical way; to him 'God' was the order and structure of the physical world. This is a variant on the pantheistic idea of God.

Einstein wrote to a correspondent "I do not believe in a personal God and

I have never denied this but expressed it clearly. If something is in me which can be called religion then it is the unbounded admiration for the structure of the world so far as our science can reveal it."[133] Richard Dawkins regrets that, by writing of God as he did, Einstein invited "misunderstanding by supernaturalists eager to misunderstand and claim so illustrious a thinker as their own."[134]

Similarly, Dawkins notes that "the dramatic (or was it mischievous?) ending of Stephen Hawking's *A Brief History of Time*, 'For then we should know the mind of God'[135], is notoriously misconstrued. It has led people to believe, mistakenly of course, that Hawking is a religious man."[136] He continues "I wish that physicists would refrain from using the word God in their special metaphorical sense. The metaphorical or pantheistic God of the physicists is light years away from the interventionist, miracle-wreaking, thought-reading, sin-punishing, prayer-answering God of the Bible, of priests, mullahs and rabbis, and of ordinary language. Deliberately to confuse the two is, in my opinion, an act of intellectual high treason."[137]

Dawkins' God

In recent years Richard Dawkins' views on God, summarised in *The God Delusion*, have been widely read particularly by non-believers eager to find support for their own beliefs (or lack of them) from a heavyweight intellectual. He starts by clarifying the God he is not talking about - "I know you don't believe in an old bearded man sitting on a cloud, so let's not waste time on that."[138] He then underlines the fact that he is "attacking God, all gods, anything and everything supernatural, wherever and whenever they have been or will be invented."[139]

Despite his target being "all gods", Dawkins can't resist taking a swipe at the God he misguidedly thinks Christians today believe in and freely worship, the God he insists believers are so deluded about. Dawkins embarks on a flight of fancy and is clearly playing to the gallery when he writes that "the God of the Old Testament is arguably the most unpleasant character in all of fiction: jealous and proud of it; a petty, unjust, unforgiving control freak; a vindictive, bloodthirsty ethnic cleanser; a misogynistic, homophobic, racist, infanticidal, genocidal, filicidal, pestilential, megalomaniacal, sadomasochistic, capriciously malevolent bully."[140]

This is the God that Dawkins doesn't believe in. He may be surprised (if not disappointed) to learn that, along with most believers today, I don't believe in that God any more than he does. John Haught points out that "the snapshot of God that [Dawkins] flashes in *The God Delusion* is a caricature that has long been offensive to theology. It seems to come almost exclusively from visiting the campsite and Web sites of creationists and ID [Intelligent Design] defenders."[141] Terry Eagleton, in characteristically colourful style, asks readers to "imagine someone holding forth on biology whose only knowledge of the subject is the *Book of British Birds*, and you have a rough idea of what it feels like to read Richard Dawkins on theology."[142]

Numerous critics have pointed out that Dawkins and his supporters seriously misread and distort the Old Testament narrative to form that view of God, and that they are seriously misguided in their view of the God that believers hold and the reasons they hold it. For example US theologian John Cornwell dismisses Dawkins' image of God as resembling "nothing so much as a megalomaniac designer-scientist. A Great Big Science Professor in the Sky."[143] English theologian Keith Ward describes it as "a biased selection of negative texts from early in a long biblical tradition, based on a tradition which contains vitally important qualifications and supplementations of those texts."[144]

Scottish pastor David Robertson tries to redress the balance; he writes "When I read the Old Testament I find a wonderful God – a God of mercy, justice, beauty, holiness and love, a God who cares passionately for the poor, for his people and for his creation. And, amazingly, it is the same God in the New Testament."[145] Like beauty, the most appropriate way of visualising God is clearly in the eye of the beholder!

The 'God Hypothesis'

Richard Dawkins constructs the arguments in *The God Delusion* around what he calls the 'God Hypothesis', which he insists is "a scientific hypothesis about the universe, which should be analysed as sceptically as any other"[146]. The 'God Hypothesis' supposes that "there exists a superhuman, supernatural intelligence who deliberately designed and created the universe and everything in it, including us."[147] As Nicholas Lash puts it, it is the belief that there is "above and beyond the familiar world with all its furniture, one more big and powerful thing."[148]

Critics have seized on the idea of a 'God Hypothesis' as a serious weak link in Dawkins' reasoning, claiming that it does no justice to either theological understanding of God or scientific understanding of the term 'hypothesis'. John Haught argues that "thinking of God as a hypothesis reduces the infinite divine mystery to a finite scientific cause, and to worship anything finite is idolatrous. The notion of a God Hypothesis shrinks God down to the size of a link in a causal chain ..."[149] Keith Ward goes further, arguing that "the God Hypothesis is neither scientific nor historical, nor does it just provide a record or prediction of my subjective experiences. It does not give rise to specific predictions, and it cannot be tested by public observation in controlled conditions."[150]

Rather curiously, despite his academic training and scientific credentials, Dawkins does not follow the normal scientific convention of testing a hypothesis by collecting evidence, analysing and testing it, then drawing conclusions informed by that analysis. Instead he treats the 'God Hypothesis' very much as a straw man, and he feels free to simply advocate a view directly contrary to it. He is convinced (and clearly determined to convince his readers) that "any creative intelligence, of sufficient complexity to design anything, comes into existence only as the end product of an extended process of gradual evolution. Creative intelligences, being evolved, necessarily arrive late in the universe, and therefore cannot be responsible for designing it. God, in the sense defined, is a delusion ... a pernicious delusion."[151]

Whilst Dawkins' notion of delusion leads to a catchy book title, Keith Ward cautions the need to keep the delusion idea in perspective, insisting that "he is setting out to defend a very recent, highly contentious, minority philosophical world-view."[152]

Origins and development of religion

It is not the intention here to trace the entire history of the idea or concept of God, which would take a separate very large book. Karen Armstrong offers detailed histories in *The Case for God*[153] and *The History of God*[154], and other useful sources include Ninian Smart's *The Religious Experience of Mankind*[155], Robert Winston's *The Story of God*[156], and Robert Wright's *The Evolution of God*[157].

Our purpose here is to identify how, when and why the idea of God emerged, to set the scene for a brief overview of religion today. Daniel

Dennett points out that "when people write books about 'the history of God' ... they are actually writing about the history of the *concept* of God, of course, tracing the fashions and controversies about God as intentional object through the centuries."[158] Karen Armstrong concludes that "the idea of God is remarkably close to ideas in religions that developed quite independently."[159]

Archaeology and anthropology have produced abundant evidence that forms of religion can be traced back to the earliest humans. The evidence also shows that whilst the detailed expressions of primitive religions (including those that persist in many remote parts of the world today) varied a great deal between cultures, places and times, they shared and continue to share some important characteristics. Historian of religion Ninian Smart[160] identifies five common ones;

[i]   The idea of a High God (a supreme spirit or god which rules over lesser ones);

[ii] The practice of totemism (use of a natural object as the emblem of a group);

[iii] Ancestor worship (veneration of the dead);

[iv] Shamans (a person who acts as an intermediary between the spirit world and the physical world); and

[v]   The use of myths and legends as ways of interpreting the world around us (for example through creation stories) and ourselves (such as stories which explain features of daily ritual).

A simple history of the idea of God would recognise three distinct phases, evidence of which can still be found in different expressions of religion around the world today.

Projection and the notion of the soul

The first phase, defined by belief in spirits, is typical of primitive religions. Ninian Smart emphasises the importance in this phase of both animism (belief in the existence of individual spirits that inhabit natural objects) and ancestor worship. These, he argued, helped primitive man to form his notion of the soul "from his own experience of dreams, where persons appear in a mysterious and immaterial fashion; from his experience of death, where seemingly the life-force departs from the body; from visions and ecstasy, where one is temporarily transported (so it seems) out of one's body."[161]

Archaeological evidence shows that over 100,000 years ago, before the emergence of the human species proper (*Homo sapiens*), Neanderthal people practiced the ritual burial of the dead, suggesting a belief in an 'invisible world' and some sort of afterlife, in which the soul survives beyond the physical body.[162] Through time it is likely that the idea of a soul distinct from the body evolved further, with primitive people projecting the idea of the soul onto the animals and objects they encountered around them. The development of ancestor worship also suggests a belief that departed spirits could exist permanently in the absence of a body, and could even take possession of living people if they chose to.[163]

Polytheism and the explanation of natural events and phenomena

The second phase sees projection replaced by explanation. Belief in departed spirits gives way to "belief in spirits whose activities explained natural events and phenomena – gods who ruled the rain, the sky, fire, and so on."[164] Thus the first gods were born. This probably began during the Neolithic period (starting about 10,000 years ago), when the first stable societies emerged as farming replaced hunting, towns and cities were built, trading began, centralised administrations and political structures evolved, and temple cults and an organised priesthood developed. Karen Armstrong notes how "there was ... no belief in a single supreme being in the ancient world. Any such creature could only be *a* being – bigger and better than anything else, perhaps, but still a finite, incomplete reality. People felt it natural to imagine a race of spiritual beings of a higher nature than themselves that they called 'gods'."[165]

This was the golden age of polytheism, in which there were gods for all seasons and all reasons. Richard Carlyon, in his *Guide to the gods*[166], gives details of more than 1,000 such gods. Some of them – such as Aphrodite (Greek Goddess of love and beauty), Neptune (Roman god of the sea), and Odin (Nordic god of battles) – are well-known, but most have only local or regional importance and are barely known outside the time and place of their origin. Examples include Thunder Bird (the Native American god of thunder), Huitzilopochtli (the Aztec God of war), Inari (the Japanese god of rice), Ganga (the Indian goddess of purification of the River Ganges),

Hapi (the Egyptian god of the Nile), and Pele (the Hawaiian goddess of volcanic fire).

Monotheism and the personal god

Phase three sees belief in multiple gods replaced by belief in one god, a single personal God.[167] This phase, which Don Cupitt calls "the coming of God"[168], began around four thousand years ago. This is the age of monotheism, the one we are living in today. It is marked by the emergence and development of the three major monotheistic traditions – the so-called Abrahamic religions – of Judaism (founded by Abraham in 2085 BC), Christianity (founded by Jesus Christ) and Islam (founded by Mohammed in 610 AD).[169]

This very simple three-phase typology masks much of the rich detail about exactly how religion has evolved, which scholars have devoted a great deal of academic research to. For example, German social scientist Max Weber traced the evolution of religion in terms of "breakthroughs", particularly through what he calls "the process of rationalisation" (the ways in which ideas are clarified, defined and ordered), as well as the processes by which cultures define their religious situation (particularly through the writing of sacred texts) and the development of religious community.[170]

New Atheist Daniel Dennett, commenting on the historic processes by which polytheism turned into monotheism, argues that "belief in God joined forces with the *belief in belief* in God to motivate the migration of the concept of God in the Abrahamic religions ... away from concrete anthropomorphism to ever more abstract and depersonalised concepts."[171] Dennett refers to this as "the intentional stance", by which he means that "the initial cause for belief in a deity is an inherited tendency to attribute agency to other people and to inanimate objects."[172]

Some historians of religion suggest that the idea of God evolved gradually and progressively, but Alister McGrath insists that "the history of religion obliges us to speak about the 'diversification', not the 'progression' of religion. The evidence simply isn't there to allow us to speak about any kind of 'natural progression' from polytheism to monotheism – and thence to atheism."[173]

The importance of myth

Myth has played important roles in the development of religion since time immemorial. We humans are story-telling animals and we have long used myth as a way of making sense of the world and our place in it. Myths are not the same as fairy tales and legends; fairy tales are "mostly wish-fulfilment stories about individual human dilemmas and situations" and legends are "stories that accumulate around well-known characters", as Kathleen Jones puts it.[174]

The popular meaning of the word myth today is a story that is not true, but Symon Hill points out that a myth is "a narrative which conveys an understanding of truth without necessarily being factual. ... myths may or may not contain literal and factual truth, but this is not the point to them."[175] J.R.R. Tolkien (author of *Lord of the Rings*) argued that myths are "symbolic stories intended to express truth" and "far from being lies, [myths] were the best way of conveying truths which would otherwise be inexpressible."[176]

Anthropologists view myth as an important tool for transmitting group experiences, and some myths recur through many cultures. Michael Shermer asks "Why is there an eternal return of certain mythic themes in religion, such as messiah myths, flood myths, creation myths, destruction myths, redemption myths, and end of the world myths?"[177] Shermer emphasises the role of myth in the development of religion, which evolved from pattern-seeking through storytelling and myth-making to morality, then on to religion and ultimately to God.[178]

This line of reasoning reflects the writings of Paul Tillich, who proposed that myths provide stepping stones towards religion. Tillich argued that "myths are always present in every act of faith, because the language of faith is the symbol" and "the symbols of faith do not appear in isolation. They are united in 'stories of the gods' which is the meaning of the Greek word *mythos*'– myth."[179]

Marcus Borg (1998) unpacks these ideas further, noting that "religious myths or sacred myths are stories about the relationship between the two worlds - the sacred and the world of our ordinary experience. In short, a myth is a story about God and us. As such, myths can be both true and powerful, even though they are symbolic narratives and not straightforward historical reports. Though not literally true, they can be really true; though not factually true, they can be actually true."[180]

Functions and benefits of religion

Whilst religion is usually defined on the basis of belief in God, even many non-believers recognise that it has a pervasive and wide-ranging influence on society, even in increasingly secular western societies. Although English philosopher Alain de Botton is not a believer, he sings the praises of religion without God in his book *Religion for Atheists*, arguing that although "the supernatural claims of religion are totally false ... religions still have some very important things to teach the secular world."[181] These include building a sense of community, making relationships last, overcoming feelings of envy and inadequacy, and getting more out of art, architecture and music.

Even confirmed New Atheist Daniel Dennett acknowledges that "according to surveys, most of the people in the world say that religion is very important in their lives. ... Many of these people would say that without their religion their lives would be meaningless." Of course, this does not necessarily mean that religion is based on reality, as the New Atheists eagerly point out. Richard Dawkins sees religion as a collective form of delusion; he agreed with Robert Pirsig, author of the best-selling cult book *Zen and the Art of Motorcycle Maintenance*[182], who wrote that "when one person suffers from a delusion, it is called insanity. When many people suffer from a delusion it is called Religion."[183] Dawkins argues that we are "psychologically primed for religion."[184]

Whether or not it is 'true', religion enhances life for people in a number of ways, which should not be under-valued in the God debate. Keith Ward argues that "religions exist largely to increase wisdom, compassion and joy, and to liberate humans from self-obsessive desire."[185]

Religion is also a powerful force for and source of social cohesion, because it binds people together through shared beliefs, customs, traditions and values, and plays an important role in shaping human identity. Daniel Dennett identifies one purpose of religion as "to encourage group cooperation in the face of trials and enemies,"[186] and Richard Dawkins notes that it "fosters togetherness in groups."[187]

Search for meaning

Even the most dedicated of atheists believes that life has some meaning, even if that is simply the challenge of coping with life and getting through it. Don Cupitt contends that "people reckon themselves to be entirely capable of knowing and fully entitled to know what it's all about. ... they think that there is a big Answer, and that they are entitled to expect it to be made known to them."[188] Religion is the route along which most people expect that knowledge to come to them.

Critical as he is about most things to do with religion and the idea of God, even Richard Dawkins acknowledges that religion "satisfies our yearning to understand why we exist ... [and] our curiosity about the universe and our place in it."[189] Fellow New Atheist Daniel Dennett suggests that the purpose of religion is "to explain things we can't otherwise explain."[190] More bluntly, radio presenter Krista Tippett insists that religion "meets the raw human urge to give meaning to our days."[191]

American neuroscientist Andrew Newberg argues that religion gives us the "ability to alleviate existential gloom and connect us with powerful spiritual forces."[192] More specifically, he points out that "faith in a higher power offers believers the assurance that their lives have meaning and purpose, that they are not alone in the struggle for survival, that powerful, benevolent forces are at work in the world, and that despite the terrors and uncertainties of existence, they should not be afraid."[193]

Alongside meaning religion offers us comfort. Again, even Daniel Dennett sees that a primary purpose of religion is "to comfort us in our suffering and allay our fear of death."[194] Richard Dawkins recognises that religion "gives consolation and comfort,"[195] despite the fact that he sees it as misguided, delusional and without foundation.

Sense of mystery

A sense of mystery is just as important as the search for meaning, and Karen Tippett notes that religion "harnesses the common human experience of mystery – our ancient and abiding intuition of meaning beyond the substance of our days."[196] William James suggests that there exists "in the human consciousness a sense of reality, a feeling of objective presence, a perception of what we may call 'something there', more deep and more general than any of the special and particular 'senses'."[197]

In their pursuit of answers to this deep-rooted and enduring mystery, Karen Armstrong insists that some people are able "to 'step outside' the prism of ego and experience the divine."[198] German theologian Friedrich Schleiermacher called this transcendent experience "the sense of absolute dependence."[199] German historian of religion Rudolf Otto called it 'the numinous' (from the Latin *numina* meaning 'spirits') sense of mystery, awe and love,[200] by which he meant "the presence of the mysterious force inherent in every aspect of life".[201] Jewish scholar Martin Buber spoke of an 'I-Thou' encounter.[202] We will explore this theme further in Chapter 8.

Karen Armstrong suggests that "the desire to cultivate a sense of the transcendent may be the defining human characteristic."[203]

Source of morality

Many people view religion as a source of morality and ethics, a guide to proper behaviour. Even agnostic Michael Shermer concedes that one of the primary purposes of religion is "the production of moral systems to provide social cohesion for the most social of all the social primates."[204]

Believers insist that religion provides absolute standards of morality for distinguishing between good and bad, between goodness and evil. Christian church leader and writer David Watson wrote quite simply that if there is no God "the universe is nothing more than random choices, and meaningless events. There is no fairness, no vindication of right over wrong, no ultimate purposes, no abstract values."[205] If God does not exist, "isn't everything permitted?" asks John Haught.[206]

This is one of the most contentious areas within the God debate, and Richard Dawkins observes that "many religious people find it hard to imagine how, without religion, one can be good, or would even want to be good."[207] New Atheists direct much of their anger about the idea of God towards claims about religion as the foundation for moral judgements since, in Christopher Hitchens' words, "religion poisons everything."[208]

Dawkins dismisses the "religious claim that, without God, morals are relative and arbitrary" as "hypothetical."[209] John Haught concedes that there is no point "in denying that people can be very moral without believing in God. Nor is there any point in denying that religions have been invoked in support of some of the most abysmal kinds of immorality."[210] This is why the New Atheists insist that "religion is evil because many bad deeds have been done by religious people."[211]

This raises two important questions about possible links between religion and morality. The first is - Do religious people have stronger morals than non-religious people? Daniel Dennett insists that he has found "no evidence to support the claim that people, religious or not, who *don't* believe in reward in heaven and/or punishment in hell are more likely to kill, rape, rob, or break their promises than people who do. The prison population in the United States shows Catholics, Protestants, Jews, Muslims, and others – including those with no religious affiliation – represented about as they are in the general population."[212] The second question is this - Would morality collapse if religion declines or disappears? Even Richard Dawkins dismisses the idea that, "should belief in God suddenly vanish from the world, we would all become callous and selfish hedonists, with no kindness, no charity, no generosity, nothing that would deserve the name of goodness."[213]

In *The God Delusion* Dawkins attempts to explain morality as a purely natural phenomenon, "the product of impersonal evolutionary invention rather than a free human response to an eternal goodness,"[214] as John Haught summarises. Dawkins believes that "our sense of right and wrong can be derived from our Darwinian past."[215] His argument is based on the proposition that acting morally, particularly acting in unselfish ways, brings evolutionary advantages. In Haught's words, according to this way of looking at things "biology indicates that we are moral because being good has contributed to human gene survival. Thus, no need for theological accounts exists. ... [and moral virtues exist because of] unintended, accidental genetic occurrences that programmed some of our ancestors to be more cooperative and altruistic than others."[216]

Haught points out, however, that Dawkins' evolutionary line of explanation is incomplete and self-contradictory, because "after all, a blind, indifferent, and amoral natural process, which is how Dawkins has always characterised evolution, can hardly explain why justice, love, and the pursuit of truth are now unconditionally binding virtues."[217] David Robertson rubs salt in the wound by pointing out that Dawkins' "absolute Darwinian philosophy cannot logically and consistently argue for morality because, to put it bluntly, there is no good or evil. ... the atheist basis of morality [is] no justice, no rhyme nor reason, no purpose, no evil, no God, just blind pitiless indifference."[218]

New Atheist writers argue that religion causes many social and political problems. This raises another important question - would the end of religion lead to an end to such things as violence, social tension and discrimination? Alister McGrath dismisses that proposition as a "simplistic belief ... [that is] sociologically naïve. It fails to take account of the way in which human beings create values and norms, and make sense of their identity and their surroundings."[219]

Health and well-being

Does religion make us healthier, live longer, or both? Richard Dawkins acknowledges, doubtless through gritted teeth, that there is reliable evidence that "religious belief protects people from stress-related diseases"[220] and prolongs life.

In recent decades scientific studies have established a variety of positive relationships between people's health and their religious beliefs and practices. For example, studies in the USA have shown that "men and women who practice any mainstream faith live longer, have fewer strokes, less heart disease, better immune system function, and lower blood pressure than the population at large."[221] It is not just physical well-being that benefits from religious engagement, because research also shows that religious individuals have lower than average rates of drug abuse, alcoholism, divorce, anxiety, depression, and suicide.[222]

These relationships between religion and well-being are likely to be indirect, working via the attitudes and behaviours that religion fosters which tend to be inherently healthy. These include more healthy approaches than in the general population to such things as promiscuous sex, drugs, and alcohol use, along with lifestyles of moderation and domestic stability.[223]

Secularisation

The word 'secular' means "worldly rather than spiritual"[224] and since the 1960s sociologists in Europe and the United States have welcomed the process of secularisation and the spread of secularism, the decline in religious belief or observance.

As Carolyn Ogden points out, the term secularism "is often used to describe the decline in overt religious observance, such as church attendance, or in adherence to a traditional, established religion, often a result of today's greater freedom from convention. It need not necessarily be assumed that religion or a sense of the divine is in decline."[225] Harvard sociologist Harvey Cox argued that "secularisation simply bypasses and undercuts religion and goes on to other things ... The gods of traditional religions live on as fetishes for the patrons of congenial groups, but they play no significant role in the public life of the secular metropolis."[226]

Religious observance in Europe started to decline dramatically during the 1960s, as increasing numbers of people stopped going to church. Organised religion was increasingly seen as old-fashioned and irrelevant, and it struggled to compete with science in offering rational explanations of how people and planet came into being, how they operate, and what the future has in store for them.

This was an era of sweeping social and cultural change in which, as Karen Armstrong reminds us, "many of the institutional structures of modernity were pulled down: censorship was relaxed; abortion and homosexuality were legalised; divorce became easier; the women's movement campaigned for gender equality; and the young railed against the modern ethos of their parents."[227] It has been argued that secularisation in industrial Western societies was in part a response to the gradual upgrading of education and diffusion of science.[228] Whilst surveys have shown that within particular countries the most educated people are often the least religious,[229] "there is no consistent relation between the degree of scientific advance in a country or culture and a reduced profile of religious influence, belief and practice."[230]

Christian sociologists Brian Walsh and Richard Middleton argue that secularism saw traditional forms of religion replaced by what they call "the gods of our age":[231]

[i]   Scientism: the belief that all truth is scientific truth and science is our best way of knowing how things really are;

[ii] Technicism: the technical mastery of nature, which "translates scientific discovery into human power"[232]; and

[iii] Economism: which "regards economics as the main factor in society"[233] and assumes that all economic choices are driven simply by the pursuit of material prosperity.

Religion was also under attack from the emergence of alternative ways of 'explaining' reality and uncovering ultimate meaning, particularly in popular culture.

Numbers and trends are quite clear. For example, historian Callum Brown describes how, "in unprecedented numbers, the British people since the 1960s have stopped going to church, have allowed their church membership to lapse, have stopped marrying in church and have neglected to baptise their children. ... Since then a formerly religious people have entirely forsaken organised Christianity in a sudden plunge into a truly secular condition."[234] Over the last 25 years in Britain the number of people describing themselves as Christian has fallen from 66 per cent to 50 per cent.[235]

What the numbers actually mean is rather less clear. Sociologists are divided over whether the statistics point to a wholesale abandonment of religion (marked by declining attendance, observance, membership, and baptism)[236] or to a move towards more privatised forms of religion (in which people continue to watch *Songs of Praise* on tv and listen to *Thought for the Day* on the radio, but stop attending church services).[237]

German philosopher Martin Heidegger[238] preferred the expression "the transition to godlessness ... the state of indecision about God and the gods"[239] to the term secularisation. This seems a better way of describing what was more a general drift of people away from organised religion than an organised walk-out or revolution.

Few who drifted away became militant atheists; most of the loss of people in church can probably be accounted for by indifference rather than hostility. The default assumption appears to be that 'religion is OK so long as it's not compulsory, or does not interfere with the lives of ordinary folks going about their business. Let the religious ones get on with their lives, and let me get on with mine.' Put simply, an increasing number of people regard the idea of God as irrelevant, either as a general proposition or as having any meaningful impact on the day-to-day reality of their lives.

CHAPTER 4

GOD IN THE DOCK

"In a world where cinemas and clubs pull in more people in an hour than most churches will see in a week, are we becoming faithless? … In a world obsessed with image, money and who's at number one in the chart this week, God simply isn't cool enough to register on most people's radar."

Leigh Ramsden (1994)

To many people the idea of God sits uneasy alongside contemporary lifestyles and ways of thinking about 'truth' and 'reality'. Credibility of belief in God is increasingly being questioned in an era in which God is seen by many people as irrelevant to their day-to-day reality.

Since the start of the twentieth century observers have commented on the decline in organised religion, and surveys have revealed declining belief and interest in God. The attack on God has, if anything, intensified over the last decade or so, as the quiet indifference that is typical of secularisation (as we saw in Chapter 3) has given way to full-frontal attacks. The most vociferous debate about and criticism of God in recent years has come from two directions - from the New Atheists, and from scientists and others who put their faith in science. We will look at these two groups in the two chapters after this one.

God on trial

CS Lewis coined the expression *God in the Dock* in an article he wrote in 1948 in defence of orthodox Christianity; he also later used it as the title of a book.[240] Lewis argued that "man is on the bench and God is in the dock,"[241] on trial because of the difficulty Christian believers face in presenting their faith effectively to modern unbelievers.

The case against God rests on two key arguments. The first is that God simply does not exist, the idea is an illusion or, as Richard Dawkins prefers, a delusion. The second is that, if God *does* exist, he cannot be a loving God (as Christians claim) if he allows the inequality, cruelty and suffering we see all around us.

In a nutshell, on the first argument the defence team argues that God does exist, while the prosecution team points to the lack of reliable evidence that would stand up in a court of law, and insists that the argument that God exists must be thrown out. On the second argument, the defence team argues that the case rests on an inappropriate understanding of the nature of God, while the prosecution team argues that God should be brought to trial for crimes against humanity. An interesting US legal test case against God was reported in 2011. It was brought by Nebraska Senator Ernie Chambers, who had sought a permanent injunction to prevent the "death, destruction and terrorisation" caused by God. Judge Marlon Polk dismissed the case, ruling that legal papers could not be served because the defendant [God] has no address.[242]

The case for the defence has been presented over the years by a large group of believers and theologians. Useful witness statements along the way include David Jenkins' short *Guide to the Debate about God* (1966) which dealt with the *nature* of God, and Martin Prozesky's *New Guide to the Debate about God* (1992) which explored the *existence* of God. Articulate and persuasive defenders of the faith today whose writings I have found particularly useful include "former nun, amateur theologian, religious intellectual, and now a self-proclaimed 'freelance monotheist'"[243] Karen Armstrong, whose *A History of God* (1994) and *The Case for God* (2009) are veritable tours-de-force, and physicist-turned-theologian Alister McGrath whose many excellent books include *The Twilight of Atheism* (2004) and *The Dawkins delusion* (2007). We will look in detail at the arguments for God in Chapter 7.

The prosecution case has been outlined in recent years by the New Atheists and championed by Richard Dawkins who (as we saw in Chapter 3) characterises the God of the Bible as "arguably the most unpleasant character in all fiction."[244] Expert witnesses called by the prosecution team include prominent twentieth-century atheists, including Bertrand Russell, Sir Alfred (Freddie) Ayer, Jean-Paul Sartre, Albert Camus, Martin Heidegger and Anthony Flew.[245] We will return to the New Atheists' arguments in Chapter 5. In the rest of this chapter we will consider other arguments against God which have been put forward particularly by philosophers over the last century or so.

Both sides in the trial are well-entrenched and see their opponents as misguided, dangerous and delusional. Philosopher Simon Blackburn describes how religious people tend to view non-believers as "materialists, egoists, relativists, nihilists, amoralists, libertines, and no doubt in the privacy of our own homes cannibals and child molesters. For only God stands between humanity and these things. In reply, the militant wing of secularism talks freely of superstition, ignorance, bigotry, self-deception, stupidity, tribalism and rank hypocrisy. It is not an edifying debate, although sometimes rather fun."[246]

It is not unknown for people to change sides in the debate, even high-profile expert witnesses, as we shall see in Chapter 9. A prominent case in point is British philosopher Anthony Flew whose writings "helped set the agenda for atheism for half a century."[247] For most of his life he was regarded as "the world's most notorious atheist"[248], but then he changed his mind and in 2007 wrote a book called *There is a God: how the world's most notorious atheist changed his mind.*[249]

God has been "in the dock" for more than a century and remains there today. There is no sign that the trial is likely to come to an end any time soon, for the jury of popular opinion to reach its final verdict in the foreseeable future, despite the best efforts of the New Atheists to kick the idea of God into the long grass.

Death of God

As Enlightenment thinking took hold from the late seventeenth century onwards and modern science emerged as a force to be reckoned with, traditional religion and the idea of God came under attack. The path towards agnosticism and atheism, which emerged during the nineteenth century, was a long and bumpy one. But a number of influential writers pointed to the way ahead.

An early challenge to traditional ideas of God came in the late seventeenth century through the writing of Jewish-Dutch philosopher Baruch Spinoza (1632-1677). In his book *Ethics* Spinoza "saw revealed religion as inferior to the scientific knowledge of God acquired by the philosopher."[250] He saw the existence of God as necessary "because it alone provided the certainty and confidence necessary to make other deductions about reality."[251] To him God represents the laws and general principles that govern all aspects of the world around us; he argued that "it's impossible for God not to exist."[252] Because he viewed God as inherent and immanent in all things, Spinoza is often accused of being a pantheist or even an atheist, but as Karen Armstrong points out "he did have a belief in God, even though this was not the God of the Bible."[253]

A century later, in 1768, French Enlightenment writer Voltaire (real name François-Marie Arouet; 1694-1778) wrote about the invention of God and gave his successors an infamous sound-bite which has been widely quoted and generally taken out of context. In 2007 New Atheist Christopher Hitchens followed fashion in quoting him, writing "though I dislike to differ with such a great man, Voltaire was simply ludicrous when he said that if god did not exist it would be necessary to invent him. The human invention of god is the problem to begin with."[254] Alister McGrath gives the full quotation of what Voltaire wrote in 1768 - "If the heavens, stripped of their noble imprint, could ever cease to reveal Him, if God did not exist, it would be necessary to invent him, whom the sages proclaim, and whom kings adore."[255]

In the early nineteenth century German philosopher Georg Wilhelm Friedrich Hegel (1770-1831) rejected the God of Judaism as "a tyrant who required unquestioning submission to an intolerable Law."[256] In *The Phenomenology of Mind* (1817) Hegel replaced the traditional idea of God with the idea of a Spirit or a life-force, which depended on the world and on people.

Equally controversial were the views of his contemporary, German philosopher Arthur Schopenhauer (1789-1860), whose book *The World as Will and Idea* was published two years later in 1819.[257] Schopenhauer believed that there is neither God nor spirit at work in the world, only human instinct and the will-to-live. He argued that, "since there was no 'God' to save us, only art, music and a discipline of renunciation and compassion could bring us a measure of serenity."[258]

German philosopher Ludwig Andreas von Feuerbach (1804-1872), a student of Hegel, developed his master's ideas further.[259] In *The Essence of Christianity* (1841) Feuerbach argued that God does not actually exist. He saw the *idea* of God as a projection of human longings, invented or dreamed up by humans to provide much-needed metaphysical and spiritual consolation, "a misguided means of comforting itself during life's dark and shadowy journey."[260] Alister McGrath emphasises Feuerbach's view that "God was not someone that humanity discovered or encountered, but 'a dream of the human soul', a pure invention, the product of a mind that could reject God with equal ease."[261] In *The Essence of Christianity* (1841) Feuerbach wrote that "to be human is divine. The idea of God is the idea of ourselves – purified, enlarged, and made 'other'."[262] He insisted that there is no God, "only ourselves and our highest moral ideals which we transfer on to that imaginary God."[263]

As the nineteenth century unfolded, these challenges to religion and the idea of God started to undermine received wisdoms. By mid-century God found himself well and truly "in the dock".

Undisputed champion of this emerging new way of thinking, which had neither need nor space for God, was German philosopher Friedrich Wilhelm Nietzsche (1844-1900).[264] In *The Gay Science* (1882) Nietzsche announced that God was dead, an expression he borrowed from Hegel. Nietzsche used the parable of a madman who, when asked where he thought God had gone, shouted out "We have killed him, - you and I! We are all his murderers!"[265] New Atheist Christopher Hitchens dismissed the pronouncement that 'God is dead' as "histrionic and self-contradictory."[266] Alister McGrath points out that Nietzsche did not base his conclusions on arguments for or against the existence of God, but noted as "a simple matter of fact that God is gradually being eliminated from modern culture. Whether this is right or wrong, good or bad, it is happening. As a matter of observable fact, Nietzsche suggested, Western culture has ceased to find belief in God plausible."[267] In his next book, *Thus Spake Zarathustra* (1883), Nietzsche "looked forward to the advent of the superman, who would completely reject Christian values such as mercy and submissiveness, and incarnate in himself the pure will to power, in a life serene and pitiless, strong and free."[268] He argued that people only believe in God because they are too afraid not to, because they are unable to manage without the comfort of the idea of God. God was born out of human weakness but became a religious trap which people slavishly fell into, and through this slave mentality people allowed God to become manipulative and oppressive.[269] But as people embrace life and live it as best they can, they become strong enough to reject God, thus they have killed him.[270]

While these German philosophers were highly influential in raising serious questions about the existence and relevance of God, they were not the only people to launch full-frontal attacks on the idea of God and the practice of organised religion.

Austrian doctor and psychiatrist Sigmund Freud (1856-1939), the founding father of psychoanalysis, saw religion as the product of wishful thinking, an illusion based on the longing for a father-figure[271]. In *The Future of an Illusion* (1927), Freud dismissed belief in God as "an illusion that mature men and women should lay aside."[272] He explained the idea of God as a projection constructed by the subconscious mind, arising from "infantile yearnings for a powerful, protective father, for justice and fairness and for life to go on for ever. God is simply a projection of these desires, feared and worshipped by human beings out of an abiding sense of helplessness."[273] Freud looked on faith as "a neurotic illusion created and accepted unconsciously by the human mind as a comfort against the pain and dread which would cripple us if we actually faced up to the facts of our existence."[274] He argued that "religious belief amounts to a kind of social neurosis … Belief in God is something of which we should be cured."[275] Like many people subsequently, Freud believed that science could and should take God's place.

Another psychiatrist, this time Swiss, had a much more sympathetic view of religion. Carl Gustav Jung (1875-1961) dismissed Freud's explanation of religion as the result of human drives "as a direct product of nineteenth-century scientific atheism which, he believed, had been responsible for misunderstanding the whole nature of the human psyche."[276] Instead, Jung's clinical experience led him to write of "the notion of the 'collective unconscious', a store of images (archetypes) common to all people, which enable them to interpret their experiences. Religion was an important factor in the life of the psyche, because it provided images that helped the individual to find personal spiritual integrity and inner peace. Religion was thus an important source of the wisdom essential for mental well-being."[277]

German philosopher and revolutionary socialist Karl Marx (1818-83) also argued that God is a product of the human mind, but created in response to social and economic alienation, not spiritual concerns.[278] Marx saw people as trapped and alienated in social, political and economic structures dictated by the class system, which repress and exploit them and mean that their well-being and happiness lie in the hand of others. Little wonder, then, that people look to religion for consolation as they daily confront painful realities. In *Contribution to the critique of Hegel's Philosophy of Law* (1843-44) Marx described religion memorably as "the sigh of an oppressed creature, the heart of a heartless world, just as it is the spirit of a spiritless situation. It is the *opium* of the people [my italics]."[279] Marx argued that the consolation is an illusion, "an expression of social distress, a turning to another world for comfort and consolation, ... [that] becomes a distraction from the real task of fighting against the causes of distress, poverty and injustice here and now."[280] Karen Armstrong points out that, to Marx, "since there was no meaning, value or purpose outside the historical process, the idea of God could not help humanity. Atheism, the negation of God, was also a waste of time."[281]

Like Feuerbach, French sociologist Émile Durkheim (1858-1917) also adopted an anthropological approach to religion and explained it in naturalistic terms. In *The Elementary Forms of the Religious Life* (1912) Durkheim described religion as "a unified system of beliefs and practices ... which unite into one moral community called a Church, all those who adhere to them."[282] He saw God not as a transcendent reality but a projection; "the 'beliefs, myths, dogmas and legends' of religion are projections on to a supernatural being which arise from collective human experience."[283] As Caroline Ogden describes it, Durkheim's idea of God was "society's projection of itself, with collective self-enhancing rituals acquiring sacredness and then being objectified into the worship of a supreme being."[284]

One of the most critical twentieth-century writers on the idea of God was German philosopher Martin Heidegger (1899-1976), who believed there is no God, just what he called Nothing (*das Nichts*). He argued that we are on our own, and must find our own way through life with all its challenges. Heidegger believed in "a sort of infinite horizon which relativises all our finite anxieties and concerns, and bundles them up into one gigantic

Angst, anxiety in the face of Nothing. ... [which] is overcome by having the courage to commit oneself to a possibility which, though bounded by death, is uniquely and authentically ours. We find our individual vocation not in relation to a tyrannical or a paternalistic god, but in relation to that unbounded horizon ... which summons each individual being to its own unique realisation."[285]

French existentialist philosopher Jean-Paul Sartre (1905-1980) shared many of Heidegger's views; both were heavily influenced by Kierkegaard's writings. As British theologian Keith Ward points out, Sartre was one of a number of continental philosophers who were "glad to be rid of God ... the hidden watcher, always observing what you were doing, so that you could never escape the censorious eye of the almighty. ... [in Sartre's view] Life is absurd, it has no meaning, objectively speaking. It is for us to give it meaning ourselves, in whatever way we choose."[286]

Radical theology

Karen Armstrong notes that, "by the end of the [nineteenth] century, a significant number of people were beginning to feel that, if God was not yet dead, it was the duty of rational, emancipated human beings to kill him."[287] Ironically, the assassination was attempted not by scientists and philosophers, but by theologians. They described their new approach as 'radical theology', arguably stretching the definition of 'radical' beyond breaking point! The enemy within struck first, it struck hard, and it struck very publicly.

US theologians Thomas Altizer and William Hamilton explain what they mean by the term 'radical theology' – "It is really that we do not know, do not adore, do not possess, do not believe in God. It is not just that a capacity has dried up in us; ... God is dead. We are not talking about the absence of the experience of God, but about the experience of the absence of God."[288] They clarify that "it is, in effect, an attempt to set an atheist point of view within the spectrum of Christian possibilities. ... The aim of the new theology is not simply to seek relevance or contemporaneity for its own sake but to strike for a whole new way of theological understanding."[289]

The cover of the 8 April 1966 edition *Time* magazine was striking; the words "Is God dead?" were printed large and bold in red, against a black background. The cover story was based on more than 300 interviews with leading theologians from around the world. As Alister McGrath comments, "although the article focused primarily on a few relatively unknown theologians who had launched a theology that everyone suspected was stillborn and was going precisely nowhere, it raised broader issues. ... Was America entering a new secular era, in which God would merely be a memory of an increasingly distant past?"[290]

Michael Shermer, an agnostic, sees the *Time* magazine article and the public debate it triggered as very much products of their day, pointing out that "by 1966 the most turbulent decade in memory was in full rage as the baby-boomer generation flexed its moral (and immoral) muscles against the conservative establishment's vision of America as a God-fearing nation. Political assassinations, campus rebellions, inner-city riots, mass demonstrations, sex, drugs, rock 'n' roll, and especially the Vietnam war led many disillusioned Americans down a nihilistic path into existential angst."[291]

To the great relief of more mainstream theologians, this brand of radical theology was short-lived and did not really catch on. Karen Armstrong dismisses it as "flawed: it was essentially a white, middle-class, affluent and – sometimes offensively – Christian theology."[292] Alister McGrath reports that "after discovering that the death of God did not, after all, mean that America had ceased to believe in God, the media lost interest in the movement."[293]

Whilst the 'death of God' discourse appeared to largely run out of steam within a matter of years, echoes of the theological ferment of the period survive. Students of the intellectual history of the 1960s will be particularly interested in the controversial but influential book *Honest to God*, published in 1963 by English theologian and Anglican Bishop of Woolwich John Robinson. Robinson suggested that Christians should abandon the traditional idea of "a God 'out there' coming to earth like some visitor from outer space [which] underlies every popular presentation of the Christian drama of salvation, whether from the pulpit or the presses."[294] He thought that, instead of thinking of God as a supernatural being somewhere 'out there' or 'up there' – the very basis of the theistic religious tradition (as we saw in Chapter 3) – it makes more sense to think of God as "that which matters most" in our personal existence.[295] This controversial idea is based on existential theologian Paul Tillich's notion of God as "the ground of our being."[296] Robinson wondered if "perhaps after all the Freudians are right, that such a God – the God of traditional popular theology – *is* a projection, and perhaps we are being called to live without that projection in any form."[297] Robinson's central message was stark: as Alister McGrath puts it, bluntly, "Christianity had to update itself – or die. There was no shortage of those expecting the latter."[298]

Another British theologian, Don Cupitt, went much further than John Robinson in arguing that religion is so badly broken that it cannot be fixed or repaired. In his controversial book *After God* (1997) Cupitt argued that "all our present major religious traditions are now coming to an end, just as the once very grand religions of ancient Mesopotamia, Egypt, and Greece came to an end in antiquity. As happened in the previous cases, we may expect that something of the great works of art will survive but virtually nothing of the doctrine."[299] He thought that "in the future we will see our religion not as supernatural doctrine but as an experiment in selfhood."[300]

Writer and biographer AN Wilson, in his book *God's Funeral* (the title borrowed from the title of a poem by Thomas Hardy written between 1918 and 1919) traces the course of this disappearing act by God in Victorian Britain in response to three sets of factors.[301] One was the influence of popular writers like Charles Dickens, George Elliot, John Ruskin, Matthew Arnold and Thomas Carlyle who were raising serious questions about whether there remained good reason to hang on to old-fashioned ideas about the existence, nature and relevance of God. Secondly, developments in science were revealing fascinating details about the world around us, and opening up intriguing new avenues of inquiry. For example, in his ground-breaking *Principles of Geology* (1830-33) Charles Lyell stretched the age of the earth back much further than the few thousand years implied in the Biblical account of creation, and in the even more ground-breaking *The Origin of Species* (1859) Charles Darwin put forward his evolutionary hypothesis, which directly contradicted that Biblical account of divine creation. The third factor was the new scholarly approaches to the Bible which were emerging, which opened up the possibility of reading the 'good book' in terms of myth, allegory, poetry, and so on, rather than just literally.

The effects were far-reaching and long-lasting. As Karen Armstrong points out, "Europeans were beginning to experience religion as tenuous, arbitrary and lifeless. ... The unthinkable had happened: everything that the symbol of God had pointed to – absolute goodness, beauty, order, peace, truthfulness, justice – was being slowly but surely eliminated from European culture. Morality would no longer be measured by reference to an ultimate value that transcended human interests, but simply by the needs of the moment."[302] Alister McGrath adds that, "politically and socially, Christianity remained highly significant in national life, and would remain so until after the First World War. Yet its ideas were increasingly seen as discredited, unattractive, and outdated by its novelists, poets, and artists. Christianity had been tried and tested at the imaginative and rational levels, and found wanting on both counts."[303]

Despite concerted efforts from a variety of directions, by the end of the twentieth century no-one had delivered the knock-out blow to God, although his opponents and critics certainly felt that they had him up against the ropes.

God as an invention

As we have seen, many nineteenth century philosophers argued that God is an invention, simply an idea dreamed up by humans as a way of helping us to cope with the difficulties, uncertainties and unknowns of living in the world. This is an article of faith of the New Atheists (as we shall see in Chapter 5) and of many of today's scientists (Chapter 6).

New Atheist Christopher Hitchens wrote that "the mildest criticism of religion is also the most radical and the most devastating one. Religion is man-made. Even the men who made it cannot agree on what their prophets or redeemers or gurus actually said or did."[304] He added that "a consistent proof that religion is man-made and anthropomorphic can also be found in the fact that it is usually 'man' made, in the sense of masculine, as well."[305] Fellow New Atheist Daniel Dennett insisted that religion is a natural phenomenon, by which he means "religion is natural as opposed to *supernatural* [his emphasis], that is it is a human phenomenon composed of events, organisms, objects, structures, patterns, and the like that all obey the laws of physics or biology, and hence do not involve miracles."[306] Richard Dawkins concluded that "religion is nothing more than a useless, and sometime dangerous, evolutionary accident."[307]

The New Atheists claim support for their view of God as an invention from scientific studies of religion, particularly those done by anthropologists trained in evolutionary theory and cognitive psychology. Examples of scientists who explain religion as a by-product of normal psychological and social processes include anthropologist Pascal Boyer in the book *Religion Explained* (2002), psychologist Justin Barrett in *Why would Anyone Believe in God?* (2004), ethnologist Robert Hinde in *Why Gods Persist* (2009), and David Lewis-Williams in *Conceiving God: the Cognitive Origin and Evolution of Religion* (2010).

Daniel Dennett argues that "Boyer lists more than half a dozen distinct cognitive systems that feed effects into this recipe for religion – an agent-detector, a memory-manager, a cheater-detector, a moral-intuition-generator, a sweet tooth for stories and storytelling, various alarm systems, and what I [Dennett] call intentional stance. Any mind with this particular set of thinking tools and biases is bound to harbour something like a religion sooner or later, he claims."[308] In his book *In Gods We Trust* (2004), American anthropologist Scott Atran argues that "religions do not exist apart from the individual minds that constitute them and the environments that constrain them, any more than biological species and varieties exist independently of the individual organisms that compose them and the environments that conform them."[309]

Believers naturally dismiss the claim that God does not actually exist, and they argue that there are sound reasons for rejecting the idea of God as a figment of the imagination. Alister McGrath concedes that to non-believers "the idea of God was an entirely understandable invention, which might even be useful in consoling weaker and foolish souls who were naïve enough to believe in it."[310] As well as consolation, he recognises that the idea of God offers humans some sense of control. He writes that "God was a human creation over which humanity had authority and control. ... God was not someone that humanity discovered or encountered, but a dream of the human soul, a pure invention, the product of a mind that could reject God with equal ease."[311]

Many critics have pointed to the lack of evidence to support the argument that God was invented. British material scientist Edgar Andrews insists that "it is not, in fact, an explanation at all. It doesn't explain religious concepts, religious experience or the almost universal religious instinct of mankind, ancient or modern."[312] American theologian John Haught accepts that "looking for an evolutionary understanding of religion is ... theologically unobjectionable. ... (For Dennett and Dawkins] a naturalistic understanding of religion leaves no meaningful room at all for plausible theological accounts of why most people are religious. ... [to the New Atheists] Science alone can tell us what religion is really all about, and it can provide better answers than theology to every important question people ask. According to Dawkins, science is even qualified to decide whether or not God exists."[313]

Alister McGrath dismisses the naturalist explanation of religion offered by Dennett and Dawkins as "highly contrived and unpersuasive."[314] He concludes that in the end it is a circular argument, which presupposes its conclusions. It begins from the assumption that there is no God, and then proceeds to show that an explanation of God can be offered which is entirely consistent with this."[315]

Dawkins in the dock

If God is an invention, why has the idea of God persisted? Why won't religion and God simply go away, if they are illusions or delusions, as the New Atheists insist?

Richard Dawkins (an evolutionary biologist by training, profession and instinct) claims to have the answer - Darwinian evolution. He argues that - even though God does not exist, the idea of God is a delusion, and religion is a natural not a supernatural phenomenon - the idea of God and the practice of religion have survived because they are passed down from generation to generation, just like physical traits such as hair colour and eye colour can be passed on from parents to children. Indeed, Dawkins goes as far as to propose a "general theory of religion" which offers "an ultimate explanation for the true origins of religion."[316]

Memes and replicators

Dawkins explanation of religion is firmly rooted in Darwin's ideas about evolution by natural selection based on competitive advantage. Darwin proposed that individuals who are better adapted to the prevailing environment are more likely to survive than those who are less well-adapted, so they are more likely to breed and pass on their genes to their successors. Ill-adapted traits tend to die out because they are not so widely inherited, since individuals with them are less likely to survive, breed and pass them on.

Dawkins' 'explanation' rests on two key ideas - a particular idea of natural replicators, and the general idea of 'accidental byproducts'. Both ideas have attracted a great deal of criticism from scientists.

A replicator is a mechanism by which things are copied and passed on from one generation to the next. In biology the gene is the key replicator, but Dawkins proposes the cultural equivalent of a gene, which he calls the meme. He first proposed the term (derived from the Greek *mimēma*, meaning "something imitated") in his 1976 book *The Selfish Gene*. He uses the term meme to describe "a unit of cultural inheritance."[317]

Dawkins visualises a meme as an idea, belief or belief system, or pattern of behaviour that spreads throughout a culture by passing from one person to another, rather like a contagious disease (such as measles). He suggests that things like tunes, catchphrases, ideas, clothes, fashions, ways of making posts or building arches, stitches in knitting, knots in ropes or fishing nets, origami folding patterns, and useful tricks in carpentry or pottery are examples of memes.

The general idea of memes has been further developed by Daniel Dennett in *Consciousness Explained* (1993) and by British psychologist Susan Blackmore in *The Meme Machine* (1999). Supporters of the Dawkins meme model argue that memes are passed on through children and their social conditioning. For example, Daniel Dennett points out that "speaking one's 'mother tongue', singing, being polite, and many other 'socializing' skills are transmitted culturally from parents to offspring ... Children grow up speaking their parents' language and, in almost all cases, identifying with their parents' religion."[318]

Dawkins compares the religion meme (which he insists exists) to a virus, in this case a 'virus of the mind' which, like a natural virus, can be spread from person to person by carriers and contact. Resorting to typically intemperate language he writes that, "once infected, the child will grow up and infect the next generation with the same nonsense, whatever it happens to be."[319]

Dawkins goes an important and equally contentious step further, arguing that religious belief and behaviour are examples of an 'accidental byproduct'. By that he means that religion is not an evolutionary adaptation in itself; the process of natural selection did not lead to the inheritance of religion *per se*, but to the inheritance of some other competitive benefit that "only incidentally manifests itself as religious behaviour."[320] This is why Dawkins argues that religious faith is "a misfiring of something useful."[321]

What was that 'something useful'? Dawkins speculates that it was the ability of our remote ancestors to detect predators. As John Haught puts it, the Dawkins' line of reasoning is that "we have inherited the kinds of brains that can easily attract and cultivate ideas about those ridiculous hidden agents we call gods or God. ... Having an excitable agency detection system makes our brains congenial hosts to the parasitic illusions of religion, even in an age of science."[322]

However it initially developed, Dawkins believes that "the meme for blind faith secures its own perpetuation by the simple unconscious expedient of discouraging rational inquiry."[323] He argues that this starts in childhood and that "natural selection builds child brains with a tendency to believe whatever their parents and tribal elders tell them. Such trusting obedience is valuable for survival. ... But the flip side of trusting obedience is slavish gullibility. The inevitable by-product is vulnerability to infection by mind viruses. ... And, very likely, when the child grows up and has children of her own, she will naturally pass the whole lot on to her own children – nonsense as well as sense ..."[324]

Critique

The notion of memes is a key pillar in Dawkins' logic in 'explaining' the development and persistence of religion. If the idea falls, then his central thesis in *The God Delusion* loses much of its intellectual rationale and foundation, and his arguments start to look very shaky. The stakes are high!

Despite Dawkins' confidence in promoting his ideas about memes, they remain what John Haught calls "novel and extremely controversial."[325] The ideas have attracted a great deal of criticism from well-informed commentators. A leading critic has been Alister McGrath, who dismisses Dawkins' idea of the meme and his view of God as a 'virus of the mind' as "two of the most unpersuasive, pseudoscientific ideas to have made their appearance in discussions of the roots of religion in recent years."[326]

The most common criticism is the lack of any direct evidence for the existence of memes. They remain just an idea, and a "highly speculative" one at that, according to Alister McGrath, who bemoans that fact that "we find speculation and supposition taking the place of the rigorous evidence-driven and evidence-based arguments that we have a right to expect."[327] With a nod towards the 'God of the Gaps' argument that we will consider in Chapter 6, David Robertson accuses Dawkins of constructing "a 'science of the gaps' just making things up as you go along in order to fit everything into your all-encompassing evolutionary theory."[328]

Critics also point to the lack of scientific credibility of Dawkins' ideas. No scientific research has been done to test the idea of memes, which challenges scientific orthodoxy. Few scientists attach any weight to the idea. Alister McGrath emphasises that "the mainstream scientific community views it as a decidedly flaky idea, best relegated to the margins."[329] David Robertson quotes Simon Conway, Professor of Evolutionary Paleobiology at the University of Cambridge, who points out that "memes are trivial, to be banished by simple mental exercises. In any wider context, they are hopelessly, if not hilariously, simplistic."[330] Even agnostic Michael Shermer points out that Dawkins offers no operational definition of a meme, or any testable model for how memes are thought to influence culture.[331] John Cornwell argues that the idea of memes "pushes the envelope more in terms of propaganda than of science."[332]

Dawkins' desire to isolate brain activity as the locus of the "religion meme" is no big deal, given that all human experience and behaviour - not just religious ones - are by definition centred in and shaped by the brain. David Robertson rhetorically asks Dawkins "if it [the idea of memes] were true, then your own ideas, including Darwinian evolution, would be considered memes as well."[333] Alister McGrath points out that "Dawkins draws an absolute distinction between rational, scientific and evidence-based ideas, and spurious, irrational notions – such as religious beliefs. The latter, not the former, count as mental viruses. But who decides what is 'rational' and 'scientific'? ... [it seems] to depend on Dawkins' highly subjective personal judgement as to what was 'rational' or not."[334]

Dawkins' proposition that the "religion meme" is a "virus of the mind" is equally difficult to defend, both because of the lack of evidence and the circular argument it relies on. Alister McGrath dismisses it as "an essentially polemical construction, devised to discredit ideas that Dawkins does not like."[335] As McGrath points out, Dawkins starts with an analogy but seamlessly turns it into a reality, writing that "the analogy – belief in God is *like* a virus – then seems to assume ontological substance. Belief in

God *is* a virus of the mind."[336] Kathleen Jones takes Dawkins to task for simplistically linking memes and viruses, reminding us that "the replication of genes, natural viruses, infections and computer viruses involve very different processes, as he must know. ... A scientist who professes the Public Understanding of Science really must know the difference between these four processes."[337]

Other challenges to Dawkins' ideas centre on his approach of deliberately collapsing complexity into simplicity to suit his pre-existing argument. For example, John Cornwell insists that "anything so complex, social, and demanding of human imagination, relationships, and choices as religion defies reducibility to a single principle."[338] He elaborates further, writing "if an idea, such as the idea of God or a god, can be thought of as parallel to a gene it would mean that beliefs come in discrete packages. But this hardly makes sense because ideas, and especially religion, are generally untidy with multiple relationships and differences in complexity, emotions, depth of intellectual rigour, associations, and so forth. The word 'god' expresses a diversity of meanings, depending on cultural, philosophical, ethnic, and historical background. Belief itself, moreover, comes in a variety of shades of assent – from absolute conviction and commitment, to vague speculation bordering on scepticism."[339] Neuroscientist Andrew Newberg points out that Dawkins' ideas make no allowance for "mystical experience ... [and] a range of unitary experiences that are often interpreted as assurances that God exists."[340] Terry Eagleton dismisses Dawkins as "an old-fashioned, crassly reductive system builder ... Such reductive systems are incompatible with the freedom which Dawkins rightly champions. In this sense, his thought is in contradiction with itself."[341]

Critics have also questioned Dawkins' ideas about cultural evolution. Alister McGrath insists that "there is no reason to suppose that cultural evolution is Darwinian, or indeed that evolutionary biology has any particular value in accounting for the development of ideas."[342] Dawkins' idea of religion as an "accidental byproduct" of evolution has also come under fire, as logically inconsistent with the Darwinian model of evolution that Dawkins is such a passionate advocate of. As Alister McGrath reminds us, Darwinian evolution by natural selection includes no notion of purpose; indeed, as Dawkins has himself written, the universe has "no design, no purpose, no evil and no good, nothing but blind pitiless indifference."[343]

It is difficult to avoid the conclusion that accepting Dawkins' idea of memes and cultural replicators requires a leap of faith every bit as large as the leap of logic Dawkins thinks is required to believe in God. Alister McGrath rejects the idea of memes as "conceptually redundant ... [because] The observational data can be accounted for perfectly well by other models and mechanisms."[344]

What Dawkins does not allow for is the possibility that evolution might have operated in a much more direct way than via the unproven route of memes and replicators. Psychologist David Geaney suggests that religion might "have achieved its ubiquitous nature by conferring evolutionary advantage to the believers themselves."[345] Such a view is compatible with the evidence that believers tend to enjoy better health and well-being, and to live longer than their unbelieving peers (as we saw in Chapter 3).

God fights back

As Mark Twain famously said after reading his own obituary, "rumours of my death have been greatly exaggerated."[346] Despite the numerous attacks on God over the last two centuries, the idea of God still affects the lives of millions of people. Michael Shermer concedes that "never in history have so many, and such a high percentage of the population, believed in God. Not only is God not dead, as Nietzsche proclaimed, but he has never been more alive."[347] Alister McGrath points out that "religion has grown globally since the high-water mark of secularism in the 1970s, even in the heartlands of the West."[348]

CHAPTER 5

DOUBT AND DENIAL

"I think humans have always wrestled with the Divine Idea – an idea that
unites and separates, creates and destroys, consoles and terrifies. It is virtually
certain that religious belief is as old as our species. And it is equally possible
that uncertainty, doubt and scepticism about God have
existed since prehistoric times."

Robert Winston (2005)

For most people in most places throughout history God was taken for
granted, part of the furniture of life. Belief in God was inherited from
parents, participation in religious rituals and traditions was part of everyday
reality, and the existence and nature of God were rarely questioned. As
British journalist John Humphreys reminds us, "it is only relatively recently
that we have been able to question the existence of God and live to argue
another day. Through much of European history it has not been wise to
admit to doubt. At best you might find yourself cut off from polite society;
at worst you might find yourself dangling from iron hooks in a dank cellar
and be cut off in a more literal sense."[349]

Wrestling with God

Why doesn't everyone believe in God? If God exists and is as powerful
and all-encompassing as believers say, surely it's not beyond God to make
everyone believe automatically, to hard-wire every person everywhere with
religious belief from the moment they are born? Why give us a choice?
The answer to that simple question is complex, but in a nutshell … God
created (invented, made) humans not as thoughtless automatons or robots,

fully pre-programmed in every way, but as thinking, feeling individuals with free will and minds to think with. We were made with the ability to choose whether or not to believe that God exists, and what sort of God we decide to believe in.

Even if we are given a choice, why does everyone not appreciate the logic of believing in God, particularly given the apparent benefits of religion that we looked at in Chapter 3, and the fact that many people are aware of direct experiences of God?

Given these two phenomena - freedom to choose and appreciating the benefits - would it not make sense for everyone to believe in God? But the fact is that belief is far from universal, as we saw in Chapter 3; recall that in 2001 there were 2.1 billion Christians, 1.5 billion Muslims and 1.1 billion non-religious people worldwide. In 2008, nearly two in five (37 per cent) people in Britain described themselves as atheists or agnostics, compared with less than one in ten (8 per cent) people in America.[350] It is not simply a matter of sitting down, thinking it through, and then making an informed choice between believing and not believing, of weighing up the pros and cons and choosing the one that appears to offer the most.

Belief is a complex matter, reflecting the interplay of many different factors including family background, cultural setting, access to information, knowledge and understanding, and experience. George Smith lists several reasons why not everyone is a believer. For example, "one may have never encountered the concept of god before, or one may consider the idea of a supernatural being to be absurd, or one may think that there is no evidence to support the belief in a god."[351] Other factors include socialisation (many people today live in secular cultures), trust in science and rationality (many people unquestioningly adopt the Enlightenment world-view), and views on religious traditions and institutions (many people view the church, for example, as out of touch with modern culture, and many have had bad experiences with church).

Some idea just how complex belief is emerges in the findings of a survey in Britain that John Humphreys asked the internet polling organisation YouGov to carry out in 2007.[352] It was designed "to find out not just how many of us believe in God but what we mean when we talk about belief."[353] Of the 2,200 people who took part:

[i]   26 per cent agreed that "I believe in 'something' but I'm not sure what";

[ii] 22 per cent agreed that "I believe in a personal God who created the world and hears my prayers";

[iii] 16 per cent agreed that "I am an atheist. The whole notion of a supernatural God is nonsense";

[iv] 10 per cent agreed that "I'm not really sure what I believe and I don't give it much thought";

[v]   9 per cent agreed that "I am an agnostic. I don't think it is possible to know if there is a God or not"; and

[vi] 5 per cent agreed that "I would like to believe and I envy those who do but cannot believe for myself."[354]

Unbelief is far from unusual, even in countries which are usually thought of as 'religious'. This is partly because census information and national surveys usually categorise people by religion on the basis of how they see themselves, and for many people in many countries 'religion' has as much to do with cultural identity and 'tribal' affiliation as it has to do with personal religious beliefs and practices. The reality is that many people do not believe in the existence of God or gods.

Whatever the reasons for not believing in God, the consequences are clear. As increasing numbers of people no longer believe in God - or, more commonly, they reject religion but remain neutral on the question of God - secularisation spreads and deepens, and God gets pushed to the margins of society and culture. In extreme cases, people adopt atheistic perspectives and practices, which can become intolerant both of the idea of God and of people who believe in God.

Dynamics and spectrum

Much of the New Atheist writing adopts a simple binary view on the question of belief in God - either people do believe in God (in which case they are believers), or they don't (in which case they are atheists). But life is rarely as simple and clear-cut as that, in two particular ways in this context - many people struggle with doubts (for and against the idea of God), and many people change their position on the idea of God through time.

Robert Winston speaks for many when he writes that "virtually all of us have, at one time or another, irrespective of our background, education, training, profession or family, wrestled with God. Often this wrestling match starts when we are children, sometimes it is profound when we are adolescents, and for some the wrestling continues for most of their lives. For some, too, the wrestling is most violent when we are frightened, dismayed or distressed – or face death."[355] Doubt is a common experience even amongst those who say they believe, as we shall see in Chapter 9.

Many people regard the idea of God as a decision that can be postponed, perhaps indefinitely. Many see God and religion as the stuff of 'old women of both sexes', along with an interest in classical music and trips to museums and art galleries. They convince themselves that it can wait until they are older; they are having far too nice a time right now and have neither any interest in nor need for all that religion stuff.

Many people who previously believed chose to give up on the idea of God. As Marcus Borg puts it, "for some, this happens consciously because the notion of God begins to seem incredible and incapable of substantiation. For others, letting go of the notion of God is more functional than consciously thought out. God becomes largely irrelevant ... [and] the notion of God in fact plays no major role in their lives although they may agree in opinion polls that 'God exists'."[356]

People have different views on not believing in God. George Smith points out that "some men consider a godless world to be a terrifying prospect; others experience it as a refreshing, exhilarating challenge. How a person will react to atheism depends only on himself [sic] – and the extent to which he is willing to assume responsibility for his own choices and actions."[357] Krista Tippett underlines the fact that "spiritual questions don't go away, nor does the sense of wonder and mystery cease, in the absence of a belief in God. Nonreligious people are some of the most fervent seekers of our age, energetically crafting lives of meaning."[358]

In terms of religion we can categorise people in various ways. One obvious distinction is between those who believe in God (or, more broadly, who are religious) and those who don't (or aren't). But this is not 100 per cent watertight because between the convinced atheists and the convinced believers sit the unconvinced agnostics, and any individual is usually free to switch from one camp to the other if they wish to.

Blaise Pascal offered a slightly different typology, dividing people into three groups – "1. Those who know God and love him; 2. Those who do not know God but seek him; and 3. Those who neither know God nor seek him."[359] This also fails to capture any element of choice or dynamics in where people stand on the question of God.

In simple terms, everyone sits somewhere along a spectrum of beliefs, from very negative (hostile) through neutral (indifferent) to positive (acceptance) or even very positive (enthusiastic adoption). This spectrum is usually divided into three broad groups of people - atheists (confirmed non-believers), agnostics (who are not convinced one way or the other) and believers. The groups are generally assumed to be discrete or watertight, but in reality each group typically contains individuals with a range of different 'beliefs'. At either end of the spectrum sit the fundamentalists (both atheists and believers), and between them and the agnostics in the middle sit the liberals (again both atheists and believers).

Doubting God - agnosticism

Richard Dawkins is champion of the 'binary school' of religious belief, insisting on presenting a choice between only two positions (evolution versus belief in God) even though other positions are logically possible. Michael Poole calls this the "fallacy of the excluded middle"[360] and Krista Tippett writes of "the vast middle ... [where] faith is as much about questioning as it is about certainties. It is possible to be a believer and a listener at the same time, to be both fervent and searching, to nurture a vital identity and to wonder at the identities of others."[361]

The middle ground is occupied by agnosticism, which holds that the existence of God can be neither proven nor disproved. It represents "a religious orientation of doubt; a denial of ultimate knowledge of the existence of God"[362], and it means the same thing as scepticism (the belief that the truth of all religious claims is "unknown and unknowable"[363]). The word agnostic was coined by Thomas Huxley in 1869 from the Greek *agnostos*, from *a*- (not) and *gnostos* (to be known);[364] it literally means "not knowing."

Agnosticism describes uncertainty about the existence of God, and it contrasts with confident belief that God does not exist (atheism). Atheist George Smith points out that, "properly considered, agnosticism is not a third alternative to theism and atheism because it is concerned with a different aspect of religious belief. Theism and atheism refer to the presence or absence of belief in a god; agnosticism refers to the *impossibility of knowledge* [his emphasis] with regard to a god or supernatural being."[365]

In other words, agnostics hold that it is impossible to believe that anyone can be sure about whether or not God actually exists. Viewed this way, drawing conclusions about the existence of God is not a matter of intelligence, knowledge or insight, it's simply not possible. Many people share this view. Celebrity agnostics who have declared themselves to be agnostic include author Mark Twain, American investor Warren Buffett, media personalities Larry King and Brad Pitt, philosopher Bertrand Russell, former UK Prime Minister Clement Attlee, natural history presenter Sir David Attenborough, and scientists Charles Darwin and Stephen Jay Gould.[366]

John Humphreys received many letters from listeners in response to his BBC radio series *Humphreys in Search of God*, about which he writes "what surprised me is how many think of themselves as neither believers nor atheists but doubters. They, too, are sincere. Devout sceptics, if you like. And many of them feel beleaguered. I'm with them."[367] Humphreys declares himself to be a "failed atheist" … he gave his book *In God We Doubt* (which is based on the radio series and findings of the YouGov survey) the sub-title *confessions of a failed atheist*.[368]

Richard Dawkins concedes that "there is nothing wrong with being agnostic in cases where we lack evidence one way or the other. It is a reasonable position."[369] He distinguishes two kinds of agnosticism, which he calls TAP (Temporary Agnosticism in Practice) and PAP (Permanent Agnosticism in Principle). He explains his thinking - TAP "is the legitimate fence-sitting where there really is a definite answer, one way or the other, but we so far lack the evidence to reach it," whereas PAP "is appropriate for questions that can never be answered, no matter how much evidence we gather, because the very idea of evidence is not applicable."[370] Eager to dismiss agnosticism as a pale shadow of his favoured atheism, he insists that "agnosticism about the existence of God belongs firmly in the temporary or TAP category. Either he exists or he doesn't. It is a scientific question; one day we may know the answer, and meanwhile we can say something pretty strong [in his view] about the probability."[371]

Denying God - atheism

While agnostics believe it is not possible to say one way or the other whether God exists, atheists are convinced that God does not exist. The word atheism comes from the Greek *atheos*, from *a-* ("without") and *theos* ("a god"), so it literally means "without a god" or godless. The term is used in two slightly different ways - to mean the belief that there is no God or gods, or the rejection of belief in the existence of God or gods.

As we saw in Chapter 3, Peter Lundstrom defined atheism as a "non-theistic belief system"[372] while Scottish theologian John Baillie prefers to see atheism as "the intellectual denial of the reality of God."[373] Although George Smith agrees that "atheism ... is the absence of theistic belief ... [he insists that] atheism, in its basic form, is not a belief: it is the absence of belief."[374] Whether or not it amounts to a belief, atheism is generally a conscious decision not a default assumption; atheists have made a deliberate decision to hold the views they do. Alister McGrath emphasises that "atheism is not about the suspension of judgement on the God Question; it is a firm and principled commitment to the nonexistence of God, and the liberating impact of this belief. The very idea of God is declared to be outdated, enslaving, and a downright self-contradiction."[375] New Atheist Christopher Hitchens applauds atheism as "a finer tradition [than theism]: the resistance of the rational."[376]

Whilst most non-believers prefer to call themselves atheists, some prefer the term 'freethinker' or even 'libertine' ... not, as Michael Onfray points out, "in the sense of one leading a dissolute life but rather in the sense of one who doubts or denies religious dogma."[377] Daniel Dennett refers to fellow atheists as 'brights', although fellow New Atheists Christopher Hitchens and Sam Harris refuse to use the term, even though Hitchens writes of "the intelligence and curiosity of the atheist."[378] Richard Dawkins uses the term 'brights' with relish to support his claim that atheists understand better than believers that there is no other reality than material reality. Dawkins dismisses all talk of spiritual things as nonsense, and looks down on believers as emotionally needy, lacking in intelligence, and easily deceived into believing nonsense.

Leaving the idea of God out of the picture altogether, atheists believe that "although there is only one kind of stuff in the universe and it is physical, out of this stuff come minds, beauty, emotions, moral values – in short the whole gamut of phenomena that gives richness to human life."[379] George Smith points out that "by severing any possible appeal to the supernatural – which, in terms of human knowledge, means the unknowable – atheism demands that issues be dealt with through reason and human understanding; they cannot be sloughed-off onto a mysterious god."[380]

Richard Dawkins explains how atheists believe "there is nothing beyond the natural, physical world, no *super*natural [his emphasis] creative intelligence lurking behind the observable universe, no soul that outlasts the body and no miracles – except in the sense of natural phenomena that we don't yet understand. If there is something that appears to lie beyond the natural world as it is now imperfectly understood, we hope eventually to understand it and embrace it within the natural."[381]

Put simply, atheists insist that the material world is all there is, and all the rest is delusion or illusion. As a consequence, they insist that rationality and science are the only ways of 'knowing'. People of faith know or have good reasons to believe otherwise.

Alister McGrath traces the mind-set of modern atheism to "the three great pillars of the golden age of atheism ... [Feuerbach, Marx, and Freud, who we looked at in Chapter 3] who between them turned a daring revolutionary hypothesis into the established certainty of an age, placing Christianity constantly on the defensive."[382] He traces the birth of "intentional atheism"[383] - "as opposed to mere cultural indifference to religion" - to the late 1790s and the emergence of the Romantic Movement in England, particularly through the poets William Wordsworth, Percy Bysshe Shelley and John Keats who saw nature as "affirming the transcendent without God."[384]

Dawkins writes of "atheist pride. Being an atheist is nothing to be apologetic about. On the contrary, it is something to be proud of, standing tall to face the far horizon, for atheism nearly always indicates a healthy independence of mind and, indeed, a healthy mind."[385] He also writes about 'coming out' as an atheist, and of his dream that his book *The God Delusion* "may help people to come out. Exactly as in the case of the gay movement, the more people come out, the easier it will be for others to join them. There may be a critical mass for the initiation of a chain reaction."[386]

Many atheists are happy to get on with their lives and to co-exist peacefully with believers, but some can't resist the urge to take a swipe at religion and dismiss it as irrational and founded on illusions and delusions.

One such writer is Michel Onfray, who seeks to discredit religion as a means of promoting his beloved atheism. He regards all religions, but particularly the three monotheisms, as anti-intellectual, legalistic and rooted in aversions. He writes of religion's "hatred of reason and intelligence; hatred of freedom; hatred of all books in the name of one book alone; hatred of sexuality, women, and pleasure; hatred of the feminine; hatred of the body, of desires, of drives."[387] He bemoans the fact that theists "live exclusively by prescriptions and constraints: things to do and things not to do, say and not to say, think and not to think, perform and not to perform. Forbidden and authorised, licit and illicit, agreed and not agreed: the religious texts abound in existential, dietary, behavioural, ritual, and other codifications."[388]

Just as atheism as a perspective or belief system sits at one end of the spectrum running from belief to unbelief, so within atheism people can be placed in particular positions; it is not a single homogeneous group. James Medd suggests three categories:[389]

[i] Hardcore atheists - such as Stephen Fry and Richard Dawkins, who spend their lives "writing about atheism, joking about it, or presiding over societies proclaiming it";

[ii] New atheists - such as Jonathan Edwards, who was "once a loudly Christian athlete ... [but has] recently – and vocally – converted to atheism. You need something to believe in, even if it's to believe in nothing"; and

[iii] Part-time atheists - like Ricky Gervais or Chris Addison for whom "it's not a big deal. Atheism is something you only think about once a year", at Christmas.

As in religion, within atheism there are shades of fundamentalism, extremism and intolerance. Symon Hill reminds us that "in the same way that religious fundamentalists refuse to see anything good or truthful in any religion but their own, there is a form of atheist fundamentalism that refuses to see anything good or truthful in any religion. ... Just as religious fundamentalists accuse many members of their religions as having sold out, so the New Atheists attack other atheists for being insufficiently hostile to religion."[390]

New Atheism

The term New Atheism appears to have been first used, in public at least, in an article entitled 'The church of the non-believers' that appeared the November 2006 edition of an American online magazine called *Wired*[391]. The term emerged suddenly, out of the blue, but it was catchy and memorable, and once coined it was quickly adopted and widely used.

Empowered by the growing secularisation of Western society over the last century, emboldened by the experience of the Death of God movement nearly half a century earlier (which we looked at in Chapter 3), and inspired by the growth of religious fundamentalism in recent decades, New Atheism is very much a product of its time.

The principal standard-bearers of this new, bold, anti-religious rhetoric are the writers Sam Harris, Daniel Dennett, Christopher Hitchens, and Richard Dawkins. Whether they genuinely represent the voices of a generation, or are just angry not-so-young men – for men they all are - is a matter for debate. American writer Roy Varghese has noted how "the proponents of a look-back-in-anger, take-no-prisoners type of atheism were out in force." [392]

The first spokesman of New Atheism to appear in print was Sam Harris, a young American philosopher and neuroscience graduate student at Stanford University[393], whose *The End of Faith: Religion, terror and the future of reason* was published in 2004.[394] That book, which challenged religious dogma and its role in American life and politics, was a polemic against religious fundamentalism and extremism, especially as expressed through terrorism post-9.11. It railed against things done 'in the name of God'. James Welsh thought that Harris, in crediting religious faith as the source of much of the violence in the world today, "was effective in a kind of outraged, dumbfounded, *vox populi* way".[395]

American psychologist Daniel Dennett took the anti-religion theme further in his 2006 book *Breaking the Spell: religion as a natural phenomenon*, in which he argued that "religion is like the liver fluke, a dreadful parasite that should be sought out and eradicated"[396] He explains his book's enigmatic title: "the spell that I say *must* be broken is the taboo against a forthright, scientific, no-holds-barred investigation of religion as one natural phenomenon among many."[397]

The End of Faith paved the way for a similarly influential book published in 2007 by Christopher Hitchens, a British journalist based in the USA[398]. The book's title, *God is not Great*, and particularly its sub-title *How Religion Poisons Everything*, convey its central message. Hitchens sees "religion as an original sin", as he titles one of his chapters. He finds it difficult to restrain his contempt for religion, which he dismisses as "violent, irrational, intolerant, allied to racism and tribalism and bigotry, invested in ignorance and hostile to free inquiry, contemptuous of women and coercive towards children."[399] John Humphreys adds, somewhat mischievously, "and it probably gives you dandruff and bad breath too."[400] Hitchens insists that religion "is ultimately grounded on wish-thinking."[401]

We have already encountered Richard Dawkins - poster-boy of New Atheism, and its self-appointed high priest (indeed, he even refers to himself as *A Devil's Chaplain*[402]) - in earlier chapters. He is the best-known of the New Atheism writers and has done more than the others to popularise its themes. His attack on religion and religious believers is the most intolerant of the bunch. His target audience was those "who have been brought up in some religion or other, are unhappy about it, don't believe it, or are worried about the evils that are done in its name."[403] As a man on a mission, Dawkins is explicit and unashamed about his objective in writing *The God Delusion*: he admits "if this book works as I intend, religious readers who open it will be atheists when they put it down."[404] Thomas Martin makes clear that the purpose of the book is "to help closet atheists 'come out' and to convert borderline theists to atheism."[405]

Dawkins views religion as at best a profound misunderstanding and at worst a form of madness. His central thesis is that humans invented God as a way of coping with uncertainty in the world around them, and that this idea has been passed on from generation to generation by an evolutionary process through 'cultural genes' that he calls memes, as we saw in Chapter 4.

The books by all four New Atheism writers are out-and-out attacks on organised religion and how it makes apparently otherwise sensible people behave. None says much about God *per se*. In fact it is worth noting that the New Atheist writers largely attack organised religion, rather than God. Reviewing them, American writer Roy Varghese was struck by how "what was significant about these books was not their level of argument – which was modest, to put it mildly – but the level of visibility that they received both as best sellers and as a 'new' story discovered by the media. The 'story' was helped even further by the fact that the authors were as voluble and colourful as their books were fiery."[406]

Core beliefs

Whilst the four leading New Atheism writers have different emphases within their books, they are bound together by a shared view of God and religion as the cause of and not the solution to many of the fundamental problems confronting humanity today. They see the idea of God as the problem not the answer, and religion as either irrelevant or a barrier to meaningful progress.

The central tenet of New Atheism, as indeed it is of traditional atheism, is that God does not exist but is a human construct. The New Atheists invest a great deal of time and effort sketching out the nature of the God they don't believe in. They write about God as if he was some form of super-man, and they judge God to be cruel, nasty and spiteful for allowing suffering, inequality and injustice. They portray God as a vindictive spy-in-the-sky who watches over people, interferes with their lives, and prevents them from just following their instincts and getting on with life.

All four New Atheism writers share deep concerns over several key issues. A core theme, certainly for Harris, Hitchens and Dawkins, is religious fundamentalism and extremism, and how it can lead to hostility and violence. Indeed, this is perhaps the most strongly-voiced theme in their books, all written in the shadow of the 9.11 atrocities in New York and at a time of rising public concern over religiously-motivated militancy and terrorism across the world. All four writers point to the inglorious history of religious conflict, and the cruelty and inhumanity of many things that have been done 'in the name of God'. This is a particularly prominent theme in *The God Delusion*, where despite pointing to endless examples and illustrations, Dawkins thoughtfully reminds his readers that "in this book, I have deliberately refrained from detailing the horrors of the Crusades, the conquistadores or the Spanish Inquisition."[407]

Sam Harris devotes a very long chapter to "the problem with Islam", noting that "we [the USA] are at war with Islam"[408] which, "more than any other religion human beings have devised, has all the makings of a thoroughgoing cult of death"[409] particularly through the principle of jihad or holy war. Christopher Hitchens insists bluntly that "religion kills" [410] (the title of his second chapter), and he cites as examples the 9.11 Twin Towers atrocity in New York, Catholic-Protestant tensions and conflicts in Northern Ireland, conflicts between Israel and Lebanon, ethnic conflicts in former Yugoslavia, religious tensions and conflicts in Bethlehem, and conflicts in Iraq. Roy Varghese reminds us that the new atheists "train their guns on well-known abuses in the history of the major world religions. But the excesses and atrocities of organised religion have no bearing whatsoever on the existence of God, just as the threat of nuclear proliferation has no bearing on the question of whether e=mc²."[411]

Questions of ethics and morality also exercise all four writers, eager to find ways of disassociating moral standards from the divine. Richard Dawkins strongly rejects the idea that "should belief in God suddenly vanish from the world, we would all become callous and selfish hedonists, with no kindness, no charity, no generosity, nothing would deserve the name of goodness."[412] He also insists that "people who claim to derive their morals [directly] from scripture do not really do so in practice."[413]

All four writers also have things to say about justice, inequality and suffering. As John Haught points out, they "try to convince their readers that the monotheistic faiths – Judaism, Christianity, and Islam – underlie a sizeable portion of the evils human beings have afflicted on one another throughout the last three millennia."[414] Christopher Hitchens picks an extreme example in pointing out that, after the 9.11 bombings in New York, "within hours, the 'reverends' Pat Robertson and Jerry Falwell had announced that the immolation of their fellow creatures was a divine judgment on a secular society that tolerated homosexuality and abortion."[415]

What's so new about New Atheism?

The central message of New Atheism is *not* new. In fact, New Atheism simply repeats and echoes most of the core arguments of traditional atheism, but with contemporary examples and illustrations. Many well-informed commentators conclude that most of what the New Atheists say and write has been said and written before, usually better. John Haught points out that, "as far as enhancing knowledge of religion is concerned, the new atheists do little more than provide a fresh catalogue of the evils wrought by members of the theistic faiths."[416]

Haught concludes that the New Atheists are a long way off what he would call "really hard-core atheists"[417]. He argues that the latter – writers such as Friedrich Nietzsche, Albert Camus, and Jean-Paul Sartre – "generally demanded a much more radical transformation of human culture and consciousness. ... To them atheism, if one is really serious about it, should make all the difference in the world, and it would take a superhuman effort to embrace it. ... [but the New Atheists] want atheism to prevail at the least possible expense to the agreeable socioeconomic circumstances out of which they sermonise. ... They would have the God religions – Judaism, Christianity, and Islam – simply disappear, after which we should be able to go on enjoying the same lifestyle as before, only without the nuisance of suicide bombers and TV evangelists."[418]

If the content and depth of New Atheism are not particularly new, what *is* new is the tone, with its entrenched militancy, intolerance and missionary zeal.

Critiques of New Atheism

There is no shortage of books published in response to the writings of the new atheists, particularly Richard Dawkins' *The God Delusion*. The bulk of this growing body of work is very critical of New Atheism.

Critiques of Dawkins's book that I have found particularly relevant and useful include Alister McGrath and Joanna Collicutt McGrath's *The Dawkins delusion: atheist fundamentalism and the denial of the divine* (2007); John Haught's *God and the New Atheism: a critical response to Dawkins, Harris and Hitchens* (2008); Keith Ward's *Why there almost certainly is a God: doubting Dawkins* (2008); [particularly the first three]; Terry Eagleton's *Reason, Faith, and Revolution: reflections on the God Debate* (2009); Kathleen Jones's *Challenging Richard Dawkins* (2007); John Cornwell's *Darwin's Angel: an angelic riposte to The God Delusion* (2007); Michael Poole's *The 'New' Atheism: ten arguments that don't hold water?* (2009); and David Robertson's *The Dawkins letters: challenging atheist myths* (2007).

Michael Ruse captures the general consensus of most critics in his conclusion that "it is not that the [New] atheists are having a field day because of the brilliance and novelty of their thinking ... the material being churned out is second rate. And that is a euphemism for 'down-right awful'."[419]

Despite or perhaps because of its flowing and at times soaring rhetoric,

The God Delusion comes across as an intemperate rage against religious belief and believers in general, and against religious fundamentalism and fundamentalists in particular. Ironically but not surprisingly, Dawkins' fundamental brand of atheism comes across as just as intolerant, blinkered and dangerous as the religious fundamentalism he is so relentlessly critical of. John Haught notes that "intolerance of tolerance seems to be a truly novel feature of the new atheists' solution to the problem of human misery."[420]

Critics often bemoan the style and tone of the New Atheists' writing. Karen Armstrong writes simply that "it is a pity that Dawkins, Hitchens and Harris express themselves so intemperately"[421], while Terry Eagleton is blunter in his observation that neither Hitchens nor Dawkins "is afflicted with an excess of modesty."[422] Hitchens' forceful style and dogmatic message have attracted a fair amount of criticism; for example, John Humphreys thinks that he "makes the Taliban look tame".[423] As Keith Ward points out, when Dawkins "enters into the world of philosophy, his passion tends to get the better of him, and he sometimes descends into stereotyping, pastiche and mockery, no longer approaching the arguments with his usual seriousness and care."[424] John Humphreys gets annoyed that the New Atheist writers "appear to believe they are superior to religious believers not only intellectually but even, in some bizarre way, morally."[425]

Critics also point to the New Atheists' lack of theological literacy and engagement with mainstream theology, preferring instead to base their arguments on ill-informed and outmoded ideas, and often on pure ignorance and prejudice, which seriously undermines the credibility of their writing. John Haught argues that their "understanding of religious faith remains consistently at the same unscholarly level as the unreflective, superstitious, and literalist religiosity of those they criticise."[426] Karen Armstrong points out that "their polemic remains shallow and lacks intellectual depth. It is also morally and intellectually conservative."[427]

CHAPTER 6

SCIENCE AND THE CHALLENGE TO GOD

"Religion has run out of justifications. Thanks to the telescope and the microscope, it no longer offers an explanation of anything important."

Christopher Hitchens (2007)

Some of the strongest criticism of the idea of God has been based on the argument that science can explain everything without the need for anything supernatural or divine. This reflects the clash of world-views that we looked at in Chapter 2 between those who believe that naturalism/ materialism offers sufficient explanation for all that we see in the world around us, and those who allow for or believe that there are things beyond what science can study and explain.

In this chapter we will look at when and how these tensions arose, explore some of the limitations inherent in the scientific approach, and consider whether and how science and religion might be reconciled.

Rationality and the development of science

In Western culture the dominant world-view up to the seventeenth century was a religious one. The consensus was that everything we are, see and experience are the results of God's handiwork. Divine providence had created everything, and continues to do so. The Biblical 'explanation' of everything was sufficient in itself ... God did it.

Even as the roots of modern science were emerging, this religious view of the world not only survived but thrived. Krista Tippett reminds us that "even when they struggled with the church, Copernicus, Galileo, and Newton believed that their discoveries would widen human comprehension of the nature of God. The more we could understand about the world around us in all its intricacy, this reasoning went, the better we would understand the mind of its maker."[428]

Things were to change dramatically with the birth of the Enlightenment towards the end of the seventeenth century. As philosopher Robin Attfield points out, "although many of the founders of modern science in the seventeenth century saw their work as an expression of Christian piety, it nevertheless carries an unmistakably secular stamp. It had a method of its own. It was sceptical of authority. It ceased to regard the search for purpose in nature as its primary concern. Theology and science were to be separated. Science was to be based on observation and reasoning and not to be deducted from ancient authorities or scripture. Typically, the world was to be construed as a mechanism, not as a semi-divine organism."[429]

Despite the challenge of science to religion, Terry Eagleton dismisses as myth the idea that "an Age of Faith is heroically ousted by an Age of Reason." He argues that "Faith and Enlightenment were never simple opposites. ... The emergent interest in Nature was not a step outside the religious outlook, but a mutation within it. ... What happened was not that science gradually exposed the fallacies of myth and religion. ... It is not that myth gave way to fact, but that one moral outlook yielded to another."[430] This new perspective was firmly rooted in the rational approach of science but was also reflected in the development of humanism and of 'God of the Gaps' thinking (Chapter 4), and the emergence of atheism (Chapter 5) and secularism.

New Atheism writers like to think of religion as a throwback to the earliest stages of human evolution, now replaced by the more advanced thinking of modern science. Christopher Hitchens, for example, dismisses religious faith as a hallmark of 'pre-history' or what he calls "the childhood of our species"[431], portraying it as an inconvenient obstacle to otherwise inevitable progress in the development of human thinking and ability. Terry Eagleton will have none of that, insisting that "at stake here is a stupendously simple-minded, breathtakingly reductive world picture, one worthy of a child's crude drawing. There is something striving to move forward, and something intent on holding it back; and while the former is unequivocally good, the second is unreservedly abhorrent."[432] Robert Winston also rejects the idea that "at a certain point in our development, we 'started to become rational', and abandoned belief in God as a consequence. To say that would be a gross over-simplification. At certain points in evolution our brains underwent a sort of seismic shift, growing in size and giving us new abilities – such as language or tool-use. But no such shift ever occurred where the use of 'reason' was concerned; or if it did, it was back in the very distant past, not in the fifteenth, sixteenth and seventeenth centuries."[433]

Nonetheless, the growth of the natural sciences during the nineteenth and twentieth centuries created serious challenges to the idea of God, which survive today. Alister McGrath highlights three particular dimensions of science that have helped shape the thinking of many people - the general public as well as scientists themselves - over the past two centuries. One is the general assumption that rational science has liberated us from "bondage to a superstitious and oppressive past" dominated by religion. Particularly damaging have been "the belief that the natural sciences conclusively prove all their theories, in contrast to the religious retreat into irrationality and mystery in the face of the evidence" and "the pervasive notion that the Darwinian theory of evolution has made belief in God impossible, thus necessitating atheism on scientific grounds."[434]

Two main areas in which a conflict between science and religion has played out are the debate about the origin and nature of the universe, and debate about the nature and origin of life. Some would say these are the two primary battle-grounds in a never-ending war between science and religion.

On the origin and nature of the universe

Since earliest times humans have gazed up at the sky and wondered how far it stretches, what lies beyond it, and how it all came into being. Thanks to science we now know a great deal more about it than ever before, and new discoveries are being made every year. For example, in the year 2000 astronomers knew of 26 planets outside our solar system but by 2010 this had grown to 502, and the number continues to rise.[435] How many of them have conditions that might be suitable to sustain life as we know it remains a mystery, but even that is not likely to remain the case forever. We now know that the universe appears to consist of 4 per cent ordinary matter, 23 per cent dark matter and 73 per cent dark energy, yet whilst it is slowly giving up its secrets as scientists probe ever further and deeper into space, a great many things about the universe remain as yet unknown. Despite all its many successes and triumphs, science still has a long way to go in discovering, describing and accounting for everything in the material universe.

Three themes which have long attracted attention from scientists are how the earth fits into the solar system, how old the earth and the universe are, and how they both began. These are big and fundamental questions; little wonder science and religion has approached them differently, and arrived at different but not necessarily incompatible conclusions about them.

Nature and age of the universe

The received wisdom up to the seventeenth century was that the earth sits at the centre of the solar system, and all the other planets rotate around it. This was what the church taught, based on what the Bible appeared to say, and the early astronomers found no evidence to the contrary. This earth-centred (geocentric) model of the cosmos was proposed by the Greek philosophers Aristotle (384-322 BC) and Ptolemy (90-168 AD), and for many centuries it was supported by the mathematicians and astronomers working within the Roman Catholic Church. But it could not explain what Galileo Galilei (1564-1642) saw in the seventeenth century when he pointed his newly-invented telescope at the night sky; he observed moons moving around the planet Jupiter, proving that not everything orbits around the earth. Galileo's bold and controversial conclusion, which directly and defiantly contradicted church teaching, was that our planet earth might not be the centre of the universe after all. Galileo insisted that his telescope was more reliable than the Bible in telling us about the natural world. As a result he was charged with heresy, found guilty in 1633 in the Inquisition, and thrown in prison (later commuted to house arrest).

Thomas Dixon points out that the key to understanding this episode in the history of science lies in the fact that "historians have shown that the Galileo affair, remembered by some as a clash between science and religion, was primarily a dispute about the enduring political question of who was authorised to produce and disseminate knowledge."[436] A more direct attack on religion was launched over a century later by French mathematician Pierre-Simon Laplace (1749-1827). Building on the work of English physicist Isaac Newton (1642–1727), Laplace developed a mathematical model of how the solar system works, including what we now call 'black holes'. When asked why his equations did not include God, he is alleged to have replied that he had no need for that hypothesis.[437]

An equally serious attack on the idea of God came through the debate about the age of the earth and the universe. A number of well-intended attempts to date the creation of the earth based on the analysis of biblical texts appear with the benefit of hindsight to be rather fanciful. For example, in a sermon given in 1525 Martin Luther dated creation at 3961 BC; in 1640 Dr John Lightfoot (Vice Chancellor of the University of Cambridge) calculated that God had created the earth on Sunday 23 October 3929 BC; and ten years later James Ussher (Archbishop of Armagh) calculated the date as Saturday October 22 4004 BC.[438] Robert Winston has pointed out that, "sadly for Ussher, within two hundred years of his death, the wonders of ancient Egypt would be uncovered. Theologians then had to grapple with incontrovertible evidence that, at the supposed time when God had been creating the earth, a powerful, sophisticated state had built huge temples along the River Nile; had enjoyed the grain, the fruit, the wine of a highly developed civilisation; had built the pyramids at Giza in Egypt; and had invented a sophisticated form of writing. And quite similar advances had been made by other humans during the same period in Mesopotamia, India and China."[439] The biblical dating was clearly way out. New Atheist Christopher Hitchens rather unkindly dismisses the attempts as "infantile computation."[440]

Cosmologists today generally agree that the universe is 13.7 billion (thousand million) years old and the earth about 4.6 billion years old.[441] Many theologians have no problem with this 'old earth' chronology, arguing that the Bible was never intended to be a science textbook; it tells us *why* the universe came into being not *how* or *when*.[442]

In the beginning

Science and religion have long been at loggerheads over the question of how the universe came into being, assuming that it has not always existed. Did it just happen somehow, or was it created? The religious view, based on what the Bible tells us, is that the universe was created out of nothing (*ex nihilo*), by a creator God with power and intelligence beyond anything we could possibly imagine. The general consensus among scientists is also that the universe came from nothing - before it there was no matter, time or space - but it was brought into existence by a physical explosion (the so-called Big Bang) which simply happened, and which in turn gave rise to everything that ever existed across the universe.

The Big Bang theory, named in the 1930s by Fred Hoyle, is based on the idea that the universe began with one huge explosion of energy and light around 13 billion years ago that created time and space. The explosion is believed to have been caused by the accidental collision of two tiny particles, lasted a tiny fraction of a second (10^{-43} seconds), and triggered a fireball of radiation that created unimaginably large temperatures (estimated to be about a hundred thousand million degrees Centigrade). Patrick Clarke explains how, "as the earth cooled down, chemical reactions took place that eventually led to the emergence of primitive life-forms, from which all life, including human life, evolved."[443] In 1948 Fred Hoyle put forward a rival Steady State theory based on the idea that matter and energy are constantly decaying and being renewed throughout the universe, which had no apparent beginning.[444]

Although the Big Bang theory is elegant and appears to fit most of the available evidence, several critical questions remain unanswered, including - what caused the explosion, where did the particles come from, and what existed before the explosion? As Kathleen Jones puts it "If the universe can begin accidentally, there must have been some sort of activity going on before the accident which had unintended consequences. If Richard Dawkins says that the universe originated in two particles, where did the particles come from? That is not a scientific explanation. What went BANG in that first fraction of a second? Who or what made it happen?"[445]

Scientists struggle to give plausible answers to those tough questions, but much attention in recent decades has been directed to the hunt for the Higgs Boson, an elusive particle which it is believed will help explain the nature of mass and energy.[446] Because it is the best theory currently available for the origin of mass - what makes stuff stuff - it has been rather unhelpfully nicknamed the God Particle. Kathleen Jones explains that the particle "is too small to be seen, and is thought to have a life of only a few milliseconds. ... [It] may turn out to be a property of something else rather than a particle or a wave; it may turn out to be a pair of particles, or it may contain something even smaller, less visible and shorter lived. It may not exist at all."[447] The hunt has been based at the Large Hadron Collider, housed underground in a 27 km long tunnel at CERN near Geneva in Switzerland, where conditions that are believed to have been present less than a billionth of a second after the Big Bang can be recreated in a controlled environment inside giant detectors. The search involves accelerating and smashing particles into one another and closely monitoring what happens. The experiment can be repeated many hundreds of times in the hope of finding evidence of underlying patterns. The challenge is immense; one scientist on the project likens it to firing needles across the Atlantic and getting them to collide half way.[448] For many years the Higgs eluded physicists, but in mid-2012 scientists working at CERN confirmed that the experiment had found evidence consistent with the existence of the particle.

Fine-tuning

Our planet Earth is the only one in the universe known to contain carbon-based life, life as we understand it. As scientists discover more about the structure and nature of the universe, it has become apparent that a certain amount of fine-tuning must have occurred in order to create a life-friendly planet like Earth.

Scientists call this fine-tuning the Anthropic Principle (anthropic means relating to human beings). But as Michael Poole explains it has been dubbed "the Goldilocks Effect because, like Baby Bear's porridge, chair and bed, things are 'just right'."[449] For example, temperatures on Earth are neither too hot nor too cold for life to emerge and continue, because the earth is the right distance from the Sun to maintain temperatures suitable for life, whilst spinning daily on its axis and rotating around the Sun. It's not just a matter of temperature, because the fine-tuning is evident in numerous ways. For example, the earth is the only planet known to have an atmosphere with the right mix of gases (particularly nitrogen and oxygen) to sustain carbon-based life and thus be suitable for plants, animals and humans. Our moon is the ideal size and distance from the earth to create just the right gravitational pull to sustain life.

What's even more amazing, the whole universe appears to be finely tuned, not just planet Earth. Richard Dawkins proudly proclaims that "we live not only on a friendly planet but also in a friendly universe. It follows from the fact of our existence that the laws of physics must be friendly enough to allow life to arise. ... Physicists have calculated that, if the laws and constants of physics had been even slightly different, the universe would not have developed in such a way that life would have been possible."[450]

Martin Rees, former President of the Royal Society and Astronomer Royal, and a confirmed atheist, pins the fine-tuning down to six fundamental constants which are believed to hold all around the universe and which, if only slightly different, would produce major changes and could even make our universe unfriendly to life. [451] Ever the cynic, Richard Dawkins calls this the 'Divine Knob-Twiddler' argument based on the logic that "the theist says that God, when setting up the universe, tuned the fundamental constants of the universe so that each one lay in its Goldilocks zone for the production of life. It is as though God had six knobs that he could twiddle, and he carefully tuned each knob to its Goldilocks value."[452]

Former atheist Antony Flew argues that "the fact that the existing laws and constants allow the survival of life does not answer the question of the origin of life. This is a very different question ...; these conditions are necessary for life to arise, but not sufficient."[453] Michael Poole disagrees; he insists that "anthropic coincidences mean not simply favourable conditions *for life surviving* but the very preconditions *of life arising* in the first place. This would not have happened if various factors about the natural world had been different, including infinitesimal differences in the fundamental constants of nature."[454]

Given the evidence of fine-tuning across the universe, the question naturally arises of how this occurred and how it is maintained. There are two likely contenders - it is a purely random outcome of natural processes at work, or it is the work of a tuner (or designer).

Richard Dawkins accounts for the fine-tuning as a purely random outcome of natural physical processes at work, which he insists "has a faintly Darwinian feel."[455] He emphasises that "the anthropic principle, like natural selection, is an *alternative* [his emphasis] to the design hypothesis. It provides a rational, design-free explanation for the fact that we find ourselves in a situation propitious to our existence."[456]

For the apparent fine-tuning to really be a random outcome of entirely natural processes, scientists recognise that it would require countless universes for it to emerge in. As Antony Flew points out, many scientists "have speculated that our universe is one of multiple others – a 'multiverse' – with the difference that ours happened to have the right conditions for life. Virtually no major scientist today claims that the fine tuning was purely the result of chance factors at work in a single universe."[457] Dawkins clarifies that the argument is based on statistical probability, given that "it has been estimated that there are between 1 billion and 30 billion planets in our galaxy, and about 100 billion galaxies in the universe … If the odds of life originating spontaneously on a planet were a billion to one against, nevertheless that stupefyingly improbable event would still happen on a billion planets. The chance of finding any one of those billion life-bearing planets recalls the proverbial needle in a haystack."[458]

However, we mustn't lose sight of the fact that the multiple universe idea is just that, an idea, a purely theoretical speculation. There is no evidence to support it, and it is easy to be sceptical about it, even though Martin Rees prefers it to the idea of God as a possible explanation for the universe.[459] Theologian Keith Ward thinks scientists find the idea attractive because "the multiverse hypothesis looks like a properly scientific hypothesis, whereas the God Hypothesis does not."[460]

People of faith see the fine-tuning of the universe as strong evidence of the work of a tuner (God) working to a divine design. Richard Dawkins calls this the "design theory", based on the idea that "God made the world, placed it in the Goldilocks Zone, and deliberately set up all the details for our benefit."[461] He concedes that some physicists who are known to be religious "suggest that there must be a cosmic intelligence who deliberately did the tuning."[462] Thomas Dixon goes further in allowing the possibility that "a creator with an interest in producing intelligent life designed our universe."[463] Physicist Freeman Dyson admits "being a scientist, trained in the habits of thought and language of the twentieth century rather than the eighteenth, I do not claim that the architecture of the universe proves the existence of God. I claim only that the architecture of the universe is consistent with the hypothesis that mind plays an essential role in its functioning."[464]

After weighing up the arguments for and against both explanations for the fine-tuning of the universe, Keith Ward concludes that "the multiverse is not an alternative to God. The hypothesis of God actually makes the multiverse hypothesis, in some sense (the sense in which all universes exist in the mind of God), more intelligible. It also positively adds elements to explanation that a purely physical hypothesis does not. For the hypothesis of an ultimate creative consciousness explains the existence of finite consciousness, of creativity, and of purpose and value, in a universe that is not solely physical in nature."[465]

Towards a Grand Theory of Everything

As if understanding the origin and nature of the universe was not a big enough challenge in itself, scientists are working hard to develop a 'grand unified theory' or a 'theory of everything'. Einstein's dream was to find such a theory that would bring together cosmology, general relativity, quantum mechanics and genetics into one common framework; it was what he had in mind when he wrote about "the mind of God" (that we touched on in Chapter 3). Like the Higgs Boson such a theory is proving elusive. Alister McGrath calls it "the holy grail of the natural sciences" but he points out that such a theory is regarded as important "because it can explain everything, without itself requiring or demanding an explanation. ...[but] What explains the explainer?"[466]

Physicist Steven Weinberg believes that physics may indeed be on the brink of discovering such a 'final theory', and he predicts that "when physical science arrives at the basement of all being, little chance exists that any footprints of a divine Friend will be visible there."[467] Richard Dawkins, as ever, puts it much more bluntly; he writes that he is "optimistic that this final scientific enlightenment will deal an overdue deathblow to religion and other juvenile superstitions."[468]

The debate about God's role in bringing the universe into being was rekindled in September 2010 with the publication of cosmologist Stephen Hawking's *The Grand Design*.[469] This was a follow-up to his best-selling *A Brief History of Time* in which he had suggested that while physics had put constraints on when a possible God might have created the Universe, it had not ruled out his existence altogether.[470] Hawking went one step further in this new book, maintaining that physical laws are reason enough for the Universe to have come into being spontaneously. He argued that "spontaneous creation is the reason why there is something rather than nothing, why the universe exists, why we exist. It is not necessary to invoke God to light the blue touch paper and set the universe going."[471] Richard

Dawkins was jubilant at the publication of *The Grand Design*, insisting that "Darwinism kicked God out of biology but physics remained more uncertain. Hawking is now administering the coup de grace."[472]

Inevitably, Hawking's conclusion that there is no need for God in explaining why everything exists and how it came into being caused quite a stir. Such a stark conclusion (based on a mathematical solution not on observations or experimentation) was not supported or endorsed by all physicists, even those who had worked with him in his research. For example Don Page, a Physics Professor who carried out research with Stephen Hawking and co-authored scientific papers with him, noted in a letter to *The Times* that "our universe (or multiverse) in all its details may be a logical consequence of [the laws of physics] ... but that does not exclude the possibility that behind the universe and its laws is a personal God as Creator. A grand design suggests to me as a Christian a Grand Designer, who could be simpler and more perfectly powerful and good than the superbly designed universe that I believe He has created."[473]

On the origin and nature of life

The debate between creation and evolution as ways of explaining the origin and nature of life has been shorter, sharper, and more focussed than that surrounding the origin and nature of the universe, but no less controversial. It has also played out very prominently in public, whereas the cosmological discourse has remained largely away from the public gaze in the privileged domain of physicists and other natural scientists.

The religious explanation, certainly as professed by the three Abrahamic religions (Judaism, Christianity and Islam), rests on the narrative of creation as recorded in the first chapter of the Bible, the book of Genesis. The passage is well-known. It opens with the words "In the beginning, God created the heavens and the earth"[474], then progresses through the separation by God of light (day) and darkness (night) and of water and land, and continues with the creation of vegetation, the sun and the moon, all creatures in the sea and on land, and finally humans. It closes by reporting that "God saw all that he had made, and it was very good."[475]

This was the story of a benevolent God creating the universe and everything in it, a unique act of divine creation, and for many thousands of years it shaped people's understanding of the world around them. It clearly suggested that there was nothing that God had not created, and God had not left out anything that matters; hence "it was very good". The story also gave the impression of an initial burst of creative activity when everything that we see around us came into being, but it says nothing about what happened next in terms of creation ... hinting that things were made that way for all time and nothing has changed since. The text speaks of the whole of creation being completed within seven days, which literalists maintain means seven actual periods of 24 hours, whereas most believers these days are content to see it as seven (possibly very long) periods of time.

The seeds for challenging and ultimately threatening (some would even say undermining) the biblical account of creation were sown by English naturalist Charles Darwin (1809-1882) during his five-year scientific survey of the coast of South America on board HMS Beagle, between 1831 and 1837. His geological observations made him question the received wisdom at that time of an earth that was only a matter of a few thousand years old. He saw the immense power of volcanic eruptions which could dramatically change landscapes over very short periods of time, but he also studied complex layers of sediment, some containing fossil remains, which suggested a much longer timescale. If that was the case, the 'young earth' model did not seem appropriate. But his most important observations were biological ones, particularly of birds. He noted, for example, how birds appeared to have adapted to the different conditions on different islands within the Galapagos, even ones close together; finches displayed variations in the shape of their heads and beaks which he explained as adaptations to different food sources. If that was the case, then species were not fixed as the Genesis account implied but were able to adapt through time and from place to place.

Darwin realised that his observations and explanations were a real challenge to the biblical account of creation, but at that stage in his life he had no strong desire to take on religion, and particularly to take on the church. He spent the next two decades thinking, reading, observing and experimenting, trying to work out what the evidence revealed, and how he might best explain it. He published his evidence and explanations in November 1859 in the book *The Origin of Species*, and the rest - as they say - is history. The book's full title - *On the Origin of Species by Means of Natural Selection or, The Preservation of Favoured Races in the Struggle for Life* - is a catchy précis of Darwin's main line of reasoning, in which he outlined his theory of evolution by natural selection.

In a nutshell, Darwin's idea was that "within any population of a species, individuals are not identical in every respect. Populations generally produce more offspring than are required to replace their parents. On average, population numbers remain stable over time; no population can increase in numbers indefinitely. Competition for breeding opportunities, food and other resources must occur among offspring, only some of which survive long enough to breed. Survivors are those best adapted to the environment (ie the fittest)."[476] Hence his theory of the gradual evolution of biological species through natural selection operating over successive generations over exceedingly long periods of time.

The challenge of Darwin's theory of evolution to biblical ideas of creation was obvious and stark. Thomas Dixon explains how, in Darwin's view, "the adaptation of organisms to their environment, and the origins of separate species, should be explained not in terms of the creative acts of Paley's designer [which we will look at in Chapter 7], but by geographical distribution, random heritable variation, competition for resources, and the survival of the fittest over vast aeons of time."[477] The implications were clear, as Karen Armstrong spells out - "God has certainly not created the world exactly as we knew it. Instead, it seemed clear that the species had evolved slowly over time, as they adapted to their immediate environment. During this process of natural selection, innumerable species had indeed perished."[478]

The biblical account implied that God had created every creature (species) separately, but a key part of Darwin's evolutionary theory was the assumption that through natural processes everything has evolved from a common ancestor. This had serious implications for humans, which the Bible explained as unique among animals and given special status by God, a special creation made in God's image. Darwin once again took his time working out what he wanted to say, aware that the implication was controversial in the extreme. In 1871 he published *The Descent of Man* in which, as Karen Armstrong explains, he suggested "that *Homo sapiens* had developed from the progenitor of the orang-utan, gorilla and chimpanzee. Human beings were not the pinnacle of a purposeful creation; like everything else, they had evolved by trial and error and God had had no direct hand in their making."[479] Patrick Clarke points out that "man [sic] was now reduced to the product of an evolutionary process that began with a single life-form. In this process, man was continuous with the animals, not different from them."[480]

With Darwin's theory of evolution it was now possible to account for the emergence and disappearance of species, and for variations within and between species, by purely natural processes, without any need for divine intervention. God and creation were kicked into the long grass as redundant in explanatory terms, as God's hand had effectively been removed from creation.

Darwin's books were widely read and the church had much to lose from a swing in public opinion and belief. The heated debate held in Oxford in 1860, at which Thomas Huxley put forward the case for evolution as an irrefutable fact, while Samuel Wilberforce (Bishop of Oxford) staunchly defended creation, is well known and it illustrates how high the stakes were and how entrenched the two sides started out and remained.[481] Kathleen Jones reckons that Richard Dawkins seems to be trying to replay this debate in the twenty-first century.[482]

Darwin was inevitably caught in the eye of the storm of the controversy between evolution and creation, and much has been written or speculated about his own religious beliefs. His grandfather, father, and elder brother "had all rejected Christianity, adopting either Deism or outright freethinking unbelief."[483] Karen Armstrong points out that, although "Darwinian theory … undermined the design-based theology that had become the mainstay of Western Christian religion … Darwin … had no desire to destroy religion."[484] John Cornwell adds that, "for all his latter-day scepticism, at no time did Darwin suggest, in his private writings or in public, that religious belief was incompatible with the scientific imagination; nor did he judge religionists to be contemptible or dangerous."[485]

For much of his life Charles Darwin saw himself as a theist. He wrote in his *Autobiography* "I feel compelled to look to a First Cause having an intelligent mind in some degree analogous to that of man, and I deserve to be called a theist."[486] He was a theist when he wrote *The Origin of Species*, but later in life he preferred to call himself an agnostic. He wrote "I have never been an atheist in the sense of denying the existence of God. I think that generally (and more and more as I grow older) but not always, agnostic would be the most correct description of my state of mind."[487] This was not because of the implications of this theory of natural selection but largely because of the problem of reconciling the notion of a loving God with the suffering he saw throughout the natural world, including the tragic death of his own daughter Annie, which affected him deeply. We will return to Darwin's loss of faith in Chapter 9.

Thomas Dixon points out that, "among those who have resisted Darwinism for religious reasons over the last century and a half, some have done so on the grounds of its conflict with a literal interpretation of scripture. For many others, however, their resistance has been to the theory of evolution's apparent incompatibility with belief in free will, moral responsibility, and a rational and immortal human soul."[488]

Other critics point out that Darwin's theory of evolution only explains how life has diversified, not how it originated in the first place. Richard Dawkins contends that the origin of life, being a highly improbable event on the natural scale, is therefore unlikely to be intended; he rules out that it can have anything other than a natural explanation.[489] As we shall see in Chapter 7, others argue differently, and insist that 'creation' and evolution are not mutually exclusive processes.

Competing truth claims

The common view is that science and religion are in competition with each other as ways of explaining the world around us. But is that really true? John Cornwell reminds us that "not surprisingly the scientific and the religious imagination find themselves at odds, in competition even, especially in the realms of explanation, where both at times trespass on each other's territories."[490]

Scientists and atheists view physical reality as all there is. From their naturalistic perspective they explain everything (including thought, feeling, mind and will) in terms of physical matter and natural causes and events. Such an intellectual framework neither needs nor allows for God. Modern science acknowledges only natural explanations, and rejects any explanations which cannot be investigated empirically through observation or properly conducted scientific experimentation.

It is a short step for scientists to dismiss the idea of God and to rubbish any talk of God. As John Haught puts it, "since God does not fall within the realm of 'evidence' that science deals with, any reasonable, scientifically educated persons must therefore repudiate belief in God."[491] Such a way of looking at things can lead to a rather colourless and soul-less view of reality. Keith Ward suggests that it paints us as "computational, inefficiently designed and largely malfunctioning, physical entities without any larger purpose or meaning within the blind, pointless, freak accident of a wholly physical universe."[492]

People of faith view things differently, allowing for supernatural as well as natural explanations. James Sire explains how science has no time for the supernatural, by which he means "anything above or beyond what one holds to be natural and exists outside natural law and the observable universe. Science limits its explanations for phenomena to natural explanations ... and cannot consider supernatural explanations, as they cannot be investigated empirically."[493]

Believers also respect the integrity and authenticity of religious texts (such as the Bible) although, as Thomas Dixon points out, "the monotheistic religions ... are all united by the idea that God is the author of two books – the book of nature and the book of scripture – and that the individual believer will find their understanding and their faith strengthened through a careful reading of both books."[494] Ecologist and Christian Sam Berry emphasises that, "if God did indeed write Books of both Words [scripture] and Works [nature], it follows that they cannot conflict with each other. The problem for us is that they are written in different languages and mixing the languages of 'philosophy', science and divinity is an excellent recipe for confusion."[495]

Knowing the mind of God

A glimmer of hope in reconciling the naturalist and supernaturalist perspectives was offered when Albert Einstein concluded that "Science without religion is lame. Religion without science is blind."[496] Hopes were raised when he wrote about "knowing the mind of God" (as we saw in Chapter 3), but as Krista Tippett clarifies, it turns out he "didn't believe in a personal God who would interfere with the laws of physics. But he was fascinated with the ingenuity of those laws and expressed awe at the very fact of their existence."[497]

In his own words, Einstein was moved by "a knowledge of the existence of something we cannot penetrate, of the manifestations of the profoundest reason and the most radiant beauty. It is this knowledge and this emotion that constitute the truly religious attitude. In this sense, and in this alone, I am a deeply religious man. I cannot conceive of a God who rewards and punishes his creatures, or has a will of the type of which we are conscious in ourselves. Enough for me, the mystery of the eternity of life and the inkling of the marvellous structure of reality, together with the single-hearted endeavour to comprehend a portion, be it ever so tiny, of the reason that manifests itself in nature."[498]

More recently, Stephen Hawking concluded in *The Grand Design* that there is no need for God in explaining the universe. This disappointed many people who assumed that Hawking probably believed in God, largely on the basis of the final sentence in *A Brief History of Time* where he wrote "If we discover a complete theory, it would be the ultimate triumph of human reason – for then we should know the mind of God."[499] But Hawking was using the term 'God' in the same way that Einstein had, as an original creating force not a God who created the universe and everything in it (the central tenet of deism) or a personal God who was and remains interested in humans (the central tenet of theism).

Richard Dawkins regrets the way in which physicists make use of the word God metaphorically, and regards the confusion this causes as 'an act of intellectual high treason'."[500]

Nonetheless, scientists have not always totally excluded God from explanations of how the universe came into being. As Christopher Hitchens reminds us, in the past "many scientists and philosophers and mathematicians took what might be called the default position and professed one or another version of 'deism', which held that the order and predictability of the universe seemed indeed to imply a designer, if not necessarily a designer who took any active part in human affairs."[501] Richard Dawkins, softening his position slightly to even allow for the vague possibility of a divine creator, draws comfort from the fact that, "compared with the Old Testament's psychotic delinquent, the deist God of the eighteenth-century Enlightenment is an altogether grander being: worthy of his cosmic creation, loftily unconcerned with human affairs, sublimely aloof from our private thoughts and hopes, caring nothing for our messy sins or mumbled contritions. The deist God is a physicist to end all physics, the alpha and omega of mathematicians, the apotheosis of designers; a hyper-engineer who set up the laws and constants of the universe, fine-tuned them with exquisite precision and foreknowledge, detonated what we would now call the hot big bang, retired and was never heard from again."[502]

Keith Ward shares Dawkins' view of God as "the physicist to end all physics", but not surprisingly he does so from the opposite viewpoint. Ward writes that "the mind of God would not be like any human mind. Human minds are dependent on brains, on a physical environment, and on being given information. A divine mind would be totally independent. Its information would not come from outside, but would be part of its own being. Human minds depend on many external and contingent factors for their knowledge, and act on many different and often irrational principles. But in God, the knowing subject and the things known are parts of the same being, and do not depend on anything external. The things known (in the first place, all possible states) are necessarily what they are."[503]

The nature of science

How does science work? Science is driven by the search for objectivity, and scientific 'knowledge' is based on logic, observation, and experimentation. The scientific method - the mode of operation that all scientists work by, no matter what field of science they are working in - is designed to make the search for that knowledge as objective as possible.

In essence, scientists start with ideas then test them rigorously and repeatedly against evidence. The usual starting point is a set of physical laws or findings from carefully controlled experiments or observations. They then formulate a theory or a hypothesis, such as an idea about how a particular part of nature operates or functions, based on the laws or findings. The theory or hypothesis is then tested, typically by using it to make predictions and then comparing those with observations of what actually happened. If the observations differ from the predictions, the theory or hypothesis is revised and the comparison is done again using revised predictions. This cycle of progressive refinement is repeated many times until the predictions closely match the observations.

The scientific method requires the theory or hypothesis to be tested multiple times (in a series of experiments or measurements), often by more than one research group, to confirm its general applicability and establish that it was not a one-off event or finding. Hence the essence of the scientific method is accuracy, rigour and repeatability.

Modern science is rooted in the philosophy of empiricism, which argues that knowledge comes only or mainly from observational evidence discovered in properly-constituted experiments. It is also rooted in logical positivism, which defines "meaningful statements" as those which can be verified through sense experience or are true simply by virtue of their form and the meaning of the words used. As Roy Varghese points out, from the perspective of logical positivism, "the only meaningful statements [are] those used in science, logic, or mathematics. Statements in metaphysics, religion, aesthetics, and ethics [are] literally meaningless, because they [can] not be verified by empirical methods. They [are] neither valid nor invalid."[504]

Scientism

The claim that science provides the most reliable access to all truth is generally known as scientism. Cosmologist George Ellis dismisses scientism as "a fundamentalist atheist religion, complete with a creed: 'Science is the sole route to true, complete, and perfect knowledge.' ... it is as dogmatic and closed a belief system as any religion has ever been."[505] Nonetheless it underlies and legitimises the general public's trust in experts - people who discover, preserve and communicate 'truth', and who explain to them what is known and understood about 'reality'. As James Sire explains, experts can and often do exert undue influence over how the general public sees, understands and values things, because "their interpretations and explanations – their 'stories' – are accepted (often without question) because we respect their authority, by virtue of which we see and treat them as holding privileged positions."[506]

But, as we saw in Chapter 2, from a postmodern perspective all narratives (stories) are part of a power struggle between competing points of view and ways of explaining things. By definition they are never value-free or fully objective, because no such thing is ever possible. This is why theologian Walter Brueggemann argues that, in judging the claims of science, "we are now able to see that what has passed for objective, universal knowledge has in fact been the interested claim of the dominant voices who were able to pose their view and to gain either assent or docile acceptance from those whose interest the claim did not serve."[507]

Paradigms

Things, even intellectual things, rarely remain constant for ever. How we investigate - often referred to as a paradigm - is important in both philosophy and science, because it shapes what are generally regarded as legitimate things to study, legitimate ways of studying them, and legitimate ways of explaining the results or findings. But, as historian of science Thomas Kuhn pointed out in *The Structure of Scientific Revolutions* (1962), paradigms are always open to change.[508] Such a 'paradigm shift' can occur when a growing body of new evidence challenges or contradicts the received wisdom, and the search begins for a more suitable paradigm which better accommodates all the evidence available at that point in time.

When the paradigm shift is particularly large, a dominant world-view can be replaced by another. A well-known example from history was the replacement of Ptolemy's geocentric (earth-centred) ideas about the universe by the Copernican view that the earth spins around its axis daily and orbits around the sun annually. A more recent example was the replacement of Newtonian physics by Einsteinian physics.[509] Newtonian physics is based on the idea that the universe is made up of solid objects which are attracted towards each other by the force of gravity. Einsteinian physics is very different; it is based on the theory of general relativity, which argues that space and time are not fixed but can vary according to the matter within them.

Limitations to science

Whilst many people still carry around in their heads the image of the scientist (mad or otherwise) in the white coat, walking round with a clipboard, deep in thought, and ultra-knowledgeable about really complex things, that is very much an outdated stereotype. Whilst science claims to be "coherent, objective, unproblematic and well-bounded" and the general view persists that "scientific thought is the yardstick with which to measure the validity of everyday thinking,"[510] historian of science Jerry Ravetz insists these are based on old assumptions about science.

Terry Eagleton insists that science "trades on certain articles of faith like any other form of knowledge. ... science, like any other human affair, is indeed shot through with prejudice and partisanship, not to speak of ungrounded assumptions, unconscious biases, taken-for-granted truths, and beliefs too close to the eyeball to be objectified. Like religion, science is a culture, not just a set of procedures and hypotheses."[511] Developing this theme further, Alister McGrath clarifies that "every intellectual tool that we possess needs to be calibrated – in other words, to be examined to identify the conditions under which it is reliable. The question of whether science has limits is certainly not improper, nor does a positive answer to the question in any way represent a lapse into some kind of superstition. It is simply a legitimate demand for calibration of intellectual accuracy."[512]

Like all other branches of knowledge, science has its fair share of limitations. Michael Poole argues that "the limitations of science lie not so much in the territory it explores ... but rather in the methods it uses, the questions it can answer and the types of explanations it gives. Science can deal with spectral wavelengths, but not the beauty of a sunset; with pair-bonding, but not love. Furthermore, science cannot tell us whether courses of action are right or wrong, only what are their likely consequences."[513]

It is beyond the bounds of science to deal with important areas of concern for humans, such as ethics, aesthetics, and meaning. George Ellis describes them as "outside the competence of science because there is no scientific experiment which can determine any of them. Science can help illuminate some of their aspects, but it is fundamentally unable to touch their core."[514] John Cornwell points to the fact that, "while science explores the material universe it is only a partial description of a reality, from which consciousness, value, and purpose are missing."[515] While Peter Medawar insisted that "science is incomparably the most successful enterprise human beings have ever engaged upon,"[516] he did stress the importance of distinguishing between what he called "transcendent questions" (which are best left to religion and metaphysics) and scientific questions, "where there are no limits to the possibilities of scientific achievement."[517]

Many moral and ethical issues arise in the uses to which scientific knowledge is put. There is no denying the fact that science "has delivered the great benefits of humankind: myriad therapies for disease and suffering, greater food security, speedy means of travel, wealth, better housing, communications, entertainment, physical comfort,"[518] as John Cornwell rightly points out. But not all applications of scientific knowledge have been benign; obvious examples include military weapons and potentially dangerous technologies like nuclear energy.

Science, and the scientific understanding of things, are inevitably time-bound. We have already seen how paradigms can change, causing new questions to be asked and old answers to be revisited in the light of new evidence. Science offers the best explanations yet, that fit currently available evidence, but scientific explanations are time-specific and likely to be revised through time. Few people these days still believe that the earth is flat or that the earth is literally the centre of the universe. Thomas Dixon points out that "the history of science is a graveyard of now-abandoned theories which were once the most successful available but which posited entities we now do not believe existed. This would apply to the 18th century theory of combustion, according to which a substance known as 'phlogiston' was given off when things burned. Another example is the 'ether' of 19th century physics – a physical medium that was supposed to be necessary for the propagation of electromagnetic waves."[519] With some relish Terry Eagleton writes that "Ditchkins [his composite of Richard Dawkins and Christopher Hitchens rolled into one] does not exactly fall over himself to point out how many major scientific hypotheses confidently cobbled together by our ancestors have crumbled to dust, and how probable it is that the same fate will befall many of the most cherished scientific doctrines of the present."[520]

Science also creates the illusion of certainty, which Jerry Ravetz describes as, "along with 'objectivity', the other great falling idol of contemporary science." He argues that "certainty has been the hallmark of genuine science, for teachers and for propagandists, for a very long time indeed. … Uncertainty is not just a black hole of disbelief. It is a special state of knowing, whereby imperfections in our knowledge can be recognised, understood and used creatively."[521] As a consequence, one of the central challenges of contemporary science is managing uncertainty. For example, there are many unknowns and much uncertainty surrounding global warming and its causes and consequences, yet scientists are expected to come up with solutions which politicians find acceptable … a major challenge indeed.

Science also seeks explanations that are as simple as possible given the available evidence. That's why, for example, scientific explanations are often based on mathematical equations which look to the untrained eye remarkably straight-forward but often capture immensely complex phenomena. Perhaps the best-known (but not necessarily the best-understood) example is Einstein's equation e=mc² which describes the relationship between mass (m), energy (e), and the speed of light (c). But scientists now know that such simplicity is deceptive. Einstein himself showed early in the 20th century that light, which was then understood as an electromagnetic wave, also appeared to behave as if it were made up of tiny particles (which were later called photons). This gave rise to quantum theory, which looks at the behaviour of atomic and subatomic particles.

As Thomas Dixon points out, quantum theory "seems to overturn many of the basic assumptions of classical Newtonian mechanics. ... According to quantum theory, entities such as photons and electrons are simultaneously both particles and waves. Whether they seem to behave like one or the other depends on how the experimental apparatus interacts with them. Heisenberg's uncertainty principle further dictates that the momentum or the position of a quantum entity can be known, but never both. ... Quantum theory also undermines the idea that the physical world exists objectively and independently of human observers, since it is the act of observation, or measurement, that collapses the wave function. The solid physical world of our everyday experience and of Newtonian physics in some sense comes into existence only by being measured."[522]

As if quantum theory was not complex enough, there is ongoing debate within the philosophy of science between so-called realists and anti-realists about whether or not reality exists independently of observers and observation. Realists believe there is "an external world that exists and has properties independently of human observers, so that it is reasonable to try to discover what those properties are, whether the entities in question are directly observable by us or not,"[523] as Thomas Dixon puts it. As he points out, "arguments about realism particularly arise in connection with what scientific theories have to say about unobservable entities such as magnetic fields, black holes, electrons, quarks, superstrings, and the like. To be a realist is to suppose that science is in the business of providing accurate descriptions of such entities."[524] Conversely, anti-realists believe that "all we ever discover, either individually or collectively, is how the world appears to us. ... We can have no knowledge of the world beyond the impression it makes on us, and so, the anti-realist concludes, we should remain agnostic about the hidden forces and structures which scientists hypothesise about in their attempts to explain those impressions."[525] From this perspective, "science is in the business only of providing accurate predictions of observable phenomena."[526]

Is the existence of God a scientific question?

Richard Dawkins won few friends in either the faith or scientific communities by insisting in *The God Delusion* that "God's existence or non-existence is a scientific fact about the universe ... [and] the presence or absence of a creative super-intelligence is unequivocally a scientific question."[527] Dawkins' rhetoric often soars, but his meaning is not always clear. Quite what he means by "a scientific fact" remains unclear; presumably he is thinking of evidence that can be corroborated by the scientific method. Nicholas Lash suggests that "what [he] seems to mean is that the existence of God is an *empirical* question"[528] and Michael Dunne agrees that, "for Dawkins, the hypothesis concerning the existence of God must always be an empirical one and there is no way in which he is willing to treat of God as a being which transcends the universe. If God cannot be the object of science, then for Dawkins he has the same status as 'fairies at the bottom of the garden'."[529]

But such a position offers little credit to the integrity of legitimate scientific enquiry. It also reveals Dawkins' obsessive compulsion in believing that science can tackle any question and the scientific method can unequivocally reveal truth, even when applied to non-material matters. John Haught takes Dawkins to task for this category error, insisting that his claim that science "can decide the question of God because of its potential command of all the relevant evidence ... makes no sense for the simple reason that [the] scientific method by definition has nothing to say about God, meaning, values, or purpose."[530]

Although Dawkins has a rather idiosyncratic take on the matter, it would be wrong to assume that he is alone in proposing a scientific approach to the study of God. Five decades ago English theologian Austin Farrer suggested that "we ought to have a science about God, or (what comes to the same thing) an empirical approach to theology. It is the suggestion that there are some facts on which religious belief rests; that these facts can, and should, be looked at with an impartial eye, and by the best and most accurate means available to us; and that having made our observations, we should not use them as ammunition either in support or in defeat of existing doctrines, but rather set old theories aside while we consider what description or explanation the observed facts genuinely call for."[531] Others have accepted the challenge that Farrer threw down, and have attempted to sketch out what "the science of God" might look like. Two interesting books on the theme are *The Science of God. The convergence of scientific and biblical wisdom* (1997) by US physicist-turned-theologian Gerald Schroeder[532] and *The Science of God. An introduction to scientific theology* (2004) by British biophysicist-turned-theologian Alister McGrath.[533]

Conflict and reconciliation

One of the key arguments that atheists (particularly the New Atheists) repeatedly use is that science has replaced religion as the best way of explaining our own existence and the nature of the universe. This builds on the popular notion that, particularly over the last three centuries, science and religion have always been at war.

Richard Dawkins is a keen advocate of the view that science and religion are locked into a battle to the death, and science has already emerged the winner. It is a popular view, with unfortunate and enduring consequences. Mathew Reisz points out that this idea of never-ending conflict leads to crude stereotyping in which "scientists end up thinking that all Christians believe in a young-Earth creation, while the religious assume that any scientist at a famous university must be an atheist and hostile to religion. Neither is at all accurate."[534] Accurate or not, the view is a very common one. In an extreme form, for example, it allows Christopher Hitchens to write off religion as "a babyish attempt to meet our inescapable demand for knowledge (as well as for comfort, reassurance, and other infantile needs). Today the least educated of my children knows much more about the natural order than any of the founders of religion."[535]

Many historians of science dismiss the 'conflict model' as simplistic and distorted. Theologian Alister McGrath (who has a PhD in physics) rejects it as "a hopelessly muddled reading of things. ... [it] is now seen as a hopelessly outmoded historical stereotype which scholarship has totally discredited."[536] Historian of science Thomas Dixon agrees, insisting that "there are good historical reasons for rejecting simple conflict stories. From Galileo's trial in 17th-century Rome to modern American struggles over the latest form of anti-evolutionism, known as 'Intelligent Design', there has been more to the relationship between science and religion than meets the eye, and certainly more than just conflict."537 Physicist and theologian John Polkinghorne helpfully points out that "there is no real conflict between science and Christianity, though there are puzzles about how they relate to each other, as there are similar puzzles about the relationship between the different sciences."538

God of the Gaps

A common view is that, as science fills in progressively more and more of the gaps in our knowledge of the world around us, what was once mysterious has become more understandable. As a result, God - the traditional way of explaining the mysterious - seems to have been pushed progressively to the margins and into smaller and smaller crevices of understanding, as a residual way of explaining the bits that science cannot yet explain.

This so-called God of the Gaps argument came to prominence during the eighteenth and nineteenth centuries. The term God of the Gaps was introduced by Scottish evangelical theologian Henry Drummond in a series of lectures delivered in Boston in 1893, where he spoke of those "reverend minds who ceaselessly scan the fields of Nature and the books of Science in search of the gaps – gaps which they will fill up with God. As if God lived in the gaps?"539 As the idea took hold and became a useful argument for scientists and their supporters to use against religion and its believers, serious questions began to be asked about whether there was in fact any need for God at all, both as an initial designer and creator, and since then as absentee retired landlord or ever-present controller and guide.

The roots of the argument can be traced back to the end of the seventeenth century, when English physicist Isaac Newton (1642-1727) wrote his ground-breaking book *The Principles of Natural Philosophy* (1687). Newton saw God as essential in explaining how the universe operates; in his view nature is passive and God makes things happen. He developed mathematical equations to describe the relations between the different parts of the universe, which he regarded as proof of God's existence.540 But, as Thomas Dixon explains, "when confronted with questions such as why the planets in our solar system remained in their orbits rather than gradually slowing down and being drawn towards the sun, or why the distant stars were not all drawn towards each other, [Newton] was prepared to hypothesise that God must intervene from time to time in order to keep the stars and planets in their proper positions."[541] To make his explanation fit the available evidence, Newton needed God to intervene "every now and then to put the orbits back on an even keel", as Christopher Hitchens gleefully explains.[542] German natural philosopher (scientist) G.W. Leibniz rejected the idea that God apparently needed "to *wind up* his watch from time to time" and "to *clean* it now and then" and even "to *mend* it, as a clockmaker mends his work; who must consequently be so much the more unskilful a workman, as he is oftener obliged to mend his work and to set it right."[543] Instead, he argued that God got it right in the first place and made a universe that worked properly from the very beginning, without the need to keep tinkering with it.

Many people today, scientists and the general public alike, would argue that the Enlightenment project has replaced God and has no need for him. There's no denying the fact that science has not only helped us to understand and explain the world about us much better but has also given us increasing mastery over it. Keith Ward reminds us, for example, that "since 1953 we have become able to identify the mechanisms of human heredity, and possibly create our own successors in genetic laboratories. We have uncovered the structure of the brain, and can map just how it operates to produce perception and thought. We have built computers that may in future simulate exactly every human thought-process."[544] Yet Ward also points out that "no special divine effects have ever been recorded in the laboratories of science, and science explains the world very well without God. So that God, the God who ought to be another fact that we can record and document, seems to have disappeared from the modern world."[545]

The view that science has pushed God to the margins, there to explain what we do not yet know, has not disappeared altogether. Michael Poole gives some contemporary examples of how people use the God of the Gaps argument, arguing for example that "scientists trace the origins of the universe to a Big Bang ... but they don't understand how the Big Bang itself started. God did that. Cosmologists know that stars were made by hydrogen collecting under gravity – but they'll never unravel the mystery of black holes. That's God's secret. The human genome sequence has been completed – but they will never be able to make things live. Only God can do that!"[546]

There are plenty of other things that science cannot yet explain and for which God is often held responsible, such as miracles and other apparently supernatural phenomena and events. Nonetheless, few people today would disagree with Dawkins' statement that we get nowhere by labelling our ignorance God[547] and few theologians give any credence to the idea of a God of the Gaps. Alister McGrath regrets what he calls "the forced relocation of God by doubtless well-intentioned Christian apologists into the hidden recesses of the universe, beyond evaluation or investigation. Now that's a real concern."[548] He dismisses the God of the Gaps argument as "a foolish move [which] was increasingly abandoned in the twentieth century."[549] To John Polkinghorne it was "a sort of Cheshire Cat deity, fading away with the advancement of knowledge. ... If God is the god of truth, then the more truth we have, the greater understanding we have, the more we are actually learning about God."[550]

Human progress, through science or other routes, does not in itself mean that God doesn't exist and never did. Neither does it necessarily mean that God might have been active in the past but is now redundant and surplus to requirements; a kind of *deus emeritus* (God in retirement). The God of the Gaps line of reasoning has echoes of a story I stumbled across when writing my first book *Ecology and Environmental Management* three decades ago. The story centred on why dragons, once so prominent in mythology and literature, have apparently become extinct in recent centuries. Many causes had been suggested for the lack of physical remains or recent sightings, including climate change, loss of habitat, competition for food, and overkill by saints and brave knights in armour, but the most likely explanation seems to be loss of credibility.[551]

Reconciling religion and science

Has science killed the idea of God and replaced religion? The New Atheists certainly think so, and would like the rest of us to think so too. Christopher Hitchens was convinced that "all attempts to reconcile faith with science are consigned to failure and ridicule."[552] He and his fellow New Atheists see it as an either/or between religion and science, and they are not alone in holding that view. Alister McGrath asks rhetorically "has science disproved God?"[553] though he remains far from convinced that it has.

To crusading atheist George Smith "the controversy between naturalism and supernaturalism is not a contest between two rival modes of explanation; it is not a matter of which provides a better explanation. Rather, it is an issue of explanation versus no explanation whatsoever. It is an issue of the knowable versus the unknowable."[554] It is interesting that Smith characterises and dismisses the supernatural as "unknowable" rather than non-existent!

Science is not the enemy of faith. Klaus Klostermaier bemoans the fact that "a died-in-the-wool materialist like Dawkins cannot accept the notion of non-material reality. Consciousness/mind/soul do not figure as 'reality' in the vocabulary of a science that recognises only 'objects' as real."[555] John Haught insists that it is scientific naturalism and not science "that has dislodged the personality of God from nature. ... Scientific naturalists believe – since they cannot prove – that science is the privileged way to encounter the real world, that only scientifically available evidence counts, and that only scientific understanding and knowledge can be trusted."[556] As Marcus Borg puts it, "a material understanding of reality is a product of the inference that only that which can be known scientifically may be regarded as real."[557]

To many people, science and religion appear to have mutually exclusive ways of thinking, seeing, and explaining. Kathleen Jones reminds us that "scientists and theologians frequently debate the same issues, but in different languages. In both fields, it is recognised that the scope and grandeur of the universe are beyond our comprehension."[558] Despite the obvious differences between science and religion, Krista Tippett points out that, "in the middle of our ... modern culture, scientific and religious truths coexist and intertwine for the most part peaceably. ... the insights of science and of theology are complementary disciplines that can mutually enrich and illuminate the deepest questions and frontiers of human life and of faith."[559]

During his visit to London September 2010 Pope Benedict XVI said that while the human and natural sciences provide us with an "invaluable understanding" of aspects of our existence, the sciences "cannot satisfy the deepest longings of the human heart, they cannot fully explain to us our origin and our destiny, why and for what purpose we exist; nor indeed can they provide us with an exhaustive answer to the question 'Why is there something rather than nothing?'."[560]

One interesting attempt to reconcile science and religion is the proposal by respected US scientist Stephen Jay Gould that "science and religion are not in conflict, for their teachings occupy distinctly different domains."[561] Gould called these domains 'magisteria' and he argued that science and religion occupy Non-Overlapping Magisteria (NOMA). From this perspective there is no real overlap between "their respective domains of professional expertise— science in the empirical constitution of the universe, and religion in the search for proper ethical values and the spiritual meaning of our lives. The attainment of wisdom in a full life requires extensive attention to both domains."[562] In considering Gould's ideas, Richard Dawkins is more than happy "to cite the old clichés, science gets the age of rocks, and religion the rock of ages; science studies how the heavens go, religion how to get to heaven."[563]

Gould's ideas about separate magisteria look promising as a way of reconciling science and religion, but they have been roundly rejected by both camps. Daniel Dennett points out that "although Gould's desire for peace between these often warring perspectives was laudable, his proposal found little favour on either side, since in the minds of the religious it proposed abandoning all religious claims to factual truth and understanding of the natural world (including the claims that God created the universe, or performs miracles, or listens to prayers), whereas in the minds of the secularists it granted too much authority to religion in matters of ethics and meaning."[564] Richard Dawkins rejected the suggestion that "the competence of the scientist might be restricted to a specific field of inquiry and that others might be experts in their own field.", as Michael Dunne puts it. He adds that "what Dawkins will not concede is that a theologian (or any theist) has any authority to speak because there is only one magisterium, that of science and of its servants."[565]

Alister McGrath suggests that rather than accepting or rejecting Gould's NOMA proposition fully, "there is, of course, a third option – that of 'partially-overlapping magisteria' (a POMA, so to speak), reflecting a realisa tion that science and religion offer possibilities of cross-fertilisation on account of the interpenetration of their subjects and methods."[566] McGrath suggests that Francis Collins (former head of the Human Genome Project), who writes of "a richly satisfying harmony between the scientific and spiritual world-views,[567] is an obvious exponent of the POMA perspective.

A common view today is that, whilst they are not necessarily always at loggerheads nor inherently incompatible, science and religion ask different questions and seek answers in different ways. Michael Shermer seizes on the fact that "science and religion are, at present, largely separate spheres of knowledge divided by, more than anything else, a difference in methodologies. ... attempts at reconciling science and religion always fail for the fundamental reason that religion ultimately depends on faith."[568] Lord Sacks (Chief Rabbi in the UK) adopts a broader perspective, pointing out that "Science is about explanation. Religion is about interpretation. Science takes things apart to see how they work. Religion puts things together to see what they mean. They are different intellectual enterprises. They even occupy different hemispheres of the brain. Science – linear, atomistic, analytical – is a typical left-brain activity. Religion – integrative, holistic, relational – is supremely a work of the right brain."[569]

Although science and religion remain two different "intellectual enterprises", this does not necessarily mean that individuals cannot straddle them and embrace both. Richard Dawkins acknowledges that many leading scientists of the past were religious. Indeed he lists the Argument from Admired Religious Scientists as one of the arguments for the existence of God. Examples he points to include the Italian mathematician and astronomer Galileo Galilei (1564-1642), the father of modern observational astronomy; English mathematician and astronomer Isaac Newton (1642-1727), founder of classical mechanics; German mathematician and astronomer Johannes Kepler (1571-1630), discoverer of the laws of planetary motion; English scientist Michael Faraday (1791-1867), who demonstrated the existence of electromagnetic fields; Scottish mathematical physicist James Clerk Maxwell (1831-1879), who formulated classical electromagnetic theory; and British mathematical physicist William Thomson (Lord Kelvin) (1824-1907), a key player in the development of modern physics. Thomas Dixon underlines the fact that "pioneers of early modern science such as Isaac Newton and Robert Boyle saw their work as part of a religious enterprise devoted to understanding God's creation. Galileo too thought that science and religion could exist in mutual harmony."[570]

But that was then; what about today? Perhaps not surprisingly, Dawkins takes a dim view on the matter. In his unapologetically highly partisan view, "great scientists of our time who sound religious usually turn out not to be so when you examine their beliefs more deeply. This is certainly true of Einstein and Hawking."[571] Later in *The God Delusion* he argues that "the efforts of apologists to find genuinely distinguished modern scientists who are religious have an air of desperation ... [and] religious apologists might be wise to keep quieter than they habitually do on the subject of admired role models, at least where scientists are concerned."[572]

Not everyone sees things this way. For example, Alister McGrath dismisses Richard Dawkins' insistence that "real scientists do not believe in God" as "a viewpoint that can only be sustained by the relentless use of selective attention and turbocharged shock-and-awe rhetoric, rather than evidence-based argument."[573] McGrath points out that few scientists share Dawkins' view "that the natural sciences are an intellectual superhighway to atheism." He adds that "most unbelieving scientists of my acquaintance are atheists on grounds other than their science; they bring those assumptions *to* their science, rather than basing them *on* their science. ... [Dawkins'] petulant, dogmatic insistence that all 'real' scientists ought to be atheists has met with fierce resistance from precisely the community that he believes should be his fiercest and most loyal supporter."[574]

Thomas Dixon points out that there are a large number of "religious scientists who continue to see their research as a complement rather than a challenge to their faith"[575] One of these is Sam Berry, former Professor of Genetics at the University of London, who has collected together the stories of a number of them in his 2009 book *Real Scientists, Real Faith*.[576] Berry's contributors include Professor Alister McGrath, a molecular biologist and theologian; Reverend Professor John Polkinghorne FRS (Fellow of the Royal Society), a theoretical physicist and theologian; Professor Sir John Houghton FRS, an atmospheric physicist and former head of the UK Meteorological Office; Professor Sir Ghillean Prance FRS, a botanist and former director of the Royal Botanic Gardens, Kew; and Professor Francis Collins, a chemist and former Director of the Human Genome Research Institute in the USA.

A large-scale study of religious belief, identity and practice among 1,700 natural and social science academics in the USA was carried out in 2010.[577] One third of those who took part said they agreed with the statement 'I do not believe in God', and 30 per cent claimed to be agnostic. Younger scientists proved more likely than their older peers to believe in God and to attend religious services, and the proportion of younger scientists with religious beliefs was found to have increased relative to a comparable survey 35 years earlier. A large proportion of the scientists did not identify with orthodox faith but saw themselves as spiritual, looking for ways to hold science and faith together but free from the constraints of traditional religion.

My own understanding and thinking in this area of science and faith has been strongly shaped by the writings of John Polkinghorne and Alister McGrath. Polkinghorne believes that "both science and religion are needed to interpret and understand the rich, varied, and surprising way the world actually is."[578] He believes that "reality is very rich and many-layered. Science, in a sense, explores only one layer of the world. It treats the world as an object, something you can put to the test, pull apart and find out what it's made of. And, of course, that's a very interesting thing to do, and you learn some important things that way. But we know that there are whole realms of human experience where testing has to give way to trusting."[579]

As a teenager Alister McGrath saw atheism as "the natural resting-place for a scientifically informed person" like himself, and he viewed God as "a baleful relic of the past, revealed as a delusion by scientific advance."[580] As an undergraduate in chemistry at Oxford, after reading Peter Medawar's book *Limits of Science*, "having realised that a love of science allowed much greater freedom of interpretation of reality than I had been led to believe, I began to explore alternative ways of looking at it. ... By the end of November 1971, I had made my decision: I turned my back on one faith [atheism], and embraced another [Christianity]. ... I suddenly found that the entire scientific enterprise made a lot more sense than I had ever appreciated. It was as if an intellectual sun had risen and illuminated the scientific landscape, allowing me to see details and interconnections that I would otherwise have missed altogether."[581]

Looking back, the story of my own journey through life (touched upon in Chapter 2) echoes many of the themes we have looked at in this chapter. It begins with a natural childhood curiosity in the world around me, which developed into an unquestioning belief in the ability of science to answer all questions that matter. After taking a science degree and launching forth on a career as an academic, I embarked on a journey of discovery which included reading widely about such things as creation and evolution, the age of the earth, and how the universe was formed, and reading books by trusted scientists who are also men of faith (because they were all men).

Coming to a personal faith as a Christian was greatly helped by this reading, but only in an intellectual way. The real breakthrough for me was spiritual, as God made his presence and character obvious to me through a range of very personal encounters and experiences. From that point on, half a life ago, it has been abundantly clear to me that faith and science are not an either/or, but they belong together and can both amplify and enrich my understanding of the world around me. I can view that world through each lens (faith and science), and through that gain a much richer, deeper and more meaningful understanding of how things are, and why they are the way they are.

CHAPTER 7

ARGUMENTS FOR GOD

"For thousands of years the greatest minds of every generation have worked diligently to prove the existence of God, and for thousands of years great minds have produced valid refutations of those proofs."

Michael Shermer (2000)

English Christian writer David Watson bemoaned "our human arrogance which assumes that God must somehow justify his existence and explain his actions before we are prepared to consider the possibility of believing in him."[582] However much we might regret that arrogance, the fact remains that a great many people today are unwilling to believe that God exists without having good grounds for doing so. Inevitably, therefore, a great deal of attention has been devoted to the search for plausible arguments for the existence God and good reasons for believing in God.

Is anyone there?

Former Bishop of Durham David Jenkins argues that "there has always been a debate about God, not only about what He is like, but about whether He exists at all."[583] From that perspective, in an ideal world everyone would believe without question that God exists; there would be no debate over the matter. But of course that's not the case and increasingly the default position for many people, particularly in western society, is that there is no God, and if there is a God it is a pale reflection of the Abrahamic God that is worshipped in Judaism, Christianity and Islam.

Why is God so elusive? Why doesn't God make himself blindingly obvious to everyone? If God is as ubiquitous and all-knowing as believers say he is, why doesn't he simply make everyone know and believe that he exists, and that would be the end of the matter? As David Jenkins puts it, "it might be supposed that God, if He existed, would be bound to have an existence so certain and so really real that anyone who was capable of thinking about Him at all would be bound to see that He really exists."[584] In a nutshell, why does God play a cosmic game of 'Where's Wally'? From a believer's perspective one answer is that God does not impose himself on us, but rather he grants us an element of choice and free will.

Believers would argue that we see God through a window into a different world, or in different 'levels of reality' (material and spiritual) as we saw in Chapter 2. Perhaps surprisingly, even New Atheist Sam Harris concedes that there is a "world beyond reason ... [in which] a certain range of human experience can be appropriately described as 'spiritual' or 'mystical' – experiences of meaningfulness, selflessness, and heightened emotion that surpass our narrow identities as 'selves' and escape our current understanding of the mind and brain."[585] Harris brings the argument back down to earth with a bump in concluding that "the problem with religion is that it blends this truth so thoroughly with the venom of unreason."[586]

Fellow New Atheist Daniel Dennett views "the goal of either proving or disproving God's existence [as] a quixotic quest – but also for that very reason not very important. ... The important question is whether religions deserve the continued protection of their adherents."[587] Presumably with Richard Dawkins in mind, Dennett points out that many atheists devote much time and energy "to looking at the arguments for and against the existence of God ... hacking away vigorously at the arguments of the believers as if they were trying to refute a rival scientific theory. But not I. I decided some time ago that diminishing returns had set in on the arguments about God's existence, and I doubt that any breakthroughs are in the offing, from either side."[588]

Dennett may well be right about the lack of "breakthroughs", but given the amount of time and effort that have been devoted over many centuries to constructing arguments for God's existence, it is only fair to give them an airing.

Nearly 200 years ago Hegel commented that "God does not offer himself for observation,"[589] so we have to find indirect ways of establishing at least the likelihood of God's existence. As we shall see, these tend to rely more on lines of argument than on proof or tangible evidence, so weighing up the nature and credibility of different arguments is not without challenge. Ultimately, belief in the existence and nature of God is a matter of faith, which we will explore in more detail in Chapter 9.

Approaches

To help us better understand the essence of many of the arguments for God it is important to clarify two important things - sources of data and types of argument.

As David Jenkins points out "there are two sources of data which can supply the actual content of Christian belief or, at least, lead to its acceptance. These are commonly and shortly described as Reason and Revelation."[590] Reason is important because it is through reason - the search for a cause, explanation or justification for something - that we think about the world about us, the world that science tries to study objectively. Natural theology uses reason (including philosophical arguments) to establish the existence of God. Revelation - the making known of a previously unknown fact, often in a dramatic way - is very different from reason. Revealed theology goes further than natural theology and reason; believers argue that it provides additional 'truths' which are not accessible to reason (such as the doctrine of creation, the doctrine of the Trinity [the view of God as father, son and spirit] and the incarnation [Jesus as the son of God]). We will look at revelation in more detail in Chapter 8.

Arguments for God's existence fall into two main categories – *a priori* and *a posteriori* arguments. *A priori* (meaning literally 'before' the fact) arguments are deductive; they argue from first principles, based on reason not experience. Philosopher Richard Swinburne points out that in *a priori* arguments "the premises are conceptual truths, viz. propositions which would be true whether or not there was a universe of material or spiritual beings other than God."[591] Anselm's Ontological Argument (below) is the most famous of the *a priori* arguments for the existence of God. *A posteriori* (meaning literally 'after' the fact) arguments, on the other hand, are inductive; they are based on experiences and observations of how things really are, then reasoning back from facts or particulars to general principles. In *a posteriori* arguments "the premises report what are (in some very general sense) features of human experience – eg evident general truths about the world or features of private human experience,"[592] as Swinburne puts it. Aquinas's Five Ways (below) are *a posteriori* arguments.

Anselm's Ontological Argument

Anselm was an eleventh century English Christian philosopher and theologian who became Archbishop of Canterbury (1033-1109). As Francis Collins points out, Anselm was a devout Christian who was also interested in understanding the rational foundations of what he believed.[593]

He developed what has become known as the Ontological Argument, an *a priori* argument. The name is derived from the Greek *ontos*, meaning 'being'. Keith Ward describes the argument as "absolutely infuriating" and notes that "since Anselm's time it has taken many forms, all circling around the one central idea of necessary existence."[594]

Anselm's argument is based on two ideas. The first is that if God exists at least in the mind, then God must also exist in reality. Merely thinking of God, even to deny his existence, proves that he exists. Given that God does exist in the mind of both believers and non-believers, then God does indeed exist.[595] This is called the argument of necessary existence because, as Carolyn Ogden points out, Anselm believed that "God could not be conceived not to exist, for a being that can be thought not to exist is not as great as one that cannot be thought to exist. In other words, existence is necessary to the idea of God."[596]

Secondly, Anselm thought of God as the most perfect being imaginable, or in his words "that than which nothing can be conceived." This is because "a being which could only be conceived in the mind would always be inferior to a being which also existed in reality. Therefore 'that than which nothing greater can be conceived' must exist in reality,"[597] as Patrick Clarke explains. As Karen Armstrong puts it, "since existence is more 'perfect' or complete than non-existence, the perfect being that we imagine must have existence or it would be imperfect."[598]

Peter Vardy points out that Anselm's Ontological Argument "is totally different from any of the other arguments on several grounds: 1. It does not start from experience as a starting point. 2. It claims to arrive at the existence of God by analysing the idea of God and this idea does not depend on experience – it is therefore an *a priori* argument. 3. If the argument succeeds, then the existence of God is logically necessary and, as a matter of logic, it simply does not make sense to doubt that God exists."[599]

Richard Dawkins dismisses Anselm's argument as "infantile" and argues that "the very idea that grand conclusions could follow from such logomachist trickery offends me aesthetically."[600] Dawkins points out that several eighteenth century philosophers refuted the argument, including David Hume (1711-76) and particularly Immanuel Kant (1724-1804), who recognised the "slippery assumption that 'existence' is more 'perfect' than non-existence."[601] Theologian Keith Ward accepts Dawkins' argument "that you cannot establish the existence of something just by the analysis of concepts,"[602] but reminds us that "the function of the ontological argument … is not to prove God, but to remind us of the uniqueness and incomparability of the divine being. It spells out what it is to be a being of supreme perfection."[603]

Seventeenth century French scientist and philosopher René Descartes (1596-1650) developed Anselm's idea a little further. He believed that the idea of God itself proves the existence of God, using the simple logic of causality, because the idea must be caused by God and so God must exist. As Andrew Pessin explains, "if nothing comes from nothing then the idea of an infinite being could only be caused by an actually infinite being. But nothing causes anything unless it exists. So an actually infinite being exists. So God exists."[604]

Aquinas's Five Ways

The medieval philosopher and theologian Thomas Aquinas (1225-1274) rejected Anselm's Ontological Argument, arguing that "had it been convincing, the existence of God would be self-evident to everyone,"[605] which it quite clearly isn't.

Aquinas took a different approach, an *a posteriori* approach based on arguing from what we can see of the world about us and tracing back to the causes of it. He was convinced that the world contains enough evidence to show that God exists, using the logic that if God did not exist then there is no way of explaining the world as we experience it. Richard Dawkins summarises the essence of Aquinas's argument; Aquinas believed that "there must have been a time when no physical thing existed. But, since physical things now exist, there must have been something non-physical to bring them into existence, and that something we call God."[606] Aquinas explained his reasoning through five what he called 'ways', or arguments.

This is still a philosophical approach to the question of God's existence, using arguments which as Michael Poole points out "may be seen as possible pointers rather than proofs."[607] The arguments would not stand up in a court of law, but that should not be the basis on which to judge them. Similarly, the evidence is not particularly persuasive to atheists and scientists like Richard Dawkins, but that says more about their partial notion of reality than about the integrity of Aquinas's thinking.

It is important to keep in mind what Aquinas was trying to do, and why he was trying to do it. Karen Armstrong reminds us that Aquinas "was not trying to convince a sceptic of God's existence. He was simply trying to find a rational answer to the primordial question: 'Why does something exist rather than nothing?' All the five 'ways' argue in one way or another that nothing can come from nothing."[608]

The first three of Aquinas's Five Ways, taken together, are often referred to as the Cosmological Argument. His Fourth Way is often called the Ontological Argument, and his Fifth Way the Teleological Argument.

Prime Mover – what was there at the beginning?

Aquinas's First Way, the first part of his Cosmological Argument, is also known as the Prime Mover Argument or the Unmoved Mover Argument. It argues from the fact of motion or change, and is based on the idea that everything in the universe is in motion, but nothing can be in motion unless it is moved by something else.[609] In Aquinas's words, "it is necessary to arrive at a first mover, moved by no other; and this everyone understands to be God."[610] Aquinas was not the first person to argue this way. As Andrew Pessin explains, the ancient Greek philosopher Aristotle (384-322 BC) believed that "wherever and whenever there is motion … there must exist God. And if the world has always existed and always will, and has been and always will be in motion, then so too God has always existed and always will."[611]

Generalising from motion and its cause, the Prime Mover Argument is about something (such as the universe) moving from 'possible' to 'actual'. As Keith Ward points out, "if all states that come into being are made actual by something actual that contains the idea of their potentiality, then there must be at least one actual state that does not come into being. The simplest hypothesis is that there is one unchanging mind that contains all potential states of the universe."[612]

First Cause – what started it all?

Aquinas's Second Way, the second part of his Cosmological Argument, is also known as the Uncaused Cause Argument. It is based on the idea that there must be a beginning; nothing can cause itself, and everything is an effect that needs to be explained by a prior cause. Hence Aquinas argued that "it is necessary to admit a first efficient cause, to which everyone gives the name of God."[613]

This is a similar argument to the Prime Mover one, but as Keith Ward points out it "amplifies [it] by drawing attention not just to change, but to the origin or coming into being of things. ... there must be some 'first cause'. That first cause does not just happen not to come into being. It could not possibly come into being, because it is timeless and eternal."[614] Aquinas understood the 'first efficient cause' (God) as the explanation of the origin of the universe, with no cause before it.

Contingency – why is there something rather than nothing?

Aquinas's Third Way, the third part of his Cosmological Argument, is also known as the Argument from Contingency. It builds on the first two Ways, and seeks to explain why there is something rather than nothing.

This is a fundamental question with obvious implications. Philosopher Ludwig Wittgenstein believed that "it is not how things are in the world that is [the mystery], but that it exists."[615] Martin Rees has said that "the preeminent mystery is why anything exists at all. What breathes life into the equations of physics, and actualised them in a real cosmos? Such questions lie beyond science, however: they are the province of philosophers and theologians."[616] Apparently philosopher Bertrand Russell declared that the universe is there because it is just there, which led John Cornwell to comment that it "seems as arbitrary as to say that dogs are there just because they are there."[617]

The argument is really about the difference between possibility and necessity. As Michael Shermer points out, in nature it is possible for things to be or not to be, but not everything could be in the realm of the possible, for then there could be nothing.[618] This gives rise to the idea of necessary existence, or as Aquinas puts it a Necessary Being, a being which is not only possible but "necessary, having of itself its own necessity ... this all men speak of as God."[619]

John Cornwell argues that Richard Dawkins ridicules the question 'Why is there anything rather than nothing?' because he does not seem to understand it, which "is shown by the fact that [he] actually think[s] that this 'argument for God' is an argument for the ludicrous anthropomorphic deity that rightly appals [him]."[620] Keith Ward also takes Dawkins to task for misreading Aquinas's Third Way, "possibly ... because he has not read it. Certainly the version of it he gives in his book is nothing like Aquinas's argument (which, of course, comes from Aristotle). Aquinas's argument is actually about the possibility of necessary existence, or of 'what must be'. The heart of it is the claim that, if everything in the universe is contingent, then there might well have been nothing at all. But to suppose that the universe could originate from nothing is to give up all hope of a final explanation. So a truly final explanation must postulate the existence of a first cause that is necessary, that could not fail to exist or to be other than it is."[621]

Cornwell insists that "the question 'why is there anything rather than nothing?' is not a final bid for evidence but a quest for meaning or sense that has begun in a moment of wonder that there is anything at all."[622] Thomas Dixon points out that "science is unable to tell us why there is something rather than nothing. Cosmological theories can try to explain how the something that does exist works and how it is related to other cosmic somethings ... But physical science cannot go beyond that to explain why the things that we call matter-energy and laws of nature ever came to be. Here we have an unclosable gap in our scientific knowledge, and one which all theists agree is filled by God."[623]

Perfection - God must be the best of all

Aquinas's Fourth Way, his Ontological Argument, is also known as the Argument from Degree. Aquinas noted that in nature there is a spectrum of goodness; some things are good and others things less so. He then suggests that there must be some maximum standard of goodness to compare everything against, and he argues that "therefore there must be something which is to all beings the cause of their being, goodness, and every other perfection; and this we call God."[624] Richard Dawkins explains it like this - "we notice that things in the world differ. There are degrees of, say, goodness or perfection. But we judge these degrees only by comparison with a maximum. Humans can be both good and bad, so the maximum goodness cannot rest in us. Therefore there must be some other maximum to set the standard for perfection, and we call that maximum God."[625]

Keith Ward explains the Fourth Way from a more spiritual perspective: he writes that it "makes explicit that an eternal mind will not only contain all possible states of affairs. It will discriminate between them, and choose to realise in itself the highest forms of value. It will be the supreme Good, worthy of admiration and reverence for its unique perfection."[626]

Design - and the need for a designer

Aquinas's Fifth Way, his Teleological Argument (from the Greek *telos* meaning 'end' or 'purpose'), is also known as the Argument from Design. It is based on three things - the fact that there appears to be evidence of order, purpose and design in the universe and in life; the belief that this cannot simply be the result of chance and needs explaining; and the conclusion that the universe and life must have been designed, so they must be the product of a designer (God) at work.[627]

Keith Ward argues that the interpretation that, because things look as though they have been designed so they must have been designed "is not quite the point of the argument. ... [It] is concerned with the idea of final causes ... [and the view] that every substance has a goal, a state that fulfils its proper potentiality, towards which it tends by its nature. This sort of goal-directedness is just part of the nature of things. It is not designed or intended by anyone."[628]

Theologian John Baillie clarifies that the essence of the argument "is not that the works of God's hands prove His existence but that they reveal certain aspects of His nature."[629] Philosopher of religion Peter Vardy concedes that "at most the Teleological Argument may show that there is some intelligence responsible for the universe, but what form this intelligence takes and whether it can be identified with the Christian God the argument may not be able to demonstrate."[630]

Conclusions about the Five Ways

Dawkins is quick to dismiss the Five Ways, insisting that they "don't prove anything, and are easily ... exposed as vacuous."[631] Alister McGrath argues that Dawkins "is clearly out of his depth, and achieves little by his brief and superficial engagement with these great perennial debates, which often simply cannot be resolved empirically."[632] Keith Ward also takes Dawkins to task, arguing "I think he has not got the patience to see what is going on, or how similar [this explanation] is to proper scientific enquiry, admittedly at the end of human understanding."[633] Michael Dunne is more pointed in his criticism; he says Dawkins "could have at least copied them down accurately."[634]

Although Dawkins' dismissal of Aquinas's arguments is ill-informed and partisan, Karen Armstrong points out that "these proofs do not hold water today. Even from a religious point of view, they are rather dubious, since, with the possible exception of the argument from design, each proof tacitly implies that 'God' is simply an-other being, one more link in the chain of existence."[635] Alister McGrath explains that "the general consensus among philosophers of religion is that, while such arguments cast interesting light on the questions, they settle nothing. Although traditionally referred to as 'arguments for God's existence', this is not an accurate description. All they do is show the inner consistency of belief in God ..."[636]

The Argument from Design

Despite the inherent limitations in Aquinas's arguments in general, the Argument from Design continues to have enduring attraction and is still widely used today. It takes various forms and is expressed in a variety of ways. Although McGrath insists that it is, strictly speaking, not an argument for God's existence, many people's views of God are heavily shaped by it. To give but one example, church leader David Robertson has written "to stare at the stars is for me one of the major if not *the* major reason for believing in God. I found it difficult to believe that this vast universe existed by itself, or as the result of an accident."[637] He is not alone in marvelling at the tidy order of things; Michael Shermer points out that "the Number One reason people give for why they believe in God is a variation on the classic cosmological or design argument: The good design, natural beauty, perfection, and complexity of the world or universe compels us to think that it could not have come about without an intelligent designer."[638]

Eighteenth century Scottish philosopher David Hume (1711-1776) urged caution in believing that the universe must have some intelligent designer or maker behind it. He argued that "the intelligent designer may be neither intelligent nor a designer", on four grounds:[639]

[i]   Even if the universe is designed, it need not have been designed by God;
[ii] For all we know, the universe is unique, and there is no evidence that universes need designers;
[iii] For all we know, matter may have an inner tendency towards order (only artificial constructions such as clocks or watches need intelligent designers); and
[iv] For all we know, the universe may be the result of pure chance.

English Christian philosopher William Paley (1743-1805) took the opposite view to David Hume. He saw all around him in the natural world evidence of intelligent design, and was convinced that the Argument for Design provided irrefutable proof for the existence of God. Paley explained his reasoning in the book *Natural Theology* (1802), where he compared design in nature with design in a man-made object like a watch.

Karen Armstrong summarises Paley's argument - "just as the intricate machinery of a watch found in a desert place bespoke the existence of a watchmaker, the exquisite adaptations of nature revealed the necessity of a Creator. Only a madman would imagine that a machine came about by chance, and it was equally ludicrous to doubt that the wonders of the natural world – the intricate structure of the eye, the minute hinges of an earwig's wing, the regular succession of the seasons, or the intermeshing muscles and ligaments of the hand – pointed to a divine plan, in which every detail had its unique place and purpose."[640]

Paley's explanation proved very popular and influential, but it has not been without its critics. Our old friend Richard Dawkins has argued that if indeed there is a cosmic watchmaker, he must be a blind one given the many natural problems that exist. Dawkins went as far as naming one of his first books *The Blind Watchmaker*.[641]

Laws of Nature

Many people are impressed if sometimes puzzled by the fact that all of nature appears to operate in such a well-regulated and orderly way, thanks to the 'laws of nature'. Scientists spend much time and effort trying to describe and explain this order and these laws, often with great success. For example, Sir Isaac Newton worked out an equation for gravity that explains why apples fall and why the planets remain in orbit, and Albert Einstein formulated an equation which explains how mass and energy are related. Recall from Chapter 6 the apparent fine-tuning of the universe and the so-called Goldilocks Zone. Nobel Prize-winning physicist Richard Feynman was moved to write "why nature is mathematical is a mystery...The fact that there are rules at all is a kind of miracle."[642]

Thomas Dixon urges caution in how we think of the laws of nature because of the need not to view them as "entities or forces that somehow constrain all of reality. Instead, they can be interpreted in a more modest way as the best empirical generalisations we have so far arrived at to describe the behaviour of particular systems in particular contexts ... Nor are we obliged to believe that the laws of, say, physics are more 'fundamental' than the knowledge acquired through biology, sociology, or everyday experience."[643]

Who wrote the laws of nature? Charles Darwin commented that "whether the existence of a conscious God can be proved from the so-called laws of nature ... is a perplexing subject, on which I have often thought, but cannot see my way clearly."[644] The pioneers of modern science, such as Isaac Newton and Robert Boyle, were also believers in God, and they looked on their research and discoveries as the search for proof of God's handiwork. Thomas Dixon describes how "they envisaged nature as an orderly system of mechanical interactions governed by mathematical laws. And they hoped that people would see in this new vision the strongest possible evidence of divine power and intelligence."[645]

More recent scientists have tended to push God from centre-stage towards the margins in terms of explaining how nature works. But as Anthony Flew explains "Einstein, the discoverer of relativity, was not the only great scientist who saw a connection between the laws of nature and the Mind of God. The progenitors of quantum physics, the other great scientific discovery of modern times, Max Planck, Werner Heisenberg, Erwin Schrödinger, and Paul Dirac, have all made similar statements ..."[646]

But note that they generally used the expression 'the mind of God' in a non-theological way, and recall (from Chapter 6) Stephen Hawking's conclusion that "it is not necessary to invoke God to light the blue touch paper and set the universe going."[647]

Keith Ward supports the argument that the laws of nature provide good evidence of God at work. He contends that "God would not be superfluous ... if God explained just why the laws of nature are as life-conducive as they actually are. The explanation would be what I have called a personal explanation – the laws are chosen by God precisely in order to generate intelligent life. If that is so, the existence of a designing God would certainly raise the probability of the laws of nature being such as to lead to the existence of intelligent life. It would make the existence of such laws virtually certain. So the God Hypothesis is not superfluous after all. It is a very good explanation."[648]

There is a chicken-and-egg dimension to the link between design and belief in God, however, which raises the inevitable question 'which came first'? Cardinal John Henry Newman had no doubt which came first in his experience; he wrote "I believe in design because I believe in God; not in a God because I see design."[649]

The challenge of infinite regress

Critics of Aquinas's Prime Mover Argument and the broader Argument from Design are quick to seize on the problem of what is generally called regress, tracing back to a former state, ideally an original state, with a view to finding a way of explaining how things started in the first place.

As we shall see, a number of the common arguments for the existence God include the idea of infinite regress, the possibility of tracing things back forever, with no obvious beginning. Keith Ward emphasises that "an infinite regress of causes would leave the universe without a final explanation. So if this universe consists of chains of causes going back to one originative event (which it does), and if there is a final explanation of the universe, there must be some cause of the whole series of changes which is immutable, not capable of being changed by anything else."[650]

Critics insist that to assume "God did it", as a way of explaining the unexplainable, is a cop out. Richard Dawkins argues that "to suggest that the first cause, the great unknown which is responsible for something existing rather than nothing, is a being capable of designing the universe and of talking to a million people simultaneously, is a total abdication of the responsibility to find an explanation."[651]

Believers reply that it is logical to see God as the ultimate cause. As Thomas Dixon explains, "to avoid an endless regress, at some point posit a first cause, a 'prime mover', and ... what we know of the world suggests that this prime mover is that same God whom many have encountered through sacred texts and religious experiences. We cannot expect the natural sciences to help us with the question of a first cause."[652]

Appearance of design

The argument from design takes as given the *fact* of design and then goes on to *explain* the design as the result of a designer at work. But, as many critics eagerly point out, just because something *looks* designed doesn't mean that it *is* designed. There are three ways of accounting for the appearance of design in the world around us - it could be the result of chance, it could have arisen by natural causes, or it could be the product of intelligent design by some cosmic designer.

Philosopher David Hulme argued that the appearance of design in the universe is an illusion which might be the result of chance occurrences, but few scientists or theologians today would agree with him. Although Stephen Hawking concluded in his book *The Grand Design* that "spontaneous creation is the reason why there is something rather than nothing, why the universe exists, why we exist"[653] that only 'explains' the beginning of things and not how things have developed since. Philosophers find it easier to envisage the possibility of a universe devoid of rules. For example, Dinesh D'Souza argues that "there is no logical necessity for a universe that obeys rules, let alone one that abides by the rules of mathematics. ... [because] the universe doesn't have to behave this way. It is easy to imagine a universe in which conditions change unpredictably from instant to instant, or even a universe in which things pop in and out of existence."[654]

Design by natural causes

Natural explanations for the appearance of design are popular these days, particularly since Charles Darwin published his theory of evolution and progressive adaptation. Patrick Clarke points out that the traditional

Argument from Design "would lose much of its original force with the arrival of Darwinism in the 1850s, when 'design' was replaced by naturalistic explanations, such as natural selection."[655]

Richard Dawkins gleefully announced that "far from pointing to a designer, the illusion of design in the living world is explained with far greater economy and with devastating elegance by Darwinian natural selection."[656] He dismisses intelligent design as "not the proper alternative to chance" and argues that "natural selection is not only a parsimonious, plausible and elegant solution; it is the only workable alternative to chance that has even been suggested."[657] To Dawkins, "evolution by natural selection produces an excellent simulacrum [representation] of design, mounting prodigious heights of complexity and elegance."[658] You can tell he is a big fan of Charles Darwin!

Dawkins asks rhetorically "who, before Darwin, could have guessed that something so apparently *designed* [his emphasis] as a dragonfly's wing or an eagle's eye was really the end product of a long sequence of non-random but purely natural causes?"[659] Two things are key to his explanation of 'apparent design' - the link between complexity and probability, and the power of accumulation. Dawkins assumes that very complex things in nature are very improbable. He illustrates this with what he calls 'The Ultimate Boeing 747 Gambit', based on the argument that "the probability of life originating on earth is similar to a hurricane sweeping through a scrapyard and having the luck to assemble a 747."[660] We will look at this argument later in this chapter.

Accumulation refers to the way in which, through many generations over a long period of time, small adaptations and changes in a species can accumulate, eventually producing something that at first sight might appear to be highly unlikely. As Dawkins explains, "natural selection is a cumulative process, which breaks the problem of improbability up into small pieces. Each of the pieces is slightly improbable, but not prohibitively so. When large numbers of these slightly improbable events are stacked up in series, the end product of the accumulation is very very improbable indeed, improbable enough to be far beyond the reach of chance."[661]

This chain-reaction of progressive evolutionary change, Dawkins argues, helps explain what he calls 'irreducible complexity' (IC), which creationists wrongly believe evolution is about. Irreducible complexity refers to the existence in nature of things which look extremely complex - like the dragonfly's wing or the eagle's eye - which have apparently evolved over a long period of time by natural selection, but for which there is no surviving evidence of intermediary forms (such as an eagle with something like an eye, but one that is not fully formed and wouldn't function as an eye does). Dawkins explains how "a functioning unit [eg the eye] is said to be irreducibly complex if the removal of one of its parts causes the whole to cease functioning."[662] According to the IC argument, as he spells it out, "either the eye sees or it doesn't: either the wing flies or it doesn't: there are assumed to be no useful intermediates. But this is simply wrong. Such intermediates abound in practice – which is exactly what we should expect in theory."[663]

Darwin's theory of evolution provides a popular and intelligent natural explanation of the appearance of design in nature without invoking the need for a designer. It proposes that natural processes at work over long periods of time are sufficient to account for observed patterns and differences between species, and claims to demonstrate what the processes are and how they operate. As we shall see shortly, evolution and the idea of God are increasingly being seen as not mutually exclusive.

But even with Darwinian evolution a major challenge remains - it tells us nothing about ultimate origins, in much the same way that the Big Bang might account for the beginning of the universe but it tells us nothing about what there was before that (hence we arrive at the problem of infinite regress). As Michael Poole puts it, "Dawkins' belief that evolution is the only alternative to 'ultimate design' involves a *category mistake*. Once life has arisen, evolution provides a scientific explanation of the *adaptation* of living things to their environments. It can tell us nothing about pre-biotic states, nor whether God is responsible for the processes involved."[664]

Design by a designer

New Atheist Daniel Dennett writes, somewhat cynically, "it just stands to reason (doesn't it?) that all the wonders of the living world have to have been arranged by some Intelligent Designer? It couldn't all just be an accident, could it? And even if evolution by natural selection explains the design of living things, doesn't the 'fine tuning' of the laws of physics to make all this evolution possible require a Tuner?"[665]

Dennett's view may be jaundiced but it is not uncommon. Fellow New Atheist Richard Dawkins rejects the argument based on intelligent design which he insists offers no "bona fide explanatory work."[666] But to reject it outright, as Dawkins does and for the reason he does, might not be justified. As Keith Ward argues, "the design argument, in its seventeenth-century form – finding the existence of organic life-forms to be too improbable to have arisen spontaneously by chance – may have been superseded by Darwin. But the design argument still lives, as an argument that the precise structure of laws and constants that seem uniquely fitted to produce life by the process of evolution is hugely improbable. The existence of a designer or creator God would make it much less improbable. That is the New Design Argument, and it is very effective."[667]

Richard Dawkins points out that "the natural temptation is to attribute the appearance of design [in the universe] to actual design itself. ... The temptation is a false one, because the designer hypothesis immediately raises the larger problem of who designed the designer."[668] Who designed the designer, and who designed the designer's designer, and so on *ad infinitum*. Here we encounter the infinite regress argument once again, although Marion Ledwig argues that it is unclear why the regress cannot stop at the designer, "surely this could be possible?"[669]

Dawkins also argues against the idea of God as designer on the grounds of complexity and improbability. In his words, "however little we know about God, the one thing we can be sure of is that he would have to be very very complex and presumably irreducibly so!"[670] and "a God capable of continuously monitoring and controlling the individual status of every particle in the universe *cannot* [his emphasis] be simple."[671] Thus, he argues, "a designer god cannot be used to explain organised complexity because any God capable of designing anything would have to be complex enough to demand the same kind of explanation."[672] He goes on to say that "intelligent design suffers from exactly the same objection as chance. It is simply not a plausible solution to the riddle of statistical improbability. And the higher the improbability, the more implausible intelligent design becomes."[673]

Critics of Dawkins' argument point out that it is based on a category error, insisting that - unlike the universe, species and the rest of nature - God is not a thing or an object, so the question of complexity is meaningless. Marion Ledwig admits "it is unclear to me why an entity which is able to design something as improbable as the universe has to be even more improbable than the universe. That is, I don't see why God has to be very complex and therefore very improbable. ... even if God were irreducibly complex, this would only cause a problem if God had to be created from something, and if the laws which hold for life on earth also have to hold for God. But the latter is an unwarranted assumption."[674]

David Robertson outlines the reasoning about divine design from the perspective of a believer, concluding that "the answer to the question who made God is simply 'nobody'. God is not made. God is the Creator, not the creation. God is outside of time and space. (This is not to say that he is not also in time and space and that there is not plenty of evidence for him there.) God creates *ex nihilo*. That's what makes him God. He does not craft from what is already there. He creates time, space and matter from nothing. ... Christians and other theists do not argue that God was created. That is precisely the point. He did not come from anywhere. He has always been. He did not evolve, nor was he made. If there is a personal Creator of the Universe then it makes perfect sense to regard him as complex, beyond our understanding and eternal."[675]

Reconciling God and evolution

Not everyone believes that evolution and God are inherently incompatible and mutually exclusive as ways of accounting for the world around us, despite the forcefulness and intolerance of Dawkins' rhetoric on the matter. There is ground in the middle.

Dawkins tries to make light of attempts to reconcile evolution and God by pointing to the writings of chemist Peter Atkins, a self-confessed humanist. In his book *Creation revisited*[676], as Dawkins explains, Atkins "postulates a hypothetically lazy God who tries to get away with as little as possible in order to make a universe containing life. ... Step by step, [he] succeeds in reducing the amount of work the lazy God has to do until he finally ends up doing nothing at all: he might as well not bother to exist."[677] Marion Ledwig chips in cheerfully that "the idea of a lazy God who wouldn't have anything to do, because everything goes by evolution and natural selection doesn't seem as ridiculous to me as Dawkins proposes. I actually think it is quite rational not to waste one's energy and let the laws do the work for you."[678]

A more serious and better informed take on reconciliation is offered by well-respected scientist Francis Collins, who writes "soon after becoming a believer, I arrived at the perspective called 'theistic evolution' – the notion that God, in his awesome intention to create a universe that would support life, and most especially life in his own image that would seek out fellowship with God, used the process of evolution to achieve these goals. An amazing process, an elegant process, a process that may seem slow and even random in our minds, but for God, who is not limited in time or space, it could be achieved in the blink of an eye and in a way that wasn't random at all."[679]

Alister Hardy, former Professor of Zoology and founder of the Religious Experience Research Unit at Oxford University, was also comfortable believing in both God and evolution. Hardy described himself as "convinced Darwinian ... [with a] need to reconcile fully the Darwinian doctrine of natural selection with the spiritual side of man ... after much hard thinking and searching of the literature, I am convinced of the truth of the selection theory but ... I do not believe that all selection is just chance. Nor do I agree with the unwarranted dogma that belief in modern evolutionary theory shows that the whole process is an entirely materialistic one leaving no room for the possibility of a spiritual side to man."[680]

Dawkins is never one to miss an opportunity to dismiss the idea of God as ridiculous, but in doing so he often inadvertently displays his theological ignorance. In characteristically intolerant style, he insists that "even if we allow the dubious luxury of arbitrarily conjuring up a terminator to an infinite regress and giving it a name, simply because we need one, there is absolutely no reason to endow that terminator with any of the properties normally ascribed to God: omnipotence, omniscience, goodness, creativity of design, to say nothing of such human attributes as listening to prayers, forgiving sins and reading innermost thoughts."[681]

Despite Dawkins' outburst, one has to concede that there is a world of difference between suggesting that 'a god' did it, and establishing with any credibility that God did it. Once again we find here echoes of the God of the Gaps argument from Chapter 6. Thomas Dixon points out that a "serious problem for the theist is how to close the large gap between positing a first cause for the universe and identifying that unknown cause with the personal God of Judaism, Christianity, Islam, or any other religious tradition."[682] It is a real problem and when believers and non-believers debate it they retreat into their core territory and view their detractors as ill-informed and unwilling to recognise anything beyond their comfort zone and outside the boundaries of their own paradigm.

Creationism

One of the biggest challenges to any possible reconciliation between evolution and God comes from the rise during the twentieth century of a fundamentalist approach to creation which is usually referred to as creationism. Creation and creationism are two different things; creation is the divine act of creating the universe and creationism is a way of understanding that act. As Thomas Dixon puts it, creationism is "a term that can loosely be used to refer to any religious opposition to evolution."[683] Most believers believe in creation by God, but creationism is very much a minority view, rejected by most believers.

Creationism is based on a literal interpretation of the account of the creation as described in sacred texts (the Hebrew Scriptures, the Christian Bible or the Quran of Islam). The book of Genesis, the first book in the Bible, tells of how God supernaturally created the universe and everything in it. In particular, it tells of how God created it out of nothing, at his command, in clearly-defined stages over a six day period, at the end of which creation had been created. It tells of how humans were created towards the end of that six-day period, "in the image of God". Creationists take this account to be literally true, and allow for nothing to be added to it or subtracted from it. Thus, for example, they believe that everything that exists was created instantly in a sudden burst of divine creation, over a period of one week (six days of 24 hours each). This requires a young earth, no more than a few thousand years old (see Chapter 6 on the age of the universe). They believe that all of the scenery and landscapes we see in the world today - which geologists account for as the product of natural processes operating over vast stretches of time - were created by Noah's flood about five thousand years ago, as described in Genesis. Creationists believe that everything was created in the form we see today and has remained the same since. This requires fixity of species and allows for no adaptation, evolution, extinction or intermediate forms. This view of creation denies any prospect of common ancestry between species, including Darwin's proposal that humans have descended from apes and so have an animal ancestry.

Creationism is alive and well, particularly in some parts of North America. Robert Winston recalls a fundamentalist church service he attended in Kentucky, where people "seemed to be deeply committed Christians most of whom believed in the literal truth of every word of the Bible. Most of these people, for example, believe that the Grand Canyon was created by Noah's flood, and that God put fossils of dinosaurs in place to fool gullible men into believing evolution."[684]

Creationist views are not held lightly, and passions can be raised when those views are challenged. This was certainly the case in the USA in 1925, in an infamous court case which has come to symbolise the conflict between faith and science. Shortly after teaching Darwin's theory of evolution had been banned in state-funded high schools in Tennessee, a biology teacher called John Scopes decided to challenge the restriction and the law behind it. The court case became a high profile show trial between supporters of the right to free speech (and through that the right to teach about evolution) and conservative Christians (creationists at heart) who denounced the idea of evolution as immoral and blasphemous. Scopes lost the case and in the decades that followed many public schools across the USA gave greater prominence to teaching about creationism than about Darwin's theory of evolution.[685]

The Intelligent Design Movement

In recent decades a particularly dogmatic form of creationism has taken hold in North America. This is often referred to as Young Earth Creationism (emphasising belief in the recent creation of the universe a matter of thousands of years ago) or Creation Science or Intelligent Design (emphasising a new approach in which quasi-scientific explanations are offered in support of creationist claims based on literal reading of the sacred texts).[686]

The Intelligent Design (ID) Movement emerged in the USA during the 1990s. One of its key arguments is that, as Michael Poole puts it, "some living things are so irreducibly complex that a single missing part would stop the organism functioning ... [so] Such organisms could not have arisen by the normal evolutionary process ... [and] They must therefore have been designed by an (unnamed) intelligence – generally understood as God."[687] In confrontational mode, they point to Richard Dawkins' account in his book *River out of Eden*[688] of the evolutionary development of the eye, which requires a series of forty adaptations in sequence, only the final one of which would yield an eye that actually sees properly. They then ask rhetorically 'How could that be the result of chance or natural processes?'[689] Other examples of irreducible complexity they refer to include the development of blood-clotting, of the immune system, of the human eye, and of the bacterial flagellum (a microscopic tail-like structure that some types of bacteria have, which acts like a propeller and moves them around).

An American court case in 2005 revisited the ground covered in the 1925 Scopes trial, recast in terms of Intelligent Design or scientific creationism, not the original creationism.[690] Parents of children at Dover Area High School in Pennsylvania sued the Dover School District because it allowed teachers to include Intelligent Design as part of science lessons, arguing that this promotes religion (while the US Constitution deliberately separates church and state), and it raises doubts about evolution. Supporters of ID argued that it was being taught as an alternative scientific theory, based on valid science not religious theory. Much of the argument in court centred on whether or not there is evidence of irreducible complexity in nature. It was argued, for example, that the flagellum was too complex to have evolved so it must be the creation of an intelligent designer. This was effectively a new take on the God of the Gaps argument we looked at in Chapter 6. The court judgement went against ID, the judge declaring in summing up that ID was a religious view not a scientific one, and so it had no place in the classroom.

In their quest to discredit the idea of a designed universe, the New Atheists quickly turned their guns on any form of creationism as an easy target. Christopher Hitchens insisted that "creationism ... is *not even a theory* [his emphasis]. In all its well-founded propaganda, it has never even attempted to show how one single piece of the natural world is explained better by 'design' than by evolutionary competition."[691] Richard Dawkins dismisses intelligent design as "politically expedient fancy dress."[692]

John Haught fights back, pointing out that "a key component of the new atheists' case against God is to suppose that creationism and ID represent the intellectual high point and central core of theistic traditions. Most contemporary theologians reject creationism and ID for theological reasons, but the new atheists have decided, almost by decree, that theology does not count and should be kept out of their discussions about God."[693]

Haught continues that "most sensible theologians have no problem with the theory of evolution. Being a religious believer is not synonymous with being a creationist… Most sensible modern religious believers accept, rather, that if God wanted to make the world in the way that Darwin proposes, why should he not?"[694] John Cornwell supports Haught's position, arguing that "most sensible believers in the Book [the Bible] subscribe without demur to Darwin's theory of evolution, while reading Genesis in the light of the mystery so well articulated by Martin Rees – 'Why is there something rather than nothing?'."[695]

Alister McGrath notes that the God of the Gaps strategy "is still used by the Intelligent Design movement … It is not an approach which I accept, either on scientific or theological grounds. In my view, those who adopt this approach make Christianity deeply – and needlessly – vulnerable to scientific progress."[696]

Michael Poole develops the case against Intelligent Design further, on four grounds:

[i] "No one knows whether a natural explanation will be found tomorrow: then, on ID reasoning, 'intelligence' seems to be no longer required. Claims made a decade ago that the development of blood-clotting processes and immune systems could not be accounted for by evolution are now seen as incorrect.

[ii] It seems to overlook how intermediate components of evolutionary processes have different functions at different stages of the evolutionary process. Even the various parts of a mousetrap could be used for other purposes than catching mice; for example, the spring could keep a box-lid closed.

[iii] If only what has specified complexity points to intelligence, what about the rest of creation which is also seen as God's planning?

[iv] It is difficult to see ID as other than a contemporary version of the 'God of the Gaps'."[697]

Arguments based on design

Alongside the various threads within the popular Argument *from* Design, there are three sets of arguments for God's existence that are *based on* design. These are based on providence, beauty, and miracles.

Providence

Philosopher Richard Swinburne spells out what he calls the Argument from Providence, a variant on the classic design argument that centres on providing for human needs.[698] His premise is that we should expect a creator God, particularly one who is good, to provide for the basic needs of people and animals. And that is exactly what he sees in the world around him. As he puts it, our world "is providential in giving normally to man [sic] (and animals) the opportunity to satisfy their own biological needs for food, drink, safety, etc.; and ... the opportunity to satisfy the biological and psychological needs of other men and of animals, and so to satisfy their own psychological needs for co-operation, friendship, etc. The very general features of men's nature and circumstances ... are such as a God has reason for making, and so there is some reason for supposing that he made them."[699] Peter Vardy also comments on the Argument from Providence, noting that "nature seems to plan in advance for the needs of animals and humans. This planning cannot be accounted for by physical laws alone ... [and] there must be more than physical laws to account for the tremendously high improbability of life."[700] God is the reason why this improbable state of affairs comes about.

Beauty

Swinburne also develops the Argument from Beauty, arguing that "God has reason to make a basically beautiful world, although also reason to leave some of the beauty or ugliness of the world within the power of creatures to determine; but he would seem to have overriding reason not to make a basically ugly world beyond the powers of creatures to improve. Hence, if there is a God there is more reason to expect a basically beautiful world than a basically ugly world."[701]

This is by no means a new idea. Keith Ward points out that "belief in one God who creates this universe for the sake of the beauty and value that can only exist within it, and belief that the cosmos is an image of eternal beauty and wisdom, can be found in Plato ..."[702] The Romantic Movement that originated in Europe towards the end of the eighteenth century as a reaction against Enlightenment rationalism was in part inspired by the awe and wonder of the natural world. As Karen Armstrong explains, "the Romantics were not averse to the mysterious and indefinable. Nature was not an object to be tested, manipulated and dominated, but should be approached with reverence as a source of revelation. Far from being inactive, the material world was imbued with a spiritual power that could instruct and guide us. Since childhood, Wordsworth had been aware of a 'Spirit' in nature. He was careful not to call it 'God' because it was quite different from the God of the natural scientists and theologians ... The Romantic poets revived a spirituality that had been submerged in the scientific age. By approaching nature in a different way, they had recovered a sense of its numinous mystery."[703]

The focus of the Argument from Beauty is beauty in the natural world. Many people comment on how they can become lost in wonder at the beauty of an exotic sunrise or sunset, an attractive flower or colourful butterfly, a wild landscape or rugged seascape, exotic animals in the wild, a picture of earth from space, pictures of distant planets, microscopic images of everyday things in nature. Such images can take us out of ourselves and move us to reflect on bigger things beyond the everyday, to think about wider meanings beyond our own lives and experiences.

But the focus of the argument is not confined to the natural world. It could be argued that great writing, art, music, and other creative arts point to something intangible beyond the everyday, ultimately to the existence of God. Richard Dawkins suggests that, "if there is a logical argument linking the existence of great art to the existence of God, it is not spelled out by its proponents. It is simply assumed to be self-evident, which it most certainly is not."[704]

Dawkins dismisses the Argument from Beauty, arguing that its logic is questionable.[705] But others are more open to the idea that a creative God not only made humans to be creative ("in his image") but made them also to appreciate beauty and what it stands for. Krista Tippett reminds us that "a passion for beauty has always been at the core of human religious experience. Art, architecture, literature, and music owe everything to religion. The examples begin pouring out if you ponder this for just a second, lush and wild, not just the music of Bach, but the mandalas of Tibetan Buddhism, the calligraphy of the Qur'an, and so on and so on."[706] Even Albert Einstein was moved by beauty, particularly through music. He is reputed to have said that "Mozart is the greatest composer of all. Beethoven created his music, but the music of Mozart is of such purity and beauty that one feels he merely found it—that it has always existed as part of the inner beauty of the universe waiting to be revealed."[707]

Miracles

The Argument from Miracles (another variant on the Argument from Design) is particularly contentious. Through it believers interpret "various public phenomena in the course of human history as evidence of God's existence and activity,"[708] as Richard Swinburne points out.

A miracle is typically thought of as an improbable or extraordinary event, and the argument runs that what are viewed as miracles, along with certain unexpected events and apparent coincidences, cannot be accounted for by science or natural law so they must have as their cause a higher power, usually God.[709] Thomas Aquinas defined miracles as "things which are done by divine agency beyond the order commonly observed in nature"[710] and St Augustine saw them as "events we cannot forecast or expect with our present understanding of nature."[711] Peter Vardy distinguishes between two types of miracle - what he calls 'coincidence' miracles ("an event that is in accordance with the laws of nature but which the believer sees as being due to the action of God"[712]) and 'violation' miracles (created by "a transgression of the laws of nature brought about by God"[713]). Most people think mainly of the second type.

The Argument from Miracles is based on three premises about God:

[i]   God initially designed and created the universe;

[ii] God designed and imposed the natural laws and rules which govern how the universe operates and explain why it is usually so stable and predictable; and

[iii] From time to time God appears to temporarily suspend or alter the laws and rules, as a result of which unusual and unexpected things can occasionally happen.

Viewed this way, miracles require divine intervention in specific places at specific times. Among other things, this raises the question of how and why God decides to intervene there and then, and why God appears content to let the natural laws and rules operate without interference at other times and in other places. But this perspective is traditional, deep-rooted and enduring, particularly amongst believers. Thomas Dixon points out that "most early modern scientists … took it for granted that God, who was responsible for determining the regular way in which nature would normally operate, was also quite capable of suspending or altering that normal course of nature whenever he so chose. Nonetheless, the method they adopted was one that has favoured a view of God as designer and lawgiver rather than as interventionist wonder-worker."[714]

As Michael Dunne points out, like many other scientists today Richard Dawkins simply "does not accept the existence of miracles or supernatural events."[715] Many people regard the idea of God intervening in the world as untenable, groundless, and impossible to believe - either because they don't believe that God exists in the first place, or they view God as absent and passive (deism, as we saw in Chapter 3) rather than present and active (theism).

The word of God - The Argument from Sacred Texts

There is an Argument from Sacred Texts (or Argument from Scriptures), which argues that God exists because it can be worked out from the scriptures.[716] But this argument has a certain chicken-and-egg flavour to it, because anyone who does not believe in God is unlikely to be persuaded by evidence in sacred texts. Using texts to 'prove' or establish what they say about themselves leads to a circular argument!

All religions have sacred texts which believers accept as a major source of knowledge and insight. For example, it is more common for Christians to believe that God has revealed himself through the Bible than through revelation (which we will look at further in Chapter 8). Fundamentalists and other literalists treat sacred texts as much more than inspired by God, and treat them as literally true, as if dictated by God. As we have seen, such an approach lies at the heart of the clash in the USA between creationists and those who believe in Darwinian evolution

The problem is, as John Haught points out, that "both scientists and religious literalists share the belief that there is nothing beneath the surface of the texts they are reading … [to the scientist] Any intuition that a deeper drama might be going on beneath the surface of nature, as religion and theology maintain, is pure fiction. … [to the religious literalist] there is no reason to look beneath the literal sense, or raise new questions about the meaning of these texts when circumstances change dramatically from one age to the next. Both sides steer clear of theology."[717] He goes on to argue that "creationists are wrong to read the creation stories [in the Bible] as science, but at least they can pick up some of the religious challenge of the text ... But the New Atheists cannot even do this much. They share the untimely scientific reading with creationists, but being also deaf to the clearly transformative intent of the Scriptures, they completely disqualify themselves as interpreters of biblical faith."[718]

The question of the authority of scripture is a vexed one. Richard Dawkins argues that "ever since the nineteenth century, scholarly theologians have made an overwhelming case that the gospels are not reliable accounts of what happened in the history of the real world. All were written long after the death of Jesus ..."[719] although he writes, with a mixture of regret and scorn, that "there are still some people who are persuaded by scriptural evidence to believe in God."[720] Fellow New Atheist Christopher Hitchens proposed that "the case for biblical consistency or authenticity or 'inspiration' has been in tatters for some time, and the rents and tears only become more obvious with better research, and thus no 'revelation' can be derived from that quarter."[721]

Believers inevitably see things rather differently. Nicholas Lash takes Dawkins to task for treating "all statements about God as if they were characteristically taken, by their users, as straightforward and literal description ... [and] his curious insistence that the only way to take a biblical text seriously is to 'believe it' literally."[722] Keith Ward insists that "what Dawkins fails to point out is that early biblical texts cannot be read in isolation from the totality of the Bible. What the Bible offers is a history of the development of the idea of God in ancient Hebrew religion. ... For Christians, the teaching of Jesus [in the New Testament] puts the whole biblical teaching in a new light, making it quite clear that God's love is unlimited, and God's mercy and forgiveness are infinite."[723] Krista Tippett adds that the Bible is "not a catalogue of absolutes, as its champions sometimes imply. Nor is it a document of fantasy, as its critics charge. It is an ancient record of an ongoing encounter with God in the darkness as well as the light of human experience. Like all sacred texts, it employs multiple forms of language to convey the truth: poetry, narrative, legend, parable, echoing imagery, wordplay, prophecy, metaphor, didactics, wisdom saying."[724]

Self-awareness - The Argument from Consciousness

The Argument from Consciousness (more correctly an Argument from *the Existence of* Consciousness) centres on how and why humans are conscious beings - aware not just of their environment but also of their own existence and thoughts, feelings and sensations. Consciousness involves having a sense of one's personal or collective identity, which includes the attitudes we have, the beliefs we hold, and our sensitivities to everything around us. It may be difficult to define, but we all know what it is from direct experience. No other animals appear to have this level of self-awareness.

Perhaps surprisingly, given how profoundly important it is not just from a philosophical point of view but in shaping our day-to-day existence and understanding of things, science can tell us little about consciousness. George Ellis points out that, "despite the enormous amount scientists know about neuroscience and its mechanisms, the neural correlates of consciousness, the different brain areas involved and so on, we have no idea of how to solve the hard problem of consciousness. There is not even a beginning of an approach."[725] Daniel Dennett goes further and insists that "human consciousness is just about the last surviving mystery. A mystery is a phenomenon that people don't know how to think about – yet."[726]

In his book *Consciousness Explained* Daniel Dennett argues that conscious states are "nothing more than" brain-states and brain-behaviour, but that conclusion appears to be going beyond current scientific understanding. Consciousness takes place in the brain, certainly, but it remains a mystery how the physical and chemical properties of the brain (brain-states) can give rise to consciousness. The problem is, as Keith Ward points out, "how conscious states – thoughts, feelings, sensations and perceptions – can arise from complex physical states."[727]

From his New Atheist perspective, Dennett sees consciousness as "the result of three successive evolutionary processes, piled on top of each other, each one vastly swifter and more powerful than its predecessor."[728] The three natural processes are:

[i] Genetic evolution ("selection of particular genotypes (gene combinations) that have proven to yield better adapted individuals (phenotypes) than the alternative genotypes"[729]);

[ii] Phenotypic plasticity ("the emergence of individual phenotypes

whose innards are not entirely hard-wired, but rather variable or
plastic, and hence who can learn during their own lifetimes"[730]);
and

[iii] Memetic evolution ("the development of replicators and cultural
transmission via memes"[731]).

Richard Dawkins also looks upon evolution as a "consciousness-raising"
process and on Darwinian natural selection as a "conscious-raiser."[732] Such
a way of accounting for consciousness inevitably leaves no room for God.

From the perspective of a believer, Keith Ward argues that the scientific
view of consciousness as being wholly dependent on matter - the physical
and chemical processes that occur in the brain - is a delusion. Instead, he
writes, "consciousness is the most evident source of existence there is, and
it is not necessarily bound to matter. It will then be very natural for finite
consciousness to have an affinity with the spiritual consciousness of God, and
sharing in the divine awareness is the most natural form of existence."[733] As
Richard Swinburne explains, the Argument from Consciousness "argues that
the fact that there are conscious beings is mysterious and inexplicable but for
the action of God."[734] Swinburne explains that consciousness is a property that
humans have but other animals don't, making people "capable of marvelling
at the natural world and worshipping God, consciously rejoicing in the beauty
of the natural world and the uncreated being who, if he exists, is its source."[735]

The human brain is an amazing thing, richly complex and still only
partially understood, which drives all we are and all we do as humans.
Many mysteries about it remain, such as what happens when its natural
workings are disturbed, for example by injury or mental health problems,
or by altered states of consciousness, for example through the medicinal
or recreational use of drugs, or other stimuli including exposure to music
or art. As the gateway through which we interact with external stimuli -
including God - the mind inevitably also plays a critical role in human
experiences of God (which we will explore further in Chapter 8), through
such things as revelation, ecstatic religious experiences, and spiritual
practices and disciplines.

In many ways we are prisoners of our own minds; we are simply too tied
up in our own brains and thoughts to be able to form a clear understanding
of what consciousness means and how it works. Sam Harris writes that "the

problem is that our experience *of* our brains, as objects in the world, leaves us perfectly insensible to the reality of consciousness, while our experience *as* brains grants us knowledge of nothing else."[736]

Right and wrong - the Argument from Morality

The moral argument for God's existence, which in many ways builds on the Argument from Consciousness, is based on the belief that humans are moral beings and animals are not, and this moral drive comes from God. Eighteenth century German philosopher Immanuel Kant (1724-1804) believed that "morality does not so much 'prove' God's existence as oblige us to believe in it,"[737] as Andrew Pessin puts it.

Richard Swinburne distinguishes between two forms of the Argument from Morality - "First there is the argument from man's [sic] moral consciousness, his making moral judgements ... this is an argument from man's awareness of moral truths. ... Secondly ... there is an argument from the fact of morality itself, from the fact that there are binding moral truths (quite apart from whether men are or are not aware of them)."[738]

The moral argument is derived from what Kant called the Moral (or Categorical) Imperative - our sense of moral duty, our "absolute, or categorical imperative (obligation) to obey the moral law if we are to behave as moral creatures."[739] This, as Kathleen Jones explains, "is what distinguishes human beings from chimpanzees. This is what distinguishes human beings from computers. This is what makes us more than 'selfish genes'."[740]

The essence of Kant's idea is that each person has an inbuilt ability to know the different between right and wrong. This is not a case of slavishly following rigid rules, but rather an ability to make value judgements by listening to our consciences. Francis Collins underlines the fact that "one of the most notable and unique characteristics of humanity, across centuries, cultures, and geographic locations, is this universal human grasp of the concept of right and wrong, and an inner voice that calls us to do the right thing. We may not always agree on what behaviours are right (since those are heavily influenced by culture), but we generally agree that we should try to do good and avoid evil."[741]

Keith Ward emphasises that Kant's "great contribution to ethics was ... to argue that there are necessary and universal moral truths, and that they are innate in the human mind, not given by some external authority, not even God."[742] Richard Swinburne need hardly mention that "the religious believer ... considers the voice of conscience to be the voice of God."[743]

How likely is God? The Argument from Probability

An interesting approach to the question of God's existence is to consider how likely or improbable it is. There are a number of twists to the so-called Argument from Probability, which Richard Dawkins calls "the big one ... It is seen, by an amazingly large number of theists, as completely and utterly convincing."[744]

Hugh Montefiore, former Anglican Bishop of Birmingham in England, wrote a book called *The Probability of God* in which he argued that "the question [of God's existence] can only be rationally resolved by a considered judgment concerning the balance of probabilities. It is likely that these probabilities will be assessed differently by individuals according to their presumptions and prejudices. ... I cannot deny that the possibility that there is no God remains open. The important question is – how probable or improbable is it? *It seems to me, on as balanced a judgment as I am capable of making, exceedingly improbable* [his emphasis]."[745] Contrary as ever, Richard Dawkins concedes that "it is indeed a very strong and, I suspect, unanswerable argument – but in precisely the opposite direction from the theist's intention. The argument from improbability, properly deployed, comes close to proving that God does *not* exist."[746]

Complexity and the Ultimate Boeing 747 Gambit

Dawkins' argument rests on his assumption that "any God capable of designing anything would have to be complex enough to demand the same level of explanation in his own right. God presents an infinite regress from which he cannot help us to escape. This argument ... demonstrates that God, although not technically disprovable, is very very improbable indeed."[747] As material scientist Edgar Andrews points out, there are four steps in this line of reasoning:

[i] "By common consent, the world is a highly improbable and complex system;

[ii] If God created the world he must be more complex than the world he created; therefore

[iii] God is less probable than the world; so
[iv] God probably doesn't exist."[748]

Dawkins proudly announces that his "name for the statistical demonstration that God almost certainly does not exist is the Ultimate Boeing 747 Gambit."[749] As used in the game of chess, a gambit is an opening in which a minor piece is sacrificed in exchange for a favourable position overall. The Boeing 747 Gambit is generally attributed to astronomer Fred Hoyle, who argued that the probability of life originating on Earth is no greater than the likelihood that a hurricane, sweeping through a scrapyard, would randomly assemble a Boeing 747 from the bits and pieces lying around. Dawkins gleefully concludes that, "however statistically improbable the entity you seek to explain by invoking a designer, the designer himself has got to be at least as probable. God is the Ultimate Boeing 747."[750]

Colourful as it is, this line of reasoning has been dismissed as flawed on a number of grounds. Keith Ward suggests six particular reasons why the gambit does not succeed:[751]

[i]   "God is not complex in the way that material organisms are complex – made up of separate parts combined together.
[ii] God, being not less than pure consciousness, demands a different kind of explanation than complex physical organisms do.
[iii] That explanation is not in terms of probability.
[iv] Any final explanation of a universe must somehow explain, or make virtually certain, its own existence. The relevant criteria for a final explanation are parsimony, elegance, comprehensiveness and – most importantly – necessity.
[v]   The God hypothesis makes possible a simple and elegant reason for the existence of one or more universes, by proposing that they are actualised for the sake of their distinctive goodness.
[vi] God can unify scientific and personal explanations in a harmonious way, without reducing one to the other."

Generalising from the particulars of the Boeing 747 Gambit, Edgar Andrews asks "by what logic must we accept that one highly improbable entity exists (the universe) while another highly improbable entity

(God) does not exist – simply because he is too complex or organised to do so?"[752]

Dawkins' Argument from Probability

Dawkins tries another way of arguing that the existence of God is highly unlikely, insisting that "what matters is not whether God is disprovable (he isn't) but whether his existence is probable."[753] With his scientific perspective firmly dictating how he views everything, he is convinced that "the existence of God is a scientific hypothesis like any other"[754] in the sense that it can, at least in principle, be shown to be true or false. Thus, he concludes, "either he [God] exists or he doesn't. It is a scientific question; one day we may know the answer, and meanwhile we can say something pretty strong about that probability."[755] Dawkins reminds us that "it is a common error [of reasoning] ... to leap from the premise that the question of God's existence is in principle unanswerable to the conclusion that his existence and non-existence are equiprobable."[756] Thus Dawkins set the scene for his evaluation of the probability of God.

Dawkins proposes a "spectrum of probabilities" about the existence of God, from certainty that God exists to certainty that God does not exist. Everyone can be placed somewhere along this continuous spectrum, no matter where they stand on the question of God. He divides the spectrum into seven sections or categories based on degree and direction of certainty, and labels each category accordingly. Thus the Dawkins taxonomy, in his own words, is:[757]

[i] Strong theist. 100 per cent probability of God. In the words of C.J. Jung, 'I don't believe, I *know*.'

[ii] Very high probability but short of 100 per cent. *De facto* theist. 'I cannot know for certain, but I strongly believe in God and live my life on the assumption that he is there.'

[iii] Higher than 50 per cent but not very high. Technically agnostic but leaning towards theism. 'I am very uncertain, but I am inclined to believe in God.'

[iv] Exactly 50 per cent. Completely impartial agnostic. 'God's existence and non-existence are exactly equiprobable.'

[v] Lower than 50 per cent but not very low. Technically agnostic

but leaning towards atheism. 'I don't know whether God exists
but I'm inclined to be sceptical.'

[vi] Very low probability, but short of zero. *De facto* atheist. 'I cannot
know for certain but I think God is very improbable, and I live
my life on the assumption that he is not there.'

[vii] Strong atheist. 'I know there is no God, with the same
conviction as Jung 'knows' there is one.'

Dawkins believes that if no evidence of God's existence can be found, a
sensible person should adopt a position close to atheism. On this basis he
suggests that the low probability of God's existence leads to *de facto* atheism.
Perhaps surprisingly, given the intolerance with which he writes about the
question of God and about believers Dawkins puts himself in the *de facto
atheist* category, not the strong atheist one, apparently believing that the
existence of God cannot be disproven.[758]

This does not mean that Dawkins has hoisted the white flag in his
campaign against the idea of God. As John Corlett points out, "what
Dawkins' arguments support is the idea that a certain rather popular notion
of God is implausible, and for a variety of reasons that have been noted
(for the most part) for centuries by philosophers from at least Kant to
Hume and beyond. But this neither defeats theism itself (not even the strict
supernaturalistic theism that Dawkins claims to refute) in its more plausible
and interesting formulations nor adequately buttresses his alleged atheism –
not even his probabilistic variety."[759]

Statistical probability – Bayes theorem

The Boeing 747 Gambit and Dawkins' estimate of the probability of God
are both based on a general notion of probability, a general sense rather than a
calculation of whether something is likely or unlikely to happen or be the case.
A different approach uses the mathematical calculus of probability based on
Bayes theorem.[760] This is a statistical approach based on calculating revised
estimates of probability in the light of experience and new information, one
step at a time, using a standard set of procedures and formulae.

In what Richard Dawkins describes as "the oddest case I have seen
attempted for the existence of God"[761], risk management consultant
Stephen Unwin used the Bayes approach to calculate 'the probability of

God.' Unwin starts by assuming complete uncertainty about whether or not God exists, which gives an initial probability of 50 per cent. He then revises the probability estimate six times, each time adding to the mix a fact that might have a bearing on the existence of God, to which he attaches a numerical weighting. The 'facts' are:

[i] We have a sense of goodness;
[ii] People do evil things;
[iii] Nature does evil things;
[iv] There might be minor miracles;
[v] There might be major miracles; and
[vi] People have religious experiences.

Taking these six 'facts' into account raises the probability that God exists up from 50 per cent to 67 per cent (ie there's a one-in-three chance that God does not exist). Finally, as Dawkins puts it, Unwin "mysteriously boosts [the probability] to 95 per cent by an emergency injection of 'faith'."[762]

Serious statisticians and theologians would drive a coach-and-horses through Unwin's analysis and conclusions, but at least he was brave enough to take on Dawkins' challenge of testing the existence of God as a scientific hypothesis, even if he appears to have stacked the odds in favour of God from the outset!

Hedging bets – Pascal's wager

It is obviously difficult if not impossible to estimate the probability of God using conventional statistical techniques, and the philosophical approaches to estimating the likelihood of God clearly also have their limitations. So an alternative approach starts from a different assumption and progresses in a different direction. It takes the form of a wager or gamble, and is named after its proposer the seventeenth century French mathematician and philosopher Blaise Pascal (1623-62).

Francis Collins describes Pascal as "a passionate seeker of truth, which he believed could be achieved by incorporating reason and faith."[763] Thus, as Karen Armstrong points out, Pascal insisted that faith "was not a rational assent based on common sense. It was a gamble. It was impossible to prove that God exists but equally impossible for reason to disprove his existence."[764] But, as Patrick Clarke clarifies, Pascal "did not himself see faith as a gamble. He was a deeply religious man, who was merely trying to show the implications of faith to his unbelieving contemporaries."[765] Pascal concluded that "you can't prove that God exists, but you can prove that you should act as if He does."[766] That is the essence of his wager.

Andrew Pessin outlines Pascal's wager: "if you choose the religious life you risk a small waste of time, itself balanced by other natural goods, in order to gain an infinite reward; and if you choose the unreligious life you risk infinite punishment in order to gain a finite reward, itself balanced by other natural risks. Clearly, choosing the religious life is the right and rational, and most of all prudent, way to go."[767]

Richard Dawkins' take on the wager is characteristically colourful: "you'd better believe in God, because if you are right you stand to gain eternal bliss and if you are wrong it won't make any difference anyway. On the other hand, if you don't believe in God and you turn out to be wrong you get eternal damnation, whereas if you are right it makes no difference. On the face of it the decision is a no-brainer. Believe in God."[768]

In short, Pascal argued that believing in God is a better bet than not believing, because the expected return on believing is much greater than that of not believing. But, as Karen Armstrong points out, "the gamble is not entirely irrational, however. To opt for God is an all-win solution. In choosing to believe in God, Pascal continued, the risk is finite but the gain infinite. As the Christian progresses in the Faith he or she would become aware of a continuous enlightenment, an awareness of God's presence that was a sure sign of salvation. It was no good relying on external authority; each Christian was on his own."[769]

Putting it all together - The Cumulative Case Argument

British philosopher of religion Basil Mitchell proposed the Cumulative Case Argument for the existence of God.[770] Patrick Clarke describes it: "the method involves combining all the known arguments for God's existence to form a composite picture that becomes in the end another argument for its own separate validity."[771] Martin Prozesky points out that it "involves a process of adding together a whole set of arguments none of which wins the debate on its own but which amounts in the end to a balance of probability in favour of the believer."[772]

This argument builds on the idea of gestalt, the notion that the whole is greater than the sum of the parts. Michael Poole suggests that there are a number of key ingredients in the cumulative case for God's existence, which may include:

[i] "That there is a world. There is something rather than nothing, raising questions such as 'What brought it into existence?'

[ii] The kind of world it is. This suggests 'an argument to design from order … and, thus, a 'Designer'.

[iii] The existence of beauty and moral values, including appeals to innate ideas of obligation and fairness.

[iv] Revelation of things that we could not otherwise know.

[v] The evidential value of religious experience, including answered prayer. This, to the believer, is perhaps the most important.

[vi] Historical evidence, drawing on both secular and religious sources."[773]

CHAPTER 8

PERSONAL EXPERIENCE OF GOD

"There are particular kinds of experiences that seem to those who have them
to be experiences of the sacred. ... [thus] if the sacred - if God - can be
experienced, then God is simply not somewhere else but also right here."

Marcus Borg (1998)

The Argument from Religious Experience, also known as the Existential Argument for God, supports and confirms the other arguments for God ... for those who have had what they regard as personal experiences of God. For other people it remains part of what they think of as the 'circular-argument' about God's existence, based on the assumption you have to believe in God (or at least believe in God's existence) to experience God.

Believers and non-believers view the whole question of personal experience of God very differently. Non-believers, who struggle with the idea of God let alone the existence of God, generally find it impossible to envisage God interacting directly with individual people, and in ways that those people are aware of. Believers are generally comfortable with the idea and existence of God, but not all are convinced that personal experience of God is possible. As we saw in Chapter 3, deists believe in a passive, absent God who initially created the universe and then left it to look after itself; for them personal experience of God is out of the question. Theists, on the other hand, believe in an active, present God who continues to engage with the universe he created; from this perspective it is quite logical for individuals to expect to be able to have personal experiences of God.

Richard Swinburne argues that we should expect God to make himself known to at least some people. He writes that "one might expect certain private and occasional manifestations by God to some men" and he points out that "the argument from religious experience claims that this has often occurred; many have experienced God (or some supernatural thing connected with God) and hence know and can tell us of his existence."[774]

Personal experience can provide powerful evidence of God's existence and engagement with people, which is usually more compelling (at least for those who have such experiences) than the other arguments we looked at in Chapter 7. William James believed that religious belief "is not to be proved by arguments. It is rather grounded in enthusiastic emotion, essentially private and individualistic; its truths well up into our lives in ways resisting verbal expression. ... No philosophical theology could ever arise or prosper in a world devoid of or divorced from the individual experiences, the lived perceptions – the religious feelings – at the foundation of all religious belief."[775]

Francis Collins urges caution in putting too much emphasis on personal experience, arguing that "belief in ... a supernatural reality itself can neither be proved nor disproved by experience. The arguments for its existence are metaphysical, and to me conclusive. They turn on the fact that even to think and act in the natural world we have to assume something beyond it and even assume that we partly belong to that something. In order to think we must claim for our own reasoning a validity that is not credible if our own thought is merely a function of our brain, and our brains a by-product of irrational physical processes."[776] But the metaphysical and the existential arguments are not necessarily mutually exclusive; one might even argue that the ability to think and act is in itself a form of personal experience of God.

Divine intervention: personal

The question of personal experience of God hinges around whether or not one believes not only that God exists, but that God created the universe and continues to engage with it - for example through miracles and revelation. As we have seen, deists and theists have different ideas about this, as do atheists and secular scientists.

The key question is 'Does God act in or interfere with nature?' Atheists and scientists would insist the answer is an emphatic no, because as John Haught points out, "if the universe were open to unpredictable divine actions, miracles, or responses to our prayers, this would put limits on, and even undermine, the predictive power of science."[777] But John Cottingham insists that the idea of divine intervention and science are not inherently incompatible. He writes that "nothing in science does, or can, rule out the possibility of divine intervention. To be sure, if we do, after all, live in a wholly natural and entirely 'closed' cosmos, then there is no such thing as a supernatural realm, and [thus] no supernatural intervention. But that question, however it is to be settled, cannot be decided on the basis of anything disclosed by modern science."[778]

Not all believers accept the idea that God intervenes directly in the world. John Habgood, a former Archbishop of York, believed that such an idea "tends to raise moral questions about God's wisdom and justice. If God were to intervene indirectly, it would (a) raise questions about the adequacy of His creation and (b), more importantly, raise questions about why God should intervene here and not there (for example, why should he not ward off a natural disaster, or an evil such as the Holocaust)."[779]

Nonetheless a great many believers (me included) are comfortable with the notion of divine intervention. Cottingham explains how "the action of God surely has to be conceived as operating against the background of the cosmos as we have it – the intricate, mathematically ordered dance of the largest galaxies and the smallest particles, the vast, complex interactive rhythm of the natural order, as it has unfolded over billions of years. This is the world disclosed by science ... And this picture, so far from being a *rival* to the theistic world-view, is strikingly compatible with it."[780]

Why not always?

If God does indeed act in nature, then "why should God intervene here and not there" as John Habgood wondered? To answer the question by glibly saying that "God moves in a mysterious way" is hardly persuasive to non-believers. This is a difficult question to answer, and many non-believers point to it as one reason why they find themselves unable to believe in the idea of a loving God, who appears to allow bad things to happen to good people. One answer might be that, just because God is capable of performing miracles such as healing the sick, does not mean that he always must do them or do them when asked to (for example by people through prayer). Kathleen Jones reminds us that "God is capable of miracles; but he may not perform them on demand – or as often as some people would like to believe."[781]

Thomas Dixon takes up this theme, asking rhetorically "if God exists and has the power to intervene in nature, and on occasion apparently uses that power ... why does God fail to intervene in so many other cases of horrific injustice, cruelty, and suffering? ... [for example] why is one person miraculously cured while another of equal faith and virtue suffers and dies? ... the theologians' dilemma will not go away: divine inaction is just as hard to explain as divine action."[782]

John Cottingham argues that "it seems plain that divine intervention could not be capricious exercises of power, nor convenient responses to the would-be manipulations of believers. Rather, they would necessarily be expressions of God's characteristics: they would not be arbitrary, but rational and intelligible; they would not be mere conferring of temporary advantages to one favourite as against another, or rewards for the performance of some mechanical ritual, but true manifestations of deep love and goodness. Perhaps most important, they would be *communications* between God and his creatures: they would be *disclosures of meaning* [his emphases]."[783] Cottingham points out that "what will be brought about by the divine action, really and genuinely present in human history, is that the minds of the participants will, through grace, be 'nourished and invisibly repaired' so they can see the truth of what was really there all along."[784]

Revelation - God as knowable

God might intervene in the world but not necessarily in ways that we humans are aware of. But God can also intervene in ways that we *are* aware of, through revelation. John Baillie goes as far as concluding that God is known to us, not through argument, but directly through revelation, which "consists neither in the dictation of writings nor in the communication of information, but in personal communion – the self-disclosure of a Personality."[785]

Like many other areas relating to personal experience of God, public opinion is deeply divided over the idea of revelation. As Thomas Dixon explains, "while rationalists have rejected revelation altogether, and fundamentalists have insisted that all forms of knowledge be tested against the Bible, many more have looked for ways to reconcile their readings of God's two books [scripture and nature] without doing violence to either."[786]

Not surprisingly the New Atheists reject outright any possibility of divine revelation, dismissing it as a delusion. Christopher Hitchens, acting as their spokesperson, proclaims that "on certain very specific occasions, it is asserted, the divine will was made known by direct contact with randomly selected human beings, who were supposedly vouchsafed unalterable laws that could then be passed on to those less favoured."[787] To support his case he offers a highly selective range of examples from the Old Testament in which "people attain impossible ages and yet conceive children. Mediocre individuals engage in single combat or one-on-one argument with god or his emissaries, raising afresh the whole question of divine omnipotence or even divine common sense, and the ground is forever soaked with the blood of the innocents."[788]

The counter-view - that God can and does reveal himself to us - is put forward by David Jenkins who values "revelation as a distinct source of data. This type of data exists because God does not leave Himself to be discovered solely or even primarily by careful and reasonable attention to and reflection upon the data of science and morality. He also takes the initiative in making Himself known. This activity of God has resulted in His being known and understood in a way which even the deepest insights into natural data would not open up to men [sic]."[789] James Sire explains further how "human beings can know the world around them and God himself because God has built into them the capacity to do so and because he takes an active role in communicating with them. ... God is forever so beyond us that we cannot have anything approaching total comprehension of him. In fact, if God desired, he could remain forever hidden. But God wants us to know him, and he takes the initiative in this transfer of knowledge. In theological terms this initiative is called revelation."[790]

People of faith believe that God reveals or discloses himself to us in three main ways:

[i] Through what he created (the universe and everything in it),
     which is usually referred to as 'general revelation';
[ii] Through the sacred text he inspired (the Bible); and
[iii]Through particular events in history (most notably the
     Incarnation, the birth and life on earth of Jesus, son of God).

Swiss theologian Karl Barth (1886-1968) argued that the Bible is the only valid source of revelation and truth about God, so it is much more important than personal experience.[791] American theologian Mortimer Adler writes that "the first article of faith" in Judaism, Christianity, and Islam "is that God has revealed himself to us in Holy Writ or Sacred Scripture. This, of course, entails the affirmation that the God who has revealed himself exists. But it goes far beyond that proposition to something that can never be proved, or even argued about, something that is always and only an article of faith or religious belief: namely, the act of Divine revelation."[792]

Reformed epistemology

There are basically two ways of seeking to establish the existence of God. One approach, called natural theology, is through the use of argument and reason - the type of approach we looked at in Chapter 7 - to prove that God exists. The other approach, called reformed epistemology (the study of the nature, validity and limits of knowledge), rejects the use of reason and insists that reliance should be placed on revelation.

The aim of reformed epistemology, according to Peter Vardy, is "to show that it is *rational* [his emphasis] not to seek justification for belief in God. Reformed epistemology holds that the truth of 'God exists' is not arrived at by a process of argument. Instead, the believer is directly aware of God's presence or of God speaking to him or her through the Bible. ... Belief in God is, thus, a 'properly basic' belief which does not stand in need of justification or proof."[793]

Vardy and Julie Arliss explain how reformed epistemology "rejects the use of reason to arrive at the existence of God saying that this is an act of arrogance and pride by sinful human beings. ... Reformed epistemologists consider that God's presence is so clearly obvious to them when they pray or when they read their Bibles that the idea of asking for justification is as ridiculous as a man standing in the presence of his wife asking for proof that it actually is his wife. [They] say that they rely on the grace of God to ensure that they see the world correctly. ... The main problem with this view, of course, is that in a multi-faith world it is difficult to decide which revelation should be accepted."[794]

Revelation to individual people

There is a fourth way in which God can and does reveal himself and that is through direct revelation to individual people. Some believe that this type of revelation is confined to the distant past (particularly the period covered by the Old Testament of the Bible) and to a small number of special people (the 'chosen ones' - selected by God for particular reasons), and that it ceased when God sent Jesus as a special form of revelation.

But many believers today are convinced both from study of scripture and from personal experience that God continues to make himself known to us by direct revelation to individuals, and not just to a small number of privileged 'chosen ones'. From this perspective revelation is alive and well today and available to ordinary people. From the stories of many people in many places (including my own) it is clear that direct revelation can play a significant part in converting non-believers into believers, often through an epiphany ("an experience of sudden and striking realisation"[795]) which can be sudden and intense or progressive and cumulative.

Keith Ward argues that it would be "unreasonable to claim that God has left the world without any knowledge of God's nature and purpose, or any hope of closer knowledge of God. Only God could provide such knowledge. Revelation becomes a highly probable consequence of the existence of a supremely good God."[796] Against this background, as William James points out, "there are moments of sentimental and mystical experience ... that carry an enormous sense of inner authority and illumination with them when they come, but they come seldom, and they do not come to every one; and the rest of life makes either no connection with them, or tends to contradict them more than it confirms them."[797]

In a collective form such experiences are integral to the rise of Pentecostalism, a fundamentalism branch of Christianity in which believers seek to be filled with the Holy Spirit in the same way as the apostles were at Pentecost after the death of Jesus nearly two thousand years ago. Karen Armstrong explains how Pentecostalism first came into being: "On 9 April 1906, the first congregation of Pentecostalists claimed to have experienced the Spirit in a tiny house in Los Angeles, convinced that it had descended upon them in the same way as upon Jesus' disciples on the Jewish feast of Pentecost, when the divine presence had manifested itself in tongues of fire and given the apostles the ability to speak in strange languages. Pentecostalists felt they were returning to the fundamental nub of religiosity that exists beneath any logical exposition of the Christian faith. Within four years, there were hundreds of Pentecostal groups all over the United States and the movement had spread to fifty other countries. ... At a Pentecostal service, men and women fell into tranced states, were seen to levitate and felt that their bodies were melting in ineffable joy. They saw bright streaks of light in the air and sprawled on the ground, felled by a weight of glory. ... Pentecostalists relied on the immediacy of sense experience to validate their beliefs."[798]

Less dramatic are the experiences of revelation that occur to many ordinary people, often in very ordinary settings. It can happen in a church service but it can also happen at home or anywhere else that person happens to be at the time. It can be associated with if not triggered by a period of prayer and/or intense focus on God, but it can also occur as that person goes about their day-to-day life. People are often more acutely aware of God's presence in particular places - such as in a quiet place (including empty churches), an attractive landscape, sometimes even in a busy city centre.

There are different views on the question of whether revelation is open to everyone, whether or not they believe in God and no matter where they stand in terms of personal faith. Karl Barth believed that "no knowledge of God exists in the world save in the hearts of regenerate Christian believers,"[799] so he insisted that "prior to the acceptance by faith of the Christian revelation man has no capacity whatever for the reception of revelation, the capacity to receive it being given in and with the revelation itself."[800] Others believe from personal experience that God can and does reveal himself even to non-believers at times. Indeed, for some people the very act of revelation can be instrumental in helping them to believe, by challenging and often over-riding intellectual issues that are barriers to faith.

Like many things to do with God revelation remains surrounded by mystery, although Krista Tippett suggests that people can make themselves more sensitive to it and more aware of it happening. As she describes it, "something mysterious happens when you train your eyes to see differently, your ears to hear differently, to attend to what you have been ignoring. The experienced world actually changes shape. There are parallels to this [biblical] idea, and versions of 'eyes to see and ears to hear' in every religious tradition I've since come to know."[801]

Keith Ward explains the essence of revelations – "In most religions, some visions or inspired words are considered to be 'revelations'. This is a rare and definitive communication of important spiritual and moral truth from

God, through a human intermediary or prophet. It seems highly probable that, if there is a God, there will be some such communication of God's nature and purpose. There will be revelation, or a finite communication of divine truth through a medium of great beauty, wisdom, moral insight and spiritual power. It may be a text or a person, or a text communicated through a person who has an especially close relationship to God. ... it is reasonable to think that some humans will have an especially close and intense knowledge and love of God, or that God will take some human lives and unite them closely to the divine in knowledge and love. They will become the channels of divine revelation of what God is and of what God desires for us and for the world."[802]

Revelation is experienced by an individual person, and what is revealed is often directed specifically at that person and their needs or situation. Revelation can also be given to one person for sharing with a group, perhaps a church or more widely, through that person.

Naturally, because it relies on the experience of individuals, great care must be taken to ensure that what that person experiences is authentic and comes from God. Inevitably there is scope for getting things wrong, perhaps through a misinterpretation of what is happening or what they think is being revealed. This can happen, for example, through the person expanding or distorting what they pass on to others about the revelation, through mental confusion (perhaps associated with mental health issues), or - for those who believe in spiritual warfare - through spiritual attack designed to discredit God (the sender) or the believer (the receiver) or both. In all cases of revelation, or what is alleged or suspected to be revelation, there is a need for discernment. As Keith Ward reminds us, "if you think it is reasonable to see God as the only ultimate reality (as it is), then you will also think it is reasonable for God to reveal spiritual truth through prophets whose minds God unites closely to the divine mind. So you will be disposed to accept truth by revelation. You will not accept it blindly or without question. You must criticise, evaluate, sift and examine."[803]

Religious experience
Revelation might be a rather dramatic form of religious experience, but it is by no means the only one.

In his ground-breaking book *The Varieties of Religious Experience*

(1902), William James defined religious experience as "the feelings, acts and experiences of individual men [sic] in their solitude, so far as they apprehend themselves to stand in relation to whatever they may consider the divine."[804] Other authorities define it in much the same way but using different language. For example, Ninian Smart writes that "a religious experience involves some kind of 'perception' of the invisible world, or a perception that some visible person or thing is a manifestation of the invisible world."[805] Richard Swinburne defines a religious experience as "an experience which seems ... to the subject to be an experience of God (either of his just being there, or doing or bringing about something) or of some other supernatural thing."[806]

These definitions offer us a way of framing the notion of religious experience and identifying some of its key characteristics. First of all, as Patrick Clarke emphasises, "it is usually a solitary experience of an individual alone."[807] Secondly, it provides first-hand experience which is both more persuasive and powerful than second-hand information passed on by others. The latter is more common among religious people; William James wrote of the "ordinary religious believer ... [whose] religion has been made for him by others, communicated to him by tradition, determined to fixed forms by imitation, and retained by habit."[808] Marcus Borg describes from personal experience how religious experiences help people to "make the transition from believing in (or rejecting) second-hand religion to experiencing first-hand a relationship with the sacred,"[809] and he explains the underlying rationale: "what I come to know in my own experience can be trusted to be true in a way that what we learned second-hand from tradition cannot be trusted."[810] Thirdly, religious experience often leads to positive belief in God. Keith Ward explains how, alongside the other arguments for God, "to affirm [their] objective reality we need confirmation of some sort from experience. As in science, elegant speculation needs some sort of confirmation from experience. That confirmation may be difficult to determine, and it may not be wholly free of ambiguity. But in the end it will be what leads most people to positive belief in God."[811]

But experience on its own is rarely capable of turning a confirmed atheist or a sceptic into a believer. As David Robertson points out, although "the vast majority of Christians do not believe because they have heard a voice or seen a vision ... [nonetheless] personal experience does play a major part (after all it is the experience we know best) ... We believe because we experience and we think and reflect upon that experience. There are many other kinds of personal experience which at least point us towards God: answered prayer, a sense of God ..., experience of the miraculous, experience of the truths and truthfulness of the Bible and the experience of being filled with the Spirit, to name but a few."[812]

Many non-believers, and many believers whose faith is based on intellectual assent rather than any personal experience of God, argue that religious experience is little more than emotionalism and illusion. Karen Armstrong calmly reminds us that "today religious experience is often understood as intensely emotional ... [but] In all the great traditions ... teachers have constantly proclaimed that far from being essential to the spiritual quest, visions, voices and feelings of devotion could in fact be a distraction. The apprehension of God, Brahman, Nirvana or Dao had nothing to do with the emotions. ... In all the major traditions, the iron rule of religious experience is that it be integrated successfully with daily life. A disorderly spirituality that makes the practitioner dreamy, eccentric or uncontrolled is a very bad sign indeed."[813]

There is, of course, always the risk that religious experience is an illusion, more about mind games than about direct revelation from God. This is certainly the line taken by the New Atheists. Spokesman Sam Harris argues that "no human being has ever experienced an objective world, or even a *world* [his emphasis] at all. You are, at this moment, having visionary experience. The world that you see and hear is nothing more than a modification of your consciousness, the physical status of which remains a mystery. Your nervous system sections the undifferentiated buzz of the universe into separate channels of sight, sound, smell, taste, and touch ... This is not to say that sensory experience offers us no indication of reality at large; it is merely that, as a matter of experience, nothing arises in consciousness that has not first been structured, edited, or amplified by the nervous system."[814] On the other hand, as brain scientist Andrew Newberg points out that "if you were to dismiss spiritual experience as 'mere' neurological activities, you would also have to distrust all of your own brain's perceptions of the material world. On the other hand, if we do trust our perceptions of the physical world, we have no rational reason to declare that spiritual experience is a fiction that is 'only' in the mind."[815]

This takes us back once again to the need for discernment. As William James makes clear in the rather quaint language typical of his day, "in the history of Christian mysticism the problem how to discriminate between such messages and experiences as were really divine miracles, and such others as the demon in his malice was able to counterfeit ... has always been a difficult one to solve, needing all the sagacity and experience of the best directors of conscience."[816] Richard Dawkins seizes on such uncertainty as a reason for dismissing all claims of personal experience of God as illusions and delusions, citing as evidence such uncommon instances as convicted murderers arguing that they heard voices of Jesus telling them to kill people, politicians and leaders insisting that God told them to do certain things, and individuals in psychiatric hospitals convinced that they are a particular famous person.[817]

Religious experiences can take many forms, but they tend to fall into two broad categories - "a feeling or sense of the divine that is somehow perceived within ordinary everyday experience" and "a perceived direct encounter with the divine", as Patrick Clarke puts it.[818]

Sense of the divine

Our sense of the divine is an indirect experience of God within our everyday experience, usually devoid of drama or emotion, and experienced as an awareness of God's presence. Richard Swinburne offers the example of a person who "may look at the night sky, and suddenly 'see it as' God's handiwork, something which God is bringing about."[819]

Late eighteenth century German theologian Friedrich Schleiermacher (whom we met in Chapter 4) believed that "we all have a sense, or feeling, of total dependence if only we stop to reflect on it." He called this feeling "a sense of absolute dependence."[820] He was convinced that this basic intuition, which is deeper than the level of rational thought and which everyone is capable of developing, is what allows us to be aware of the possibility and existence of God.

More than a century later Rudolf Otto, in *The Idea of the Holy* (1917), insisted that religion is rooted in a personal experience of what he called 'the numinous', by which he meant the presence of a divinity or the supernatural. Otto argued that "we are capable of perceiving the numinous as a mysterious but real object of experience. This experience ... evokes awe and wonder, and is at once fearsome and fascinating, provoking attraction and repulsion at the same time. This perception of the holy is not the result of rational thinking or reasoning, but is a form of direct intuition. ... the experience of the numinous, or the holy, lay at the root of all religions."[821]

Marcus Borg explains how experiences "in which people report an awareness of God's presence ... do not involve visions or transformed landscapes or deep mystical union or beings of light but nevertheless seem to persons who have them to be experiences of divine presence. Though quite ordinary compared to the extraordinary character of ecstatic experiences, they stand out in the memory of the individual as remarkable."[822] Paul Tillich emphasised that "experience is not the source of the contents of the Christian understanding of God but the medium through which they are existentially received."[823]

Encounter with the divine

This second type of religious experience tends to be much more dramatic than the sense of the divine, and it can involve great emotion. As Patrick Clarke points out, "direct experience of the divine is a claim made by many individuals, and is classically exemplified by those encounters with God described in the Bible."[824]

Jewish philosopher Martin Buber (1878-1965) believed that "religion consisted entirely of an encounter with a personal God, which nearly always took place in our meetings with other human beings."[825] As Buber saw it, people have impersonal encounters with things, with which they form superficial relationships, but they have personal encounters with other people, with which they can form much deeper and richer relationships. He called these two types of encounter *I-It* and *I-Thou* (or *I-You*) encounters. As Andrew Pessin explains, in an *I-It* encounter "the other is a mere object with no intrinsic ends of its own, something we may simply use or exploit or dismiss. Here there is no direct engagement: we may think of the other any way we like, mediated by our own concepts and ideas, however it suits us."[826] An *I-You* encounter is very different; here the "relationship is characterised by intimacy, mutuality, dialogue, exchange; it is a two-way relationship in which we treat the other as a genuine person with needs and interests to be explored and respected. We are thus directly engaged with that other as those needs and interests are directly present to us."[827] Buber believed that people want to see revelation as an *I-You* encounter, an encounter with another person, a personal encounter with God. This is very different from an *I-It* encounter which, as Patrick Clarke explains, "turns the encounter into an objective relationship with a 'thing'. God can never be a thing."[828] Marcus Borg points out that "in *I-You* moments, the world is known as a '*You*' [not an '*It*']... as a presence rather than as an object. Indeed, such moments are glimpses of 'the eternal *You*', experiences of the sacred in which the world is experienced in the finite and in the here and now."[829]

Keith Ward describes Buber's approach as "a specific way of being in the world, of apprehending it, as a relational event or a series of relational events, as a form of meeting which is personal and yet so much more and so deeply other. If that sense of meeting is added to the sense of infinity, of mystery, of dread and beauty, which sometimes, and often by surprise, comes upon us, then there exists the feeling for the gods ..."[830]

William James gives examples of what he calls 'super-normal incidents', which include "voices and visions and overpowering impressions of the meaning of suddenly presented scripture texts, the melting emotions and tumultuous affections connected with the crisis of change ..."[831] Such experiences have long been part of the mystical tradition. They often serve to deepen a person's faith and can lead to a sudden, dramatic conversion from unbeliever to believer.

Three common forms of encounter with the divine are dreams, visions and near-death experiences. As Marcus Borg points out, dreams can "sometimes mediate a sense of the sacred. Not all dreams do; indeed, most do not."[832] But, as he puts it, "some dreams have a numinous quality to them in which the dream itself conveys a sense of the presence of the sacred. ... [and] it sometimes seems that dreams put us in touch with an internal wisdom that knows more about us than we know about ourselves."[833] Borg also writes about visions, which he defines as "vivid experiences of momentarily seeing into another layer or level of reality. Like a dream, they involve visual images, though they can also include photisms (experiences of light) and auditions (sounds, especially voices). ... visions have a numinous quality - a sense of the sacred and a sense that they come from God. ... Visions point to an alternate reality, a layer of reality other than (and alongside of) the world of our ordinary experience."[834]

Borg stresses that visions of this sort are not hallucinations, "delusions in which nothing real corresponds to what is reported."[835] But Keith Ward reminds us of the need for discernment, pointing to the fact that "we know that there are many fraudulent claims to have seen apparitions. There are many cases of people who hear voices telling them to do terrible things. There are many people who are deluded into thinking they have been abducted by extra-terrestrials or are really Napoleon. So we are wise to be careful. But if there are fraudulent and deluded claims, it is logically possible that there could be genuine claims by people who are not immoral, or who are not in general 'mad' (suffering from mental beliefs that make them unable to run their lives effectively or happily). If there are genuine communications from God by means of mind-constructed visual images or 'words', we might also want to say that the information they convey should extend knowledge and should have important spiritual significance. ... having made as many reality checks as we can, we must conclude that a claim to see an apparition made by a sane, moral, rational, critically aware and trustworthy person has to be considered a candidate for a genuine communication of truth from God. That is only so if belief in God is not 'mad'. It has to be a reasonable postulate. If it is, it may be confirmed by visions or voices."[836]

Whilst there are grounds for seeing near-death experiences as responses to changes in normal bodily processes, many people who have them frame them or describe them as experiences of the sacred. Borg points out that "the experiences themselves are remarkable, combining visionary elements and an out-of-body experience, and have relatively constant elements across time and cultures. They include a sense of journeying through a tunnel, leaving one's body, and encountering a being of light."[837]

Mystical experiences

Mysticism can be defined as "the knowledge of, and especially the personal experience of, states of consciousness, or levels of being, or aspects of reality, beyond normal human perception, including experience of and even communion with a supreme being."[838] Those who experience such states, perhaps through spiritual disciplines such as contemplation and self-surrender, argue that it involves a spiritual awareness of knowledge that is inaccessible to the intellect. It goes beyond what we can normally experience in our day-to-day lives.

Mystical experiences are another form of encounter with the divine, at least as hotly contested as dreams, visions and near-death experiences. They have attracted a great deal of attention by theologians and others. For example, Rudolf Otto spoke of them as experiences of "the numinous" and Mircea Eliade spoke of them as "hierophanies" (manifestations of the sacred) and "theophanies" (manifestations of the sacred as God).[839] William James described a mystical experience as being "grasped and held by a superior power"[840] and Michael Shermer called it "the ultimate close encounter with God, directly and experientially."[841]

Marcus Borg points out that mystical experiences "involve ecstatic states of consciousness in which one is vividly aware of the presence of God. ... They are 'ecstatic', which means literally to be out of oneself, or out of one's ordinary state of consciousness. Sometimes occurring spontaneously, these non-ordinary states can also be entered through ritualised means and spiritual disciplines."[842]

Brain scientist Andrew Newberg argues that "all the great scriptures make the same point: Fundamental truth has been revealed to human beings through a mystical encounter with a higher spiritual reality; mysticism, in other words, is the source of the essential wisdom and truth upon which all religions are founded."[843]

Borg also points out that in a mystical experience "the world may look new, fresh, wondrous. ... Such experiences are typically accompanied by a change in one's sense of oneself. The boundary between self and world that marks our ordinary consciousness becomes soft ... and may even disappear so that one experiences communion or union with the sacred."[844] William James gives the example of one man who reported a "state of ecstasy [that] may have lasted four or five minutes, although it seemed at the time to last much longer. ... in this ecstasy of mine God had neither form, colour, odour, nor taste; moreover ... the feeling of his presence was accompanied by no determinate localisation. It was rather as if my personality had been transformed by the presence of a spiritual spirit. ... God was present, though invisible; he fell under no one of my senses, yet my consciousness perceived him."[845] Another man described how he felt "a temporary loss of my own identity, accompanied by an illumination which revealed to me a deeper significance than I had been wont to attach to life."[846]

This state of consciousness, in which the individual's sense of self dissolves, is sometimes referred to as One Mind or a unitary state. Andrew

Newberg insists that it "must be felt to be believed by both body and mind, even though both body and mind are transcended by it. But mystics insist that it is completely possible to understand – and attain – if we set aside our subjective disbelief. ... it is described as a state without time, space, and physical sensations; with no discrete awareness of any material reality at all. Ironically ... the attainment of [it] requires a mental journey into the deepest parts of the self, yet those who have reached this ultimate state agree that subjective self-awareness vanishes once [it] has been achieved. So, to get to this state we have to use the mind to get beyond the mind. The mind has to get out of its own way. This obliteration of the self may be the most difficult concept for the rational mind to comprehend."[847]

William James identified four distinct features of individual mystical experiences:[848]

[i]   They cannot be described in words (or as he puts it, they are "ineffable"); like love, they need to be directly experienced in order to be understood.

[ii] They have a noetic quality; they are states of knowledge and not just feelings or emotional experiences. As James puts it, "they are states of insight into depths of truth unplumbed by the discursive intellect. They are illuminations, revelations, full of significance and importance and, as a rule, they carry with them a curious sense of authority."

[iii] They are transient and only last a very short time; "except in rare instances, half an hour, or at most an hour or two, seems to be the limit beyond which they fade into the light of common day."

[iv] The individual cannot control or create the experience, "it is a gift"; "the mystic feels as though his own will is in abeyance, and indeed sometimes as if he were grasped and held by a superior power." As Patrick Clarke puts it, "in the mystical state the subject is passive, in the sense of being overwhelmed by the experience."[849]

Writing of mystical states, James believed that "for the person having the experience they are so real that they cannot be denied. ...They break down the authority of the non-mystical or rationalistic consciousness, based upon the understanding and the senses alone. They show it to be only one kind of consciousness and that there is something beyond everyday awareness of physical objects."[850]

As well as this cognitive (knowing) dimension of the personal mystical experience - in which "the mystics now know something others do not know and that they did not know before"[851] - there is also an affective (feeling) dimension. Those who have such experiences report feelings of joy, peace, and well-being. Borg notes that "such experiences have occurred across cultures and throughout history. The founders of most of the world's religions are reported to have had such experiences ... But ordinary people also have them."[852]

From personal experience, Marcus Borg concludes "it seems to me that ecstatic religious experience is the primary reason for taking seriously the reality of the sacred, of God. These experiences lead to the inference that there is more than one kind of reality, more than one level of reality, and that these other levels or layers can be (and are) known. Of course, such experiences do not *prove* the reality of God or the sacred. Such a demonstration is impossible. But I find the evidential value of religious experience to be far more interesting and suggestive than the traditional 'proofs' of God's existence, which I am convinced do not work. The varieties of religious experience suggest that the sacred - God - is an element of experience, not simply an article of faith to be believed in."[853]

Scientific study of religious experience

Richard Dawkins acknowledges that "many people believe in God because they believe they have seen a vision of him – or of an angel or a virgin in blue – with their own eyes. Or he speaks to them inside their own heads. This argument from personal experience is the one that is most convincing to those who claim to have had one. But it is the least convincing to anyone else, and anyone knowledgeable about psychology."[854] Dawkins is suggesting that what people think are direct experiences of God are in reality illusions or delusions, things that take place in the head and can be explained by natural psychological processes with no need for any external trigger, such as divine intervention.

Alister McGrath challenges him head on, posing the question "are we psychologically primed for religion? This is an important question, and it clearly requires a psychological answer. It soon becomes clear that Dawkins is not qualified to give one. Dawkins shows himself to be ill at ease with psychology and neuroscience, despite the critical importance they play at this juncture with his argument. ... [Dawkins conflates] the language of information processing and brain physiology ... and seems to confuse brain mechanisms with psychological constructs. This isn't the brilliant popularisation of difficult scientific ideas that we saw in *The Selfish Gene*; it's just a confused and misleading account of someone else's area of specialisation."[855]

Despite Dawkins' ill-informed conclusion, it is the case that scientific attempts to demystify religious experience are starting to challenge the way we think about God in scientific terms.

Systematic study

A classic approach to the scientific study of religious experience is to collect and analyse a large number of observations (in this case of individual people's experiences) in the search for patterns and possible relationships. This empirical approach - based on observation rather than on theory or pure logic - is how much scientific research is conducted (as we saw in Chapter 6), and it is exactly the basis on which Charles Darwin formulated his theory on the origin of species by natural selection.

The most famous scientific study of religious experience is the work of Professor Sir Alister Hardy FRS, a former Professor of Zoology at Oxford University who looked at religion in the same way that a naturalist looks at nature. Hardy set up the Religious Experience Research Unit in the 1960s to collect and analyse evidence of people's spiritual feelings and their sense of spiritual awareness, and to study what impacts those might have on how people live. The results of his analysis are summarised in his 1979 book *The Spiritual Nature of Man*,[856] and they build on the formative earlier research of William James which was more anecdotal than systematic, and which informed his 1902 book *The Varieties of Religious Experience*.

Hardy and his colleagues collected three thousand stories from people who believed they had experienced God. Two examples will suffice. In one, a lady in her 80s had had a vision as a child when "suddenly without warning I saw right through the physical world into a realm of great beauty; I found myself saying to myself 'well this is what I suppose heaven is like'."

In another example, a lady believed she had been touched by a divine power; she reported that "out of my mouth came a few words of a tongue that I didn't recognise at all, a language; I can only describe it as something like the disciples on the day of Pentecost when they were taken for being drunk at 9 am and Peter said these people are not drunk but they are filled with the Holy Spirit. I was supernaturally happy."[857]

The most common experiences were sensory ones. More than five hundred people reported having visions, over four hundred had heard voices, and over three hundred and fifty had a sense of being physically touched. In terms of affective experiences, more than six hundred reported a sense of joy or ecstasy, and nearly two hundred reported having a sense of certainty or enlightenment.

Neurotheology - God in the head

Richard Dawkins discards the existential argument because he insists that all religious experiences can be explained or accounted for as the product of normal psychological processes at work.[858]

There's no denying the fact that experiences of God, as indeed experiences of everything, are received and interpreted in our brains. Neuroscientist Andrew Newberg points out that "our brain uses logic, reason, intuition, imagination, and emotion to integrate God and the universe into a complex system of personal values, behaviours and beliefs."[859] Newberg and his colleagues conclude that "the [scientific] evidence suggests that … religions persist because the wiring of the human brain continues to provide believers with a range of [mystical] experiences that are often interpreted as assurances that God exists."[860]

Michael Persinger took an interesting if controversial approach in seeking to better understand the link between religious experience and brain activity. He developed what he called 'The God Helmet', a rigid helmet that passes weak magnetic fields through the brain of a human wearing it. Persinger claims that he can artificially induce a religious experience in almost anyone by stimulating a particular part of the brain - the temporal lobes, which lie on either side of the brain and are associated with important functions like memory, speech, hearing and aspects of vision. Richard Dawkins took the test but claims to have had no religious experience in it or through it. Alister McGrath dismisses Persinger's hypothesis that "religious experience is associated with pathological brain activity, subtly implying that religion is itself therefore pathological", adding that readers of *The God Delusion* "ought to be aware (for Dawkins does not mention it) that Persinger's experiments have been severely criticised for their conceptual and design limitations, and that his theory is no longer regarded as plausible."[861]

A different approach, which neurologist Andrew Newberg calls 'neurotheology', is based on monitoring what happens in the brain during religious experiences, using sophisticated brain imaging technology. Newberg carried out a series of studies in which he injected volunteer Tibetan monks and Franciscan nuns with a radioactive tracer as they meditated; he then tracked the movement of the tracer in the subject's bloodstream as it moved into and through the brain.[862] In most subjects he found that the flow of blood into the parietal lobes (a part of the brain that handles all of our sensory information and uses it to create our sense of ourselves) decreased as meditation reached a peak. This is consistent with the claims made by many deeply religious people that they experience a loss of the sense of self when they meditate. Newberg concludes that the brain scans support the hypothesis "that suggests that spiritual experience, at its very root, is intimately interwoven with human biology. That biology, in some way, compels the spiritual urge."[863] His studies have also shown that practice makes perfect, in the sense that "intense long-term contemplation of God and other spiritual values appears to permanently change the structure of those parts of the brain that control our moods, give rise to our conscious notions of self, and shape our sensory perceptions of the world. … [and] contemplative practices strengthen a specific neurological circuit that generates peacefulness, social awareness, and compassion for others."[864]

Newberg is at pains to point out that his brain research has shown that "there is no 'God spot', nor is there any simple way to categorise religious beliefs. The data points to an endless variety of ways in which spiritual practices can affect the cognitive, emotional, and experiential processes of the brain, and each one of these experiences will lead to a different notion about God."[865] He admits that "brain science can neither prove nor disprove the existence of God, at least not with simple answers. The neurobiological aspects of spiritual experience support the *sense* of the realness of God."[866]

Natural or divine causes?

Despite these advances in understanding how brain states and religious experiences interact, the question naturally arises - to what extent are these experiences genuinely of God or from God? What about purely psychological explanations of religious belief?

David Geaney suggests that "religious belief may be a specific example of the [self-serving] positive cognitive bias that exists in normal individuals. Unrealistically positive views about the self, exaggerated beliefs about personal control and unrealistic optimism are the hallmarks of normal thought and are absent in mild depression. In addition to happiness and contentment, these biased beliefs are associated with other aspects of mental health such as the ability to care for and about others, the capacity for productive and creative work, and the ability to develop in response to a changing and sometimes threatening environment."[867]

Geaney touches on the subject of mental health, and a number of critics of the Argument from Religious Experience seize on the possibility (or the likelihood as they would insist) that such experiences are caused by psychiatric conditions. New Atheist Sam Harris belittles this line of reasoning in writing "it is surely an accident of history that it is considered normal in our society to believe that the Creator of the universe can hear your thoughts, while it is demonstrative of mental illness to believe that he is communicating with you by having the rain tap in Morse code on your bedroom window. And so, while religious people are not generally mad, their core beliefs absolutely are. ... In fact, it is difficult to imagine a set of beliefs more suggestive of mental illness than those that lie at the heart of many of our religious traditions."[868]

Psychiatrist Joseph Pierre is much better informed on the matter than Harris is, and he points out that there are no clear guidelines in psychiatric clinical practice to distinguish between normal religious beliefs and pathological religious delusions. Pierre argues that, "historically, psychiatrists such as Freud have suggested that all religious beliefs are delusional, while the current DSM-IV [*Diagnostic and Statistical Manual of Mental Disorders*, Fourth Edition] definition of delusion exempts religious doctrine from pathology altogether. ... Religious beliefs and delusions alike can arise from neurologic lesions and anomalous experiences, suggesting that at least some religious beliefs can be pathological. Religious beliefs exist outside of the scientific domain; therefore they can be easily labelled delusional from a rational perspective. However, a religious belief's dimensional characteristics, its cultural influences, and its impact on functioning may be more important considerations in clinical practice."[869]

The evidence that emerges from brain stimulation and brain monitoring studies is rather inconclusive. It can demonstrate that particular areas within the brain are associated with religious experiences, but cannot establish whether observed effects are the result of normal brain processes or divine intervention. The debate continues.

Robin Henig, reviewing *The God Delusion* in *The New York Times*, asks "Are the non-believers right, and is religion at its core an empty undertaking, a misdirection, a vestigial artefact of a primitive mind? Or are the believers right, and does the fact that we have the mental capacities for discerning God suggest that it was God who put them there?"[870] Krista Tippett explores the same territory, asking "the question of whether human spirituality is generated by the brain, rather than by a transcendent maker. On the other hand, some counter, wouldn't the mind behind life instil a capacity in human beings to apprehend it and communicate? Or are our most debased and transcendent instincts driven by a 'selfish gene', or a 'God gene'?"[871]

CHAPTER 9

THE NATURE OF BELIEF

"Any attempt to prove the existence of God by means of reasoned argument
has failed, and will always fail. God cannot be argued into existence,
if he wishes his creatures to approach him in faith rather
than in the certainty of knowledge." [872]

Hugh Montefiore (1985)

In Chapter 7 we looked at the most common arguments for God, and in Chapter 8 we explored personal experience of God. From what we saw in both chapters it is clear that there is much scope for disagreement over the nature, strength and validity of the evidence used to defend the idea and existence of God. Most non-believers struggle to see as credible the arguments usually put forward by believers, and believers generally struggle to accept and sometimes even to understand the arguments that non-believers put forward against God.

Believers and non-believers have access to the same evidence, but they view it, weigh it and interpret it differently. So the position one takes in any discussion about God depends partly on one's vantage point. In this case Richard Dawkins and his fellow New Atheists, along with many scientists and other atheists, are outsiders looking in, whilst others (including Alister McGrath, Marcus Borg and me) are insiders looking out.

In the light of this it is clearly important to look at the nature of belief, what it means and what it involves. In this chapter we explore the nature of and interrelationships between three key things - knowledge, belief and faith.

Reality

We need to start by considering 'What is reality?' What do we mean by the term? Dictionaries define 'reality' along the lines of "the quality or state of being actual or true ... something that is real."[872] This naturally raises the question of what we mean by 'actual', 'true' or 'real'. Defining 'reality' as the state of things as they are or appear to be, rather than as one might wish them to be, helps clarify an important quality of reality.

Philosophers define reality in terms of something that actually exists, independent of human awareness. In other words, reality exists whether or not we are aware of it. This of course raises the question of who the 'we' are - does that mean everyone everywhere, or a particular sub-set of people? The latter notion of 'we' raises the prospect of different people having quite legitimate grounds for seeing *their* take on reality as the 'true' or 'real one', and for dismissing other people's takes as not 'true' or 'real. From this perspective it is quite possible for supernatural reality to exist - at least in principle - even if not everyone recognises it.

Philosophers and scientists argue that reality is not a thing in itself, a physical object of some form, but rather the way we interpret and understand the world around us. We rely on our five senses (sight, sound, touch, smell and taste) for most of the 'hard' information we receive about that world, but of course our senses can deceive us. Illusionists and magicians rely on such deception, as do people working in such fields as virtual reality and computer-generated imagery. So, is there a reality independent of mind? Brain scientist Andrew Newberg points out that "our modern understanding of the brain's perceptual powers ... [shows that] nothing enters consciousness whole. There is no direct, objective experience of reality. All the things the mind perceives – all thoughts, feelings, hunches, memories, insights, desires, and revelations – have been assembled piece by piece by the processing powers of the brain from the swirl of neural blips, sensory perceptions, and scattered cognitions dwelling in its structures and neural pathways."[873]

Although believers and non-believers have the same senses and brain mechanisms, they often view and interpret the world very differently, reflecting their different world-views. We looked at world-views briefly in Chapter 2 but we can take this theme a bit further here. James Sire defines a world-view as "composed of a number of basic presuppositions, more or less consistent with each other, more or less consciously held, more or less true. They are generally unquestioned by each of us, rarely, if ever, mentioned by our friends, and only brought to mind when we are challenged by a foreigner from another intellectual universe."[874] Brian Walsh and Richard Middleton emphasise that "our world-view determines our values. It helps us interpret the world around us. It sorts out what is important from what is not, what is of highest value from what is least. ... world-views (just like cultures) never belong to just one individual. World-views are always shared; they are communal. ... Another person's world-view *is* like a different world or universe, and its constitutive elements are like a map to that world. This is why it is often so difficult for people of different visions of life to communicate and understand each other."[875]

The polarisation between science and religion that we looked at in Chapter 6 is rooted in radically different world-views. This helps to explain why 'the God Question' won't go away or be answered once and for all, and why both sides often argue that their opponents are uninformed, partisan and blinkered. Finding common ground is difficult when each side has different ways of looking at and thinking about 'reality', particularly in terms of:

[i] The *nature* of reality: science sees and seeks to explain only the natural (material reality), whereas religion sees and seeks to explain both the natural and the supernatural;

[ii] *Awareness* of reality: science uses reason to explain reality, whereas religion uses faith and reason; and

[iii] Proof or *evidence* of reality: science uses empirical methods (observation or experiment) to study and explain reality, whereas religion relies more on personal experience and revelation.

Inevitably, Richard Dawkins trusts only the scientific take on 'reality' and dismisses the religious take as stuff and nonsense. He sees the role of science as "to discover important truths about the real world"[876] and claims that science is "the honest and systematic endeavour to find out the truth about the real world."[877] But Dawkins does not even attempt to define truth or real; as Klaus Klostermaier points out he "presupposes that what he says is the truth and that the world as he understands it is the real world."[878]

Knowledge

If the way we see things and interpret things is strongly dependent on our world-view, how on earth can we actually *know* anything? How can we be certain about anything? How do we distinguish between what we think, what we believe, and what we know?

We start from the assumption that there are such things as facts. A fact is something that actually exists, that actually *is*. It would exist even if no-one knew about it, and its existence is beyond doubt no matter who debates it nor what world-view they view it from. The nature and quality of the fact might be open to debate but its existence is non-negotiable.

Most dictionary definitions of the verb 'to know' emphasise four things about how we relate to any particular fact - being aware of it, possessing information about it, understanding it as truth, and being certain about it. Thus we can place everything on a spectrum ranging from fact (true) to fiction (untrue), from certain (we know) to uncertain (we doubt).

Another important aspect of knowledge is the difference between knowing *about* something or someone and actually *knowing* it or them. I know about a great many famous people, but I don't know any famous person in the sense of being directly acquainted with them in the same way that I know my family and friends. Theists would argue that it is possible to *know* God, not just *know about* God.

Sources of knowledge

We get most of the information about the world around us from four sources - sense (our five senses), reason (our powers of rational thought), testimony (what others tell us), and memory (what we remember). Thomas Dixon cautions that all of these sources are fallible - "our senses can deceive us, our reasoning can be faulty, other people can knowingly or accidentally mislead us, and most of us know only too well (and increasingly with age) how partial and distorted our memories can be."[879]

For many people there is a fifth source of knowledge - revelation (which we looked at in Chapter 8) - which can never be proved and is an article of faith or religious belief. This allows us to draw a distinction between 'natural knowledge' and 'revealed knowledge'. As Dixon explains, "natural knowledge is produced by the exercise of the natural human faculties of sense and reason (these faculties can be engaged in reasoning about scripture as well as about the natural world). Revealed knowledge is produced by a supernatural uncovering of the truth – either through the medium of scripture or by a direct revelation from God to the individual believer."[880]

Another inconvenient truth is that the more we know, the more we discover there is to know. Robert Winston reminds us that "science seems to provide answers to the mysteries of our existence. Yet, whatever we hypothesise, observe, measure or record about the natural world leaves more, and increasingly more, unanswered questions. Though a very superficial view might suggest the contrary, science does not give us certainty about ourselves or our origin."[881]

Keith Ward insists that "we do not regard the existence of God as a factual matter, in any ordinary sense. We do not send out search parties ... We do not carry out experiments to find out if God is making a difference ..."[882] In terms of sending out search parties, Soviet cosmonaut Yuri Gagarin – the first person to travel into outer space onboard the spacecraft Vostok 1 for a few hours on 12 April 1961 – returned safely back to Earth and reported "I looked and looked but I didn't see God."[883] C.S. Lewis apparently responded that this was like Hamlet going into the attic of his castle looking for Shakespeare![884] Nearly fifty years later, in July 2010, US astronaut Jeff Williams joined members of his Lutheran Church in Houston Texas in a church service beamed live from the International Space Station; there was clearly no conflict of interest between faith and science for him.[885]

Ownership and reliability of knowledge

Thomas Dixon asks two important questions relating to knowledge – 'Who owns knowledge?' and 'What makes one source of knowledge more reliable than another?' In other words, why do we trust one type of knowledge more than another? Specifically in the modern world, why is scientific 'knowledge' widely regarded as more reliable and trustworthy than religious 'knowledge'?

Much of the heat in the debate between science and religion rests on how each side interprets the relative authority of different sources of knowledge. One reason why the general public often trust claims made by scientists more than those made by theologians and church leaders is that, as James Sire points out, "many scientists and technologists continue in their own confidence that science gives sure knowledge, but they seem to be the last part of the intellectual world to do so."[886] Science and scientists claim the high ground by insisting that they work only with 'sure knowledge' or objective knowledge, but this intellectual high ground is only part of the bigger picture of reality. Terry Eagleton reminds us that, for the New Atheists, "religious statements are the same kind of thing as scientific ones; it is just that they are worthless and empty."[887]

The monopoly of rationality that science claims for itself is based on two key claims which are rarely challenged or tested - 1. reason is the sole criterion for truth; and 2. measurable knowledge is the only knowledge worth having. Thus, it is argued (or more often simply assumed), science is the only route to true knowledge.[888] But, as philosopher of science Jerry Ravetz argues, we need to "get over the illusion of objectivity in science, as embodied in its supposed impersonality and value-neutrality."[889] The limits to science that we looked at in Chapter 6 are good reasons to question the objectivity that scientists often claim for their work.

The popular view today is that science has 'right' answers to all questions. But this view is based on "the illusion, unique to the English-speaking world, that there is some single set of procedures which uniquely qualify as 'scientific' and give privileged access to truth,"[890] as Nicholas Lash puts it. Terry Eagleton colourfully points out that "whereas scientists used to be regarded as unspeakable yokels from grammar schools with dandruff on their collars ... they have become in our own time the authoritarian custodians of absolute truth."[891]

Explanation

An important dimension of knowing something is having the ability to explain it, to account for it by giving a reason. Naturally, believers often invoke God as the reason and thus the best explanation for things. Conversely, non-believers invoke natural processes and dismiss any notion of supernatural causes or reasons.

Fourteenth century English Franciscan friar William of Ockham proposed a "keep it simple" principle for explaining anything, which is generally referred to as Ockham's (or Occam's) Razor. Stated simply, it says "all things being equal, the simplest explanation tends to be the right one". In other words, make as few assumptions as possible, eliminate those that appear unnecessary, and accept the first sufficient explanation. This approach is sometimes applied to the existence of God, using the logic that if the idea of God does not help explain the universe then God is not relevant and can be eliminated from the enquiry. New Atheist Christopher Hitchens seizes on the fact that "Ockham stated that it cannot be strictly proved that God, if defined as a being who possesses the qualities of supremacy, perfection, uniqueness, and infinity, exists at all."[892]

Fellow New Atheist Daniel Dennett proposed the terms skyhooks and cranes as devices for explaining things.[893] Richard Dawkins adopted the terms in his attack on the idea of God and defence of the theory of evolution by natural selection. As Dawkins puts it "skyhooks – including gods – are magic spells. They do no *bona fide* explanatory work and demand more explanation than they provide. Cranes are explanatory devices that actually do explain. Natural selection is the champion crane of all time. It has lifted life from primeval simplicity to the dizzy heights of complexity, beauty and apparent design that dazzle us today."[894] He goes on to argue that "only a crane can do the business of working up gradually and plausibly from simplicity to otherwise improbable complexity. The most ingenious and powerful crane so far discovered is Darwinian evolution by natural selection. Darwin and his successors have shown how living creatures, with their spectacular statistical improbability and appearance of design, have evolved by slow, gradual degrees from simple beginnings. We can now safely say that the illusion of design in living creatures is just that – an illusion."[895]

Not everyone shares Dawkins' confidence in rejecting all possible explanations for life on earth other than evolution. John Haught points out that, "like other scientific naturalists, the New Atheists suffer from a bad case of explanatory monism. That is, they assume that there is only one explanatory slot available, namely, the one shaped to look for physical causes, and this is enough. Scientism has shrunk their perspective to the point where it leaves only a narrow slit through which they view the complexity of the real world. The subjective, intentional, personal side of reality remains completely out of its sight."[896] Haught dismisses Dawkins's God Hypothesis because it allows for only one explanation and "tries to force the idea of God to play the role of a hypothesis just like those of science."[897]

Whilst acknowledging the important role played by science in explaining the world around us, philosopher Richard Swinburne insists that "the capacity of science to explain itself requires explanation – and the most economical and reliable account of this explanatory capacity lies in the notion of a creator God."[898] Alister McGrath supports Swinburne's argument that "the intelligibility of the universe itself needs explanation. It is therefore not the *gaps* in our understanding of the world which point to God, but rather the very *comprehensibility* of scientific and other forms of understanding that requires an explanation."[899] Lord Sacks, a former Chief Rabbi in the UK, takes a much simpler approach, pointing out that "Science is about explanation. Religion is about interpretation. ... The Bible simply isn't interested in how the Universe came into being. ... It is interested in other questions entirely. Who are we? Why are we here? How then shall we live? It is to answer those questions, not scientific ones, that we seek to know the mind of God."[900]

Despite the bold claims of scientists like Richard Dawkins, it would be wrong to assume that science alone can provide the best (most reliable) answers to most questions. As John Haught points out "there are many channels other than science through which we all experience, understand, and know the world."[901] An obvious example - the evidence that someone loves us is hard to measure, but it can still be real, or real enough for us to act on it. Great paintings, music and writing can trigger emotional responses in us, as can encounters with the beauty and wonder of nature. The world and how we experience it are about much more than molecules, forces and equations.

Evaluating truth claims

Truth can be defined as "a fact that has been verified", and the key criterion for truth is that it conforms to reality. So there is, at least in theory, such a thing as absolute truth, which does not change through time or depending on who is looking at it. But many areas of what is claimed to be truth - many things which are currently not fully understood - are contested, with different people arguing differently over the same thing, often using the same evidence. In the history of science, for example, the flat Earth model was once regarded as truthful, because it conformed to what was then known about the planet, but we now know differently.

So how do we decide what *is* true? We rarely have access to all the evidence we would like in order to make a firm decision about something, so we end up having to be content with what economists call 'satisficing behaviour' based on 'sub-optimal decision-making' (ie it's the best we can do with what we have available). For many things, the existence of compelling evidence is often regarded as enough to define something as 'the truth'. But how compelling is compelling enough to ensure sound decisions? In law different standards of proof apply in different circumstances; in the UK, for example, the standard of proof required in a criminal court is "beyond reasonable doubt", whereas that required in a domestic tribunal is lower, being "on a balance of probabilities."

Michael Poole argues that "a belief may be said to be true if, and only if, it corresponds with things as they actually are. Pointers to truth include: comprehensiveness (taking into account all known, relevant data); consistency (free from internal contradictions); coherence (holding together, making sense overall)."[902]

Philosophers talk about two main theories of truth - the so-called correspondence theory, and the coherence theory. The correspondence theory of truth maintains that "a statement is true if it corresponds to a state of affairs which it attempts to describe", as Peter Vardy puts it. He explains that "someone who holds to a correspondence theory of truth is today called a *realist*."[903] The coherence theory of truth maintains that "a statement is true if it coheres [is consistent] with other true statements ... and someone who holds a coherence theory of truth is today called an *anti-realist*."[904]

The satisficing behaviour that economists talk about reflects our willingness to make decisions that are sound but often not perfect. As well as being a pragmatic solution to the challenge of never having all the information we might like, this is also a product of how we balance different objectives. As George Ellis explains, "it is crucial to understand that our minds act, as it were, as an arbiter between three tendencies guiding our actions – the cold calculus of more and less, the economically most beneficial choice; second, what emotion sways us to do – the way that feels best, what we would like to do; and third, what our values tell us we ought to do – the ethically best option, the right thing to do."[905]

Evidence and proof
Knowledge and explanation require evidence - the facts or information on which judgements can be made in deciding whether a belief or proposition is true or valid. Is there evidence to support the existence of a particular

thing such as God, Aids or global warming? Is there evidence to support a particular way of explaining something, such as how species develop or how the universe was formed? The evidence used must be both credible and relevant. Who decides and on what grounds?

John Cottingham points out that "the term 'evidence' conjures up images of the courtroom or the laboratory, and if we have these contexts in mind then it seems clear that what are needed are the tools of detached rational scrutiny and careful quantitative measurement. But there is so much else in human experience that is not susceptible to this kind of assessment, or at least not entirely so."[906]

Once again, on the matter of evidence for or against the existence of God, there are strong views both ways. Not surprisingly Richard Dawkins privileges scientific notions of evidence and proof, insisting that "it is religion that offers the simplistic and reductionist view. A willingness to look, to question and to conceive the inconceivable through science offers a more inspiring and enlightened view of the wonderful world around us than faith. A view that is evidence-based."[907] Without using the term or claiming it as his intellectual birthright, Dawkins writes from within a scientific paradigm which, as Brian Walsh and Richard Middleton explain, "functions as the scientists' conceptual framework – their shared generalisations, values and beliefs. It provides the criteria by which theories are judged, evidence is deemed admissible, the nature of demonstration is determined, and the elements of a true conclusion are constituted. A paradigm suggests what questions should be asked and therefore which research programs will likely be fruitful."[908]

Marion Ledwig takes Dawkins to task, arguing that "evidence seems to be his sole criterion, neglecting the fact that evidence can be interpreted in different ways ... [and] that it is not only evidence that counts, but that the interpretation of the evidence should be consistent with the theory which one advances, and that that is why one needs logic to a certain extent."[909] Francis Collins is more damning in his critique of Dawkins, arguing that "to apply scientific arguments to the question of God's existence, as if this were somehow a showstopper, is committing a category error [presenting things of one kind as if they belonged to another]."[910]

Truth and viewpoint

The notion of truth is treated differently by people with different world-views, so for example modernists and scientists see it differently from postmodernists, and people of faith see it differently again.

Sigmund Freud claimed that "science alone is a reliable road to true understanding of anything"[911] although Patrick Clarke explains the limitations of the verification principle that underpins modern science; it is rooted in the belief that "a statement which cannot be verified by some form of sense experience is meaningless. ... Measured against the verification principle, statements of metaphysics (about things that lie behind the world of experience) and religion (about God and the supernatural) were classed as nonsensical or meaningless. This was because (a) they could not be verified and (b) they made no difference to how the world is since they are consistent with all possible states of affairs."[912] Postmodernists view truth as contingent (conditional and relative to other things) and contested (open to negotiation and based on personal choice), allowing everyone the freedom to believe whatever they want, without having to defend their position.

Richard Dawkins claims the philosophical high ground in insisting that "people of a theological bent are often chronically incapable of distinguishing what is true from what they'd like to be true."[913] Peter Vardy frames Dawkins' claim in anti-realist terms, pointing out that "realists maintain that claims about God are true because they correspond or refer to the reality of God which is independent of the universe God created and sustained. Anti-realists reject correspondence and instead maintain that religious statements are true within the 'story' that religious believers have created. People do not discover religious truths ... they make them."[914] Vardy explains how, "at the very most, anti-realists hold, the arguments for God's existence show that there *may* be such a God and this is too tentative a conclusion to provide grounds for religious belief."[915]

John Polkinghorne concluded that "there are good motivations for belief in God, sufficient for many of us to commit ourselves to betting our lives on them. The claim is ... that theism explains more than atheism ever could, making intelligible what otherwise would have to be treated as merely a happy accident."[916] Like many other people I find this conclusion compelling, both on grounds of personal experience and logic.

Belief

Our lives and experiences are shaped both by what we know and what we believe. As Andrew Pessin points out, "we need our beliefs to get us through the day."[917] But we all have different beliefs, and we have them for different reasons.

There are some things I definitely do believe, some things I definitely don't believe, some things I'd like to believe, some things I find hard to believe, and some things I no longer believe. Try this at home, you might find it interesting!

[i]   Three things I *do* believe – there will be a tomorrow; a US astronaut did set foot on the moon in 1969; Eric Clapton is the best guitarist in the world ... ever.

[ii] Three things I *don't* believe – the moon is made of cheese; Superman really exists; pigs can fly.

[i]   Three things I'd *like to* believe – my children and their children will enjoy long, happy, healthy and fulfilling lives; in 20 years time the *Make Poverty History* campaign will be redundant because it's objectives will have been achieved; Gwyneth Paltrow would give me the time of day if she ever came on the market again (and, my wife reminds me, if she - my wife - didn't object!).

[iii] Three things I *find hard* to believe, but for which there appears to be reliable evidence – how a huge airplane can rise in the air just by the movement of air over its wings; television pictures, phone calls and emails can be sent around the world in real time; the world's tallest man grew to 8 feet 11.1 inches (2.72 m) in height.[918]

[iv] Three things I *no longer* believe – it really does go dark when I close my eyes; my dad must be the cleverest man in the world he knew so much; my pet goldfish could survive for weeks without being fed.

This raises the question do all beliefs carry equal weight? In other words, is what I believe about Eric Clapton as important as what I believe about God, for example? Logically the correct answer is no, because some beliefs shape our behaviour more than others, and through this some beliefs can have more influence than others on such things as our quality of life and how we treat others.

Belief and knowledge

As we have seen, our knowledge of something is based on awareness of it, having information about it, understanding it as truth, and being certain about it. That might be fine for tangible things; for example, unless the photographs of it and reports about it are false, I *know* that Mount Everest exists. Similarly I know that I have four grown-up children, that it gets dark earlier in the day during winter months where I live, and that the Atlantic Ocean is very wide.

But what about things that are not tangible? There are many things that I *think* or *believe* but do not know. I think, for example, that I'd find it a great struggle to climb to the summit of Everest, but I've never (yet) tried so I don't know for certain. Similarly, I believe that my children are leading happy lives, mainly because I've seen little evidence to the contrary, but only they know if they are.

How does belief differ from knowledge? Belief is less certain than knowledge, obviously, but we still need grounds or reasons for thinking a particular way. Belief is also more personal than knowledge, because we each form our own beliefs about something based on a mixture of things; these include personal experience, knowledge, the ability to weight things up rationally, openness to being persuaded to think or see things differently, and willingness to accept things on trust, often on the authority of others.

As Terry Eagleton explains, "the relations between knowledge and belief are notably complex. A belief, for example, can be rational but not true. It was rational, given their assumptions and stock of knowledge, for our ancestors to hold certain doctrines which later turned out to be false. They thought that the sun circled the earth because it looks as though it does. … It is important to recognise that just as one can have faith but not knowledge, so the opposite is also true. … Those who demand a theorem or proposition rather than an executed body are not on the whole likely to have faith in any very interesting sense of the term."[919]

George Smith spells out three "minimum requirements that must be fulfilled before any belief can claim the status of knowledge:

[i]   A belief must be based on evidence;

[ii] A belief must be internally consistent (ie not self-contradictory);

[iii] A belief cannot contradict previously validated knowledge with which it is to be integrated."[920]

Belief and truth

Dictionaries define belief in terms of agreeing with a proposition or being convinced that a statement or allegation is true. Knowledge changes through time, as we individually and collectively discover more, learn more and communicate better. But beliefs can also change through time (again individually and collectively) as the grounds for thinking a particular way change, perhaps because of experience or improved knowledge.

The key to making sense out of beliefs (our own and other people's) and how they shape attitudes and behaviour is that we think what we believe is 'true'. Who would knowingly genuinely hold on to a particular belief if they *knew* (not just had reason to believe) it was not true? Such a position might appeal to bar-room philosophers who like a good debate, but the rest of us like a quieter life! Similarly, few people are likely to hold flatly contradictory beliefs about different things at the same time. Most of us hold coherent packages of beliefs (sometimes called belief frameworks) in which some beliefs support others, so the gestalt principle ('the whole is greater than the sum of the parts') comes into play.

This linking of belief and truth is hard-wired into our brains. As Andrew Newberg explains, "a belief can be defined as any perception, cognition, or emotion that the brain assumes, consciously or unconsciously, to be true."[921]

Nonetheless, as Michael Poole points out, "although we can believe things that may be true or false, we can only know things that are true. ... Beliefs lie somewhere on a line between knowledge and opinion. Justification depends on evidence ..."[922]

The belief-making process

How do beliefs form? Andrew Newberg explains how "our beliefs ... are an assemblage of perceptual experiences, emotional evaluations, and cognitive abstractions that are blended with fantasy, imagination, and intuitive speculation."[923] He writes about how "recent discoveries about the way the brain creates memories, thoughts, behaviours, and emotions ... [and help us to] see how all beliefs emerge from the perceptual processes of the brain, and how they are shaped by personal relationships, societal influences, and educational and spiritual pursuits."[924]

Newberg describes how we form beliefs in terms of what he calls 'the belief-making process', which is shaped by four sets of factors -

[i]   Perception: "the information we receive about ourselves and the world through our senses";
[ii] Cognition: "all the abstract conceptual processes that our brain uses to organise and make sense of our perceptions";
[iii] Emotions: which "help to establish the intensity and value of every perceptual and cognitive experience we have"; and
[iv] Social consensus: "the input [we] receive from other members of the community" without which "many of our most cherished beliefs would never emerge into consciousness."[925]

Given that all of these factors can change through time, it is logical to expect that as individuals our beliefs can change through time. Naturally an adult sees and understands things differently from when they were a child, so their beliefs will have changed as they grew up. Similarly an elderly person, with greater life experience under their belt, may well hold different beliefs from what they did decades earlier. But on the whole, as adults, our beliefs tend to be relatively conservative in the sense that we hang on to them until we have good reason to change.

As John Humphreys puts it, "once someone believes something – whether it is a religious faith or something quite different – it is very difficult to shake their belief. That need not mean (though sometimes it will) that the believer is stupid or unthinking. ... most of us want our beliefs to be confirmed rather than proved false, and we will disregard any inconvenient evidence."[926]

Most of us know from experience that we will only change our mind and our belief about a particular thing when there are good grounds for doing so, particularly when confronted with strong and persuasive new evidence (new to us, or new overall). The human ageing process also kicks in. As Andrew Newberg explains, "we may modify some of our beliefs as we go through life; but the older we get, the less they will change, in part because of the architecture of the ageing brain."[927]

Philosophers talk of basic (or properly basic or foundational) beliefs or propositions; an example would be the existence of the world. Basic beliefs have two key properties:

[i]   They do not depend on justification by other beliefs; and
[ii] From them we derive other beliefs or propositions.

Alvin Plantinga introduced the idea that theism is a properly basic belief, arguing that "belief in God is similar to belief in other basic truths, such as belief in other minds or perception (seeing a tree) or memory (belief in the past). In all these instances, you trust your cognitive faculties, although you cannot prove the truth of the belief in question. … Believers, it is argued, take the existence of God as a basic proposition."[928]

Faith in science

The central thread in Richard Dawkins' *The God Delusion* is his insistence that religious faith is based more on wishful thinking than on tangible evidence of the form that would stand up to scientific scrutiny. Yet, as many critics have pointed out, Dawkins seems blind to the fact that he lives by faith, not in God but in the rationality and objectivity of science. Although he would find it hard to recognise it in himself, his faith in science is just as strong as the most religious believer's faith in God, and his passion in defending science could match the zeal of the most committed evangelist. Like most other scientists Dawkins is blind to both his faith in scientism and what John Haught calls his "uncompromising literalism."[929]

Paradoxically, New Atheism is founded on an act of faith - faith in science, expressed through scientism. As Karen Armstrong points out, "there is an inherent contradiction in the new atheism, especially in its emphasis on the importance of 'evidence' and the claim that science always proves its theories empirically. As Popper, Kuhn and Polyani have argued, science itself has to rely on an act of faith. … Dawkins' hero Darwin admitted that he could not prove the evolutionary hypothesis but he had confidence in it nonetheless, and for decades … physicists were happy to have faith in Einstein's theory of relativity, even though it had not been definitely verified."[930]

John Haught pursues the same theme asking rhetorically if, as Dawkins insists, "faith in God requires independent scientific confirmation, what about the colossal faith our New Atheists place in science itself?"[931] He points out that "Harris's and Dawkins's own scientism, the intellectual backbone of their scientific naturalism, is a belief for which there can be no 'sufficient' evidence or empirical 'evidence' either. There is no way, without circular thinking, to set up a scientific experiment to demonstrate that every true proposition must be based in empirical evidence rather than faith. The censuring of every instance of faith, in the narrow new atheist sense of the term, would have to include the suppression of scientism also."[932]

Recall from Chapter 6 that among the widely-described limitations of science are its conditional and contingent nature (accepted explanations can change through time as new evidence comes to light) and its dependence on paradigms (ways of operating that themselves can change through time). As a result, scientific understanding is always time-specific, and works fine until a better 'story' or narrative comes along.

Faith in science and faith in God are not as different as some people would like to think. John Haught points out that "both scientists and religious literalists share the belief that there is nothing beneath the surface of the texts they are reading – nature in the case of science, sacred scriptures in the case of religion. Scientism, the scientific community's version of literalism, assumes that the universe becomes fully transparent only if it is packaged in the impersonal language of mathematics or other kinds of scientific modelling. Any intuition that a deeper drama might be going on beneath the surface of nature, as religion and theology maintain, is pure fiction."[933]

Haught argues that "scientism is to science what literalism is to faith. It is a way of shrinking the world so as to make it manageable and manipulable. It is a way of suppressing the anxiety that might arise from a more open, courageous, and wholesome encounter with mystery. We can observe the narrowing instinct at work ... in the cascade of shrinkages that the New Atheists have to push through in order to take religion out of the hands of theology and put it in the steadier hands of science where they think it really belongs. The shrinkages include:

[i] Reducing, or trying hard to reduce, the entire monotheistic religious population to scriptural literalists, dogmatic extremists, escapists, perverts, perpetrators of human suffering, and fanatics;

[i] Reducing the cultural role of theology to the systematic underwriting of religious abuse;

[ii] Reducing the meaning of faith to mindless belief in whatever has no evidence;

[iii] Reducing the meaning of 'evidence' to 'what is available to science';

[iv] Reducing the whole of reality to what can be known by science; and

[v] Reducing the idea of God to a 'hypothesis'.

He concludes that "when it comes to the topic of religion, the New Atheists mirror their extremist opponents in assuming that they are in complete and inalterable possession of the truth."[934]

Faith in God

We come to the heart of the matter, the crossroads where believers and unbelievers part company and take very different sides. To the believer, having faith in God is as natural as breathing; to the unbeliever faith in God comes into the same category as believing in Father Christmas and the tooth fairy.

Keen to expose faith in God as delusional, New Atheist Sam Harris makes a rather curious comparison - a bit like Forrest Gump's observation that "life is like a box of chocolates." Harris proposes that "faith is rather like a rhinoceros, in fact: it won't do much in the way of real work for you, and yet at close quarters it will make spectacular claims upon your attention."[935] Quick to dismiss what they don't understand and haven't experienced, Harris and his fellow New Atheists can come across as just as intolerant and closed-minded as many of the ultra-religious people they repeatedly ridicule. Those who live in glass houses shouldn't throw stones!

What do we mean by faith?

William James defined religious faith as "faith in the existence of an unseen order of some kind in which the riddles of the natural order may be found and explained."[936]

Faith is generally seen as the same thing as *belief* but, as Marcus Borg points out, "faith as belief does not mean believing a particular set of doctrines or biblical statements to be true, regardless of their intelligibility or persuasiveness. But faith does involve believing enough to respond." There are two other important dimensions to faith, as Borg explains - faith as *fidelity* or faithfulness ("to have faith is to be faithful to the relationship with God") and faith as *trust* ("to have faith in somebody is to trust them; to have faith in God is to trust God").[937]

There is a difference between *what* we believe and *how* we believe, and in this sense the different Christian traditions have tended to view faith in different ways. Patrick Clarke explains how, "in the Catholic tradition, faith has tended to be identified with the content of what is believed. In this sense, faith becomes closely identified with revelation seen as truths and dogmas. Traditionally, this has been known as *fides quae* [the content of the faith, *what* we believe]. In the Protestant tradition following the Reformation, faith came to be identified with an attitude of trust in God through Christ. This put the emphasis on the subjective response to the object of faith. This subjective aspect of faith became known as the *fides qua* [the faith by which it is believed, *how* we believe]." [938]

Blind faith

According to atheist Douglas Adams, in *The Hitchhiker's Guide to the Galaxy*, God said "I refuse to prove that I exist, for proof denies faith and without faith I am nothing."[939]

Although it was written as a send-up, this statement nonetheless contains more than a grain of truth. Believers recognise that God could have made humans with built-in faith, but he chose not to. God did so because the attention and adoration freely given by those who have faith in him is much better than it would be if they had no choice in the matter, that is, if we were all hard-wired with faith (genetically pre-programmed in Dawkins' terms) and had no option but to believe in and worship God.

Douglas Adams' statement also reflects what the Bible says about faith rather than proof. Key texts include the statements that "faith is the substance of things hoped for, the evidence of things not seen"[940]; "we walk by faith not by sight"[941]; "we look not to the things that are seen but to the things which are unseen"[942]; "blessed are they that have not seen, and yet have believed"[943]; and "now we see in a mirror dimly, but then face to face. Now I know in part; then I shall understand fully."[944]

Yet that is the very nature of faith; it rests on trust rather than on reason, logical proof or firm evidence. This inevitably gives unbelievers of all persuasions a field-day. In *The God Delusion* (2006) the high priest of atheism Richard Dawkins defines faith as "belief without evidence,"[945] echoing his earlier definition of it in *The Selfish Gene* (1976) as "blind trust, in the absence of evidence, even in the teeth of evidence."[946]

We saw above the argument that scientism requires as much faith as faith in God. This gives critics like John Haught the right to point to the logical inconsistency of the New Atheists who argue that "the fundamental problem with faith is that it is based on no 'evidence', or at best on insufficient evidence, and therefore must be rejected in all its forms."[947] Haught explains how the New Atheists "think of faith as a set of hypotheses – such as the God hypothesis or the soul hypothesis – that lack sufficient scientific or empirical evidence for reasonable people to accept. They allow that if the right kind of empirical evidence ever turns up, then reasonable people will be permitted to give assent to the God Hypothesis or the soul hypothesis. But then there will no longer be any need for faith. Knowledge will have replaced it."[948]

But the argument that faith requires belief without evidence misses the point. It presupposes several key things, including that 'evidence' means tangible evidence, that weighing up the evidence involves rational judgment using quasi-scientific criteria, and that it is all a matter of clinical judgement on objective grounds. It fails to allow for God - the very thing on which the faith rests - to have any involvement in the matter, and assumes that to argue in this way is circular and evidence of the very delusion that Dawkins talks about. But it also discounts any possibility of personal experience of God.

John Humphreys, a significantly more tolerant and open-minded atheist than Richard Dawkins, acknowledges that "faith is not a belief that certain propositions about the world are true. It is not grounded in rational argument and neither is there any good line of reasoning that can persuade one to believe. ... The Archbishop and the little old lady down the road might use a different vocabulary to try to explain why they believe, but it comes to the same thing in the end. They believe because they believe. This is not about intellect or learning: it's more basic than that. It is both more profound and more simple. ... what drives belief has little to do with the head and a great deal to do with the heart."[949]

Leap of faith

Sam Harris argues that "every religion preaches the truth of propositions for which it has no evidence. In fact, every religion preaches the truth of propositions for which no evidence is even *conceivable* [his emphasis]. This put the 'leap' in Kierkegaard's leap of faith."[950]

Danish philosopher Søren Kierkegaard (1813-55) argued "that faith (in Christ) requires an unsupported leap into the unknown. This daring leap of faith leads to the knowledge that is essential to make sense of life, and provides the enlightenment that man is looking for."[951] This 'leap' is not a matter of "wishful thinking, a blind leap in the dark or believing what you know isn't true" but more a case of "launching out into the unknown on the strength of the known,"[952] as Michael Poole points out.

As Andrew Pessin explains, Kierkegaard believed that "God, and God's mind, cannot be known at all: God is utterly inconceivable, utterly transcendent, and utterly 'other' for us. And He is especially not knowable by reason; or even expressible in the dogmatic propositions of the faith. For faith is not a matter of propositions. It is rather a way of being, of maintaining a personal relationship to this utterly unknowable object, and is utterly opposed to reason. It is to the contrary grounded in the absurd – in the paradox of the eternal, infinite, transcendent God becoming temporal, finite, and concrete in the person of the saviour. The faithful individual attains this relationship only by suspending the rational."[953]

As many believers would confirm from their own experiences, "faith is a mode of apprehension which perceives something more in the total reality with which we are confronted than is manifest, or is expected to be manifest, to the senses,"[954] as John Baillie puts it. He explains further how "faith is an act of perceiving rather than of conceiving ... [and how] the divine presence is perceived by us, never in isolation from, but always in and through some familiar human experience."[955] This builds on the belief of philosopher Augustine (354-430 AD) that we can only grasp some truths because God lets us see inside his mind. As Andrew Pessin explains, Augustine argued that "just as sunlight makes visible to our eyes ordinary objects that would not be visible in the dark, so too, a kind of divine light makes knowable by our minds certain ideas and truths that, in its absence, would not be knowable. God illuminates our minds so that we can 'see' what is in His."[956]

Because God - the focus of our faith - plays a vital role in creating and shaping our faith, faith is not simply a matter of will on our part. Marcus Borg explains how "instead ... we are led into it. It grows, and the process continues through our lifetime. It is not a requirement that we are to meet but a quality that grows as our relationship with God deepens. Yet the will is also involved. We decide to take the first step, and then another (though sometimes we are virtually pushed into this by desperation or lured into it by example or experience). The will is involved in seeking to be faithful even when our faith is not immediately verified by our experience. ... Even faith ultimately is a gift of God. It is by grace."[957]

Trust and commitment

I pointed out above that faith does not rest on firm evidence but on trust, and trust is key ... in just the same way that scientism requires trust in its premises and assumptions. Karen Armstrong reminds us that "there is a distinction between belief in a set of propositions and a *faith* which enables us to put our trust in them."[958]

Michael Poole points out that "faith, in its religious sense, is comparable to trust in a person. It includes faith *that* something is true, but it goes beyond faith that God exists or that he created the world. Faith in God means trust in, confidence in, and reliance on God. It includes dependence on God for forgiveness and help in living; it involves commitment ..."[959]

Faith as trust is really important. Andrew Newberg emphasises that "behind our drive to survive, there is another force, and the best word to describe it is faith. Faith not just in God, or in science or love, but faith in ourselves and each other. Having faith in the human spirit is what drives us to survive and transcend. It makes life worth living, and it gives meaning to our life."[960]

Richard Dawkins goes a step further and bemoans the fact that, to many people, "unquestioning faith is a virtue"[961] because "the more your beliefs defy the evidence, the more virtuous you are."[962] Claiming the moral high ground, he argues that "what is really pernicious is the practice of teaching children that faith itself is a virtue. Faith is an evil precisely because it requires no justification and brooks no argument."[963]

John Polkinghorne explains how "faith involves trusting in well-motivated beliefs, not shutting one's intellectual eyes and believing impossible things because some unquestionable authority told you so."[964] Believers would argue, from personal experience, that the ability to do this comes directly from God. Many would agree with John Baillie that faith "is a supernatural virtue, attainable only by means of a direct infusion of divine grace. This means that, in addition to the external signs by which revelation is accompanied, there is also by the grace of God a direct persuasion of its truth in the heart of the believer."[965]

Being led into faith, apparently by God, and being directly persuaded by God of the truth of divine revelation, are other ways of saying that faith is a response to a direct invitation by God. It involves more than intellectual agreement with religious texts and arguments, although both the mind and the heart are integral to it. Despite what Richard Dawkins says about the matter (below), faith is not a matter of intelligence; both C.S. Lewis and J.R.R. Tolkien were Professors at Oxford University and both were men of faith. Biographer Joseph Pearce explains how, for Tolkien, "Catholicism was not an opinion to which one subscribed but a reality to which one submitted."[966]

Paul Tillich describes faith as "an act of a being who is grasped by and turned to the infinite,"[967] underlining the fact that faith is more like something that happens to a person than something the person does for themselves. The "being" that Tillich wrote of is not kidnapped or brainwashed but rather "grasped" and transformed, in a process in which "both the rational and the non-rational elements of his [sic] being are transcended."[968] From this perspective Tillich sees faith as "a total and centred act of the personal self, the act of unconditional, infinite and ultimate concern."[969]

Terry Eagleton develops this theme further, arguing that far from being a purely intellectual exercise, faith involves "a commitment and allegiance – faith *in* something which might make a difference to the frightful situation you find yourself in … Christian faith, as I understand it, is not primarily a matter of signing on for the proposition that there exists a Supreme Being, but the kind of commitment made manifest by a human being [Jesus] at the end of his tether, foundering in darkness, pain, and bewilderment, who nevertheless remains faithful to the promise of a transformative love."[970]

This "total and centred act of the self", and the commitment and allegiance that underpins it, can lead to what William James refers to as fruits of the "faith-state."[971] James describes the calm frame of mind and body that believers can experience through God as "a paradise of inward tranquillity."[972] He wrote of "a state of mind, known to religious men, but to no others, in which the will to assert ourselves and hold our own has been displaced by a willingness to close our mouths and be as nothing in the [presence] of God."[973]

Faith and reason

One of the key arguments of the New Atheists is that "faith is irrational and demands a positive suspension of critical faculties."[974] Christopher Hitchens reckons that "to believe in a god is in one way to express a *willingness* [his emphasis] to believe in anything. Whereas to reject the belief is by no means to profess belief in nothing."[975]

Richard Dawkins won few friends outside his New Atheism clique by referring to himself and his colleagues as "brights"[976] and dismissing his opponents as "faith-heads"[977], clearly convinced that atheists are more intelligent and can see better and clearer than believers. Not all of his fellow New Atheists share such unswerving self-confidence: Christopher Hitchens writes of his own "annoyance at Professor Dawkins and Daniel Dennett, for their cringe-making proposal that atheists should conceitedly nominate themselves to be called 'brights'."[978]

In my view Dawkins has got things back-to-front, because far from being endowed with special vision or intelligence atheists have a rather impoverished and partial view of things, being only able or willing to see and understand one type of reality. The atheist emphasis on material reality, and on rationality and intellect, blinds them to other forms of reality; it's a bit like a horse wearing blinkers, or colour-blind people unable to see and appreciate the full spectrum of colours, in both cases denied the full richness of what is on offer. With such a blinkered outlook they simply miss much of the depth of reality and the full range of human experience.

Dawkins' premise, that clever people can see through religion, is at best flimsy and most likely flawed. Less well-educated people tend to have fewer and lower life chances, less power and ability to change things, poorer health and quality of life, so it should perhaps be little surprise that they are often more open to God and feel more dependent on God than those who think they can achieve great things on their own.

This is not the only blind-spot that Dawkins has, because as Terry

Eagleton points out, "even Richard Dawkins lives more by faith than by reason. There are even those uncharitable observers who have detected the mildest whiff of obsessive irrationalism in his zealous campaign for secular rationality. His anti-religious zeal makes even the Grand Inquisitor look like a soggy liberal."[979] John Haught levels a similar criticism at Sam Harris, who he claims "makes a tacit act of faith in his own critical intelligence. But he never provides us with a good reason as to why he should trust his mind to lead him and us to truth. ... he never justifies his enormous cognitional swagger. He simply believes blindly in the superior capacity of his own mind to find truth with a facility and certainty that people misguided by religious faith do not possess."[980]

The New Atheists try to polarise the debate between believers and non-believers, arguing that the latter (who rely on reason) are the intellectual good guys and the former (who rely on faith) the intellectual bad guys. But, as G.K. Chesterton wrote, "it is idle to talk always of the alternative of reason and faith. Reason is itself a matter of faith. It is an act of faith to assert that our thoughts have any relation to reality at all."[981]

The eleventh century theologian Anselm insisted that God could be known only in faith; he wrote the much-quoted statement "I do not seek to understand in order to have faith but I have faith in order to understand."[982] Karen Armstrong points out that "Anselm was not claiming to embrace the creed blindly in the hope of it making sense one day. His assertion should really be translated: 'I commit myself in order that I may understand.' At that time, the word *credo* still did not have the intellectual bias of the word 'belief' today but meant an attitude of trust and loyalty."[983]

John Haught points out that "theologians today understand faith as the commitment of one's whole being to God. But the New Atheists, echoing a now obsolete theology, think of faith in a narrow intellectual and propositional sense. The seat of faith for them is not a vulnerable heart but a weak intellect."[984] The 'vulnerable heart' comment is a reference to Pascal's conviction that "it is the heart which experiences God, and not the reason. This, then, is faith: God felt by the heart, not by the reason".[985]

The argument about reason also falls flat because it assumes or even requires that faith is a matter of choice. But believers would flatly reject the assumption that they have made a conscious decision to believe in God. David Jenkins argued that "reason will never establish that God exists. He is far too divine to be an object of reason. ... the reasons which even the most skilful theologians and philosophers can give for believing are never adequate. He would not be God if they were."[986]

Terry Eagleton captures something important in writing that "it is rather a question of being gripped by a commitment from which one finds oneself unable to walk away."[987] This commitment is faith which rests ultimately on the "authority of God who reveals," as Thomas Aquinas put it.[988] Martin Luther saw things in a similar way; he was convinced that "faith does not require information, knowledge and certainty, but a free surrender and a joyful bet on his [God's] unfelt, untried and unknown goodness."[989]

Friedrich Schleiermacher (whom we met in Chapter 4) argued that reason could only take us so far on the journey towards God; feeling must take over after that, leading towards "the feeling of absolute dependence."[990] As Karen Armstrong explains, from this perspective "feeling was not opposed to human reason but an imaginative leap that takes us beyond the particular to an apprehension of the whole."[991] Schleiermacher believed that "religion's essence is neither thinking nor acting but intuition and feeling."[992]

Richard Dawkins concludes that the arguments for God's existence - which Daniel Dennett dismisses as "intellectual conjuring tricks or puzzles rather than serious scientific proposals"[993] - "turn out to be spectacularly weak."[994] Whilst Dawkins draws comfort from that fact, he can't hide his annoyance that most people don't approach the question of God with a fully open mind. As he sees it, this is because we are "psychologically primed for religion ... [because of] native dualism and native teleology."[995] He argues that dualists "personify inanimate physical objects at the slightest opportunity, seeing spirits and demons even in waterfalls and clouds"[996] and that teleologists assign purpose to everything, so that "childish teleology sets us up for religion. If everything has a purpose, whose purpose is it? God's, of course."[997]

Most people would agree with Richard Dawkins that "believing is not something you can decide to do as a matter of policy. At least, it's not something I can decide to do as an act of will."[998] John Humphreys picks up the same theme, writing that "you cannot *decide* to believe, in the way that you can decide which horse to put your fiver on in the three-thirty at Kempton Park. ... Neither can you *make* yourself believe. Of course you can fake it ... But you can't fool God – not if he has anything like the powers we're told he has. And you can't, of course, fool yourself."[999]

Whilst faith is not in itself a matter of choice or will, it is rarely the case that someone comes to faith without being open to it, or at least not hostile to it. Being open to faith - or as William James puts it, having "the will to believe"[1000] - clearly matters. Hugh Montefiore, a former Bishop of Birmingham wrote that "unless there is a predisposition to believe, and unless there is a presumption that belief is a rational choice which has intellectual justification, the atmosphere will not be conducive to faith."[1001] 'Not conducive' is not the same as blocking or being an unsurmountable barrier to faith, and some people can have unexpected and sudden conversion experiences (epiphanies) which can move them from unbelief to belief in ways that surprise even themselves let alone their family and friends.

Doubt, uncertainty and mystery

Few people have faith which is rock-solid and unshakable in every dimension all of the time. For most people faith involves both certainties and questions, even though the balance is in favour of the certainties. Even atheists allow for some wriggle-room. A good example is the 2009 advertisement campaign by the British Humanist Association using posters on public buses in Westminster, London, which announced "There is probably no God. Now stop worrying and enjoy your life."[1002] How interesting that they include the word 'probably'!

The New Atheists write in such dogmatic terms that they come across as having no uncertainties or doubts about their own ways of seeing things. Alister McGrath takes Richard Dawkins to task for being "resistant to the calibration of his own certainties, seeing them as being luminously true, requiring no defence. He is so convinced that his own views are right that he could not bring himself to believe that the evidence might legitimate other options – above all, *religious* options."[1003] Kathleen Jones points out that "if the evidence for a religious view of the world is not scientific in the sense of being observable and provable, he [Dawkins] will have nothing to do with it – though there is a great deal in the scientific field, from the Big Bang to dark energy, which he is well aware is neither observable nor provable. Science is allowed its mysteries, religion is not."[1004]

Absolute certainty about the existence of God, one way or the other, is an unreachable goal, but that is not necessarily a bad thing. As Karen Armstrong points out, "our scientifically-oriented knowledge seeks to master reality, explain it, and bring it under the control of reason, but a delight in unknowing has also been part of the human experience. Even today, poets, philosophers, mathematicians and scientists find that the contemplation of the insoluble is a source of joy, astonishment and contentment."[1005] Armstrong notes the "long religious tradition that stressed the importance of recognising the limits of our knowledge, of silence, reticence and awe."[1006]

It might surprise and would probably disappoint Richard Dawkins and his fellow atheists to know that doubt is not unusual amongst believers. John Baillie explains that "although there may be few of us who have ever denied God's reality outright, yet there must be many of us who have experienced from within something of the nature of this doubt."[1007] But doubt does not necessarily mean an end to faith, or a crumbling of a person's strength of faith. Paul Tillich was convinced that "'doubt isn't the opposite of faith; it is an element of faith."[1008] Timothy Keller has a nice take on this; he argues that "a faith without some doubts is like a human body without any antibodies in it."[1009]

Francis Collins insists that "doubt is an unavoidable part of belief. … If the case in favour of belief in God were utterly watertight, then the world would be full of confident practitioners of a single faith. But imagine such a world, where the opportunity to make a free choice about belief was taken away by the certainty of the evidence. How interesting would that be?"[1010]

Whilst doubt within faith might be inevitable, it can have serious consequences. Andrew Newberg wrote of the psychiatrist Victor Frankl who was imprisoned in a Nazi death camp until the end of World War II and wrote that "the single most important thing that kept a survivor alive was faith. If a prisoner lost faith in the future, he was doomed, because the will to live seldom returned."[1011] This was very much the experience of Jewish Holocaust survivor and 1986 Nobel Peace Prize Winner Elie Wiesel. In the book *Night* Wiesel describes his experiences of torture and depravity as a Jewish prisoner in the Nazi death camps at Auschwitz and Buchenwald, and how witnessing such inhumanity seriously affected his faith. He wrote "Never shall I forget those moments that murdered my God and my soul and turned my dreams into ashes."[1012] He explained to interviewer Cathleen Falsani how "there was never a question of whether God exists. I never doubted God's existence. I doubted his justice, his presence, his kindness, his compassion, his love, all the attributes I loved."[1013] Wiesel told another interviewer, Krista Tippett, how he was drawn to "an idea first described by the Jewish philosopher Martin Buber, that in certain historical periods there is an 'eclipse of God'. Perhaps, he imagines, the Holocaust was so massive and unbearable that God turned his face away."[1014]

Religious faith as journey

It is simplistic, unreasonable and unrealistic to expect the strength of a person's faith to remain constant through time. Experience shows that for most people it can vary a great deal through time, even if the substance of their faith remains relatively unchanging. As William James puts it, "nothing is more common in the pages of religious biography than the way in which seasons of lively and of difficult faith are described as alternating. Probably every religious person has the recollection of particular crises in which a direct vision of the truth, a direct perception, perhaps, of a living God's existence, swept in and overwhelmed the languor of the more ordinary belief."[1015]

James Fowler suggested that a typical person's faith evolves through six stages as they grow from childhood to adulthood, and in doing so learn to trust, commit and relate to other people and the world around them.[1016] Three of these stages (imitation, literalism, and conformity) usually occur during childhood and adolescence, and some people never get beyond the third stage. Most people who reach the fourth stage (criticality) do so as adults. Few people reach the two final stages, where they learn to be "open to the strange truth of others" and eventually where "faith creatively takes a truly universal and inclusive form."[1017]

Fowler's model suggests that the journey through life for most people is straightforward, linear and one-directional, but that is not always the case. For many people life has its twists and turns, and the journey becomes as important as the destination. So too, the way people view God. John Cornwell points out that "a religious believer's idea of God, throughout a lifetime, from childhood to old age, is bound to be one of expanding, and sometimes contracting, associations, including original ideas, concepts and metaphors, some of which have been initiated by the believer rather than received. ... a person's idea of God ... develops imaginatively, creatively, and dynamically with the ebb and flow of relationships, reading, chance encounters, age, and life experience."[1018] He concludes that "it's possible that belief in some souls is like an on-off switch – all or nothing – rather than a dimmer-switch constantly expanding and contracting, sometimes shading into total darkness."[1019]

The fact is that there is great permeability between different positions and categories of belief, running through from convinced atheist through agnosticism to convinced believer. There is also a range of positions within the 'belief' end of the spectrum, from rock-solid through some doubt to major doubt. But it is important to note two key things:

[i] We are not born into any particular category but our views are
     heavily shaped by our family and cultural background and by our
     experiences; and
[ii] We can change our religious allegiance - move into or out of
     religion, switch from one religion to another, and/or change
     our level of commitment to and engagement within a particular
     religion - through time. Nothing is fixed in stone.

We can move usually freely and by choice between categories along this spectrum, travelling in either direction. It is usually a matter of conscience, understanding and personal choice, though there is often a great deal of personal inertia and social and cultural barriers to rapid or repeated movements.

Finding faith

Some people adopt the religion of their family without ever having to think about it, as a form of intellectual and spiritual inheritance. This happens particularly in families in which belief in God is taken for granted (for example amongst Muslims, Jews and Catholics) and family life is steeped in religious tradition, teaching and practices. In such circumstances the individual never has to make any deliberate choice about what religion if any they will adopt and follow, it comes as part of their birthright, part of the package of values, attitudes and practices they are born into.

But today most people in most countries are not born into religious families, so they can or have to make their own choices as far as religion is concerned. This includes the option to reject religion outright, as well as the option to use religion as a defining cultural characteristic. Thus, for example, most people in the UK would tick the 'Christian' box on the census more because they live in a Christian country than because they are a practicing Christian. But it also includes the option to adopt a particular religion, or convert to it. As Andrew Newberg emphasises, "for those who embark on a spiritual journey, God becomes a metaphor reflecting their personal search for truth. It is a journey inward toward self-awareness, salvation, or enlightenment, and for those who are touched by this mystical experience, life becomes more meaningful and rich."[1020]

William James defines 'conversion' in typically archaic but colourful language: "to be converted, to be regenerated, to receive grace, to experience religion, to gain an assurance, are so many phrases which denote the process, gradual or sudden, by which a self hitherto divided, and consciously wrong inferior and unhappy, becomes unified and consciously right superior and happy, in consequence of its firmer hold upon religious realities. This at least is what conversion signifies in general terms, whether or not we believe that a direct divine operation is needed to bring such a moral change about."[1021] He quotes "Professor Starbuck of California" who argued that conversion involves self-surrender in which "the personal will must be given up. In many cases relief refuses to come until the person ceases to resist, or to make an effort in the direction he desires to go."[1022]

James gives examples from personal testimonies that demonstrate "how real, definite, and memorable an event a sudden conversion might be to him [sic] who has the experience. Throughout the height of it he undoubtedly seems to himself a passive spectator or undergoer of an astonishing process performed upon him from above. There is too much evidence of this for any doubt of it to be possible. Theology, combining this fact with the doctrines of election and grace, has concluded that the spirit of God is with us at these dramatic moments in a peculiarly miraculous way, unlike what happens at any other juncture of our lives. At that moment, it believes, an absolutely new nature is breathed into us, and we become partakers of the very substance of the Deity."[1023] This is the "new creation" that the apostle Paul talked about in the Bible, in which "the old has gone, the new has come."[1024] It is also the reason why evangelical Christians speak of being "born again".

The result of such conversion, James explains, is four important and beneficial changes in the individual:

[i]   "The state of assurance (the loss of all the worry, the sense
      that all is ultimately well with one, the peace, the harmony,
      the willingness to be, even though the outer conditions should
      remain the same);

[ii] The sense of perceiving truths not known before;

[iii] The objective change which the world often appears to
      undergo"[1025]; and

[iv] "The ecstasy of happiness produced."[1026]

There is no shortage of testimonies offered by former atheists and agnostics
who developed a belief in God. We have already heard a little about Alister
McGrath's conversion in Chapter 6, and I've sketched out mine in the
Introduction and Chapter 6.

Russian writer Leo Tolstoy (1828-1910) wrote an account of his
conversion in his 1886 book *What I Believe*: "Five years ago I came to believe
in Christ's teaching and my life suddenly changed; I ceased to desire what I
had previously desired, and began to desire what I previously did not want.
What had previously seemed to me good seemed evil, and what had seemed
evil seemed good. It happened to me as it happens to a man who goes out
on some business and on the way suddenly decides that the business is
unnecessary and returns home. All that was on his right hand is now on his
left, and all that was on his left hand is now on his right."[1027]

A different picture is painted by English philosopher of religion John
Hick (1922-2012) - "As a law student at University College, Hull, at the
age of eighteen, I underwent a powerful evangelical conversion under the
impact of the New Testament figure of Jesus. For several days I was in
a state of intense mental and emotional turmoil, during which I became
increasingly aware of a higher truth and greater reality pressing in upon
me and claiming my recognition and response. At first this was highly
unwelcome, a disturbing and challenging demand for nothing less than
a revolution in personal identity. But then the disturbing claim became a
liberating invitation. The reality that was pressing in upon me was not only
awesomely demanding . . . but also irresistibly attractive, and I entered with
great joy and excitement into the world of Christian faith."[1028]

Hick's story shares some elements with that of the English academic and
writer C.S. Lewis. Lewis was brought up in a Christian family in Belfast

and abandoned his early belief as a border at Wyvern College. When he was 17 years old he wrote to a friend – "I believe in no religion. There is absolutely no proof for any of them, and from a philosophical standpoint Christianity is not even the best."[1029] His biographer Joseph Pearce describes how, "by the summer of 1929 he had renounced agnosticism and professed himself a theist, believing in the existence of God but renouncing the claims of Christianity."[1030] Lewis rediscovered faith through an interest in Norse mythology and conversations with fellow academic J.R.R Tolkien. In his 1955 autobiography *Surprised by Joy*, after "feeling, whenever my mind lifted even for a second from my work, the steady, unrelenting approach of him whom I so earnestly desired not to meet,"[1031] Lewis describes how "in the Trinity term of 1929 I gave in, and admitted that God was God, and knelt and prayed: perhaps, that night, the most dejected and reluctant convert in all England. ... a prodigal who is brought in kicking, struggling, resentful, and darting his eyes in every direction for a chance of escape."[1032]

Yet a different spiritual journey was taken by scientist Francis Collins who was Director of the Human Genome Research Institute in the USA. Collins was an atheist until his late twenties when he converted to Christianity.[1033] The son of atheists, he went to university as an agnostic and this continued through his doctorate in physical chemistry at Yale, and the first two years of medical school. During his third year he had more contact with people with serious, often life-threatening, illnesses, some of whom talked openly about their faith. When one asked him directly 'What do *you* believe, doctor?' he said he didn't really know, but it "caused me to recognise that I didn't have an answer based on a proper examination of the evidence ... And so began a two-year effort to try to understand what the world religions have to say, and what God must be like if he exists."[1034] A local Methodist minister gave him a copy of C.S. Lewis's *Mere Christianity* to read, and "within an hour or two of sitting down with it, I realised that my arguments about faith were completely naïve; there was much more substance to faith than I had ever dreamed. ... It probably took me three or four months to get all the way through that little book because it was so unsettling to see the foundations of my atheistic world-view falling apart page by page and leaving me in a position to potentially having to accept the idea of God's existence. Ultimately that resulted – to my great surprise and with a good deal of resistance on my part – in my becoming a Christian at age twenty-seven."[1035] Collins describes how "on a beautiful fall day, as I was hiking in the Cascade Mountains during my first trip west of the Mississippi, the majesty and beauty of God's creation overwhelmed my resistance. As I rounded a corner and saw a beautiful and unexpected waterfall, hundreds of feet high, I knew the search was over. The next morning, I knelt in the dewy grass as the sun rose and surrendered to Jesus Christ."[1036]

One of the most high profile conversions from atheism to belief was that of world-famous philosopher Anthony Flew, which he describes in his book *There is a God: how the world's most notorious atheist changed his mind* (2009).[1037] Flew, whose father was a preacher, was raised in a Christian home and attended a private Christian school. He wrote that "by the time I reached my fifteenth birthday, I rejected the thesis that the universe was created by an all-good, all-powerful God,"[1038] partly because of the problem of evil, particularly the German hostility towards the Jews in the years before World War II which he witnessed first-hand. In 2004 Flew announced that he had changed his mind about God after more than six decades of atheism, and had moved from atheism to deism. To the annoyance of Richard Dawkins and fellow scientists, Flew changed his mind *because of* not *despite* what modern science was revealing about the world around us, particularly about three key questions - "The first is the question that puzzled and continues to puzzle most reflective scientists: How did the laws of nature come to be? The second is evident to all: How did life as a phenomenon originate from non-life? And the third is the problem that philosophers handed over to cosmologists: How did the universe, by which we mean all that is physical, come into existence?"[1039] Flew stressed that "my discovery of the Divine has proceeded on a purely natural level, without any reference to supernatural phenomena. It has been an exercise in what is traditionally called natural philosophy. It has had no connection with any of the revealed religions. Nor do I claim to have had any personal experience of God or any experience that may be called supernatural or miraculous. In short, my discovery of the Divine has been a pilgrimage of reason and not of faith."[1040] Ever the philosopher, he emphasised that "I have followed the argument where it has led me. And it has led me to accept the existence of a self-existent, immutable, immaterial, omnipotent, and omniscient Being."[1041]

Losing faith

The dynamics of faith run both ways, and it is possible for people to lose faith as well as find faith, through the process of what William James calls "counter-conversion ... the transition from orthodoxy to infidelity."[1042] Believers can become agnostics or atheists, but often the process is driven more by growing indifference and a mounting sense of irrelevance than by specific rational arguments. As Dennett asks, "what do people do when they discover that they no longer believe in God? Some of them don't do anything; they don't stop going to church, and they don't even tell their loved ones. They just quietly get on with their lives, living as morally (or immorally) as they did before. Others, such as Don Cupitt (who we met in Chapter 4)... feel the need to cast about for a religious creed that they can endorse with a straight face. They have a firm belief that *belief in God* is something to preserve, so when they find the traditional concepts of God frankly incredible they don't give up. They seek a substitute. And the search, once again, need not be all that conscious and deliberate."[1043]

Don Cupitt became an Anglican priest in 1960 but stopped officiating at public worship in the early 1990s and ceased to be an active member of the church in 2008. Cupitt "rejects all ideas of gaining salvation by escaping from this world of ours. 'All this is all there is', he says and he now sees true religion in terms of joy in life and an active attempt to add value to the human lifeworld. 'Life' is all that there is and all we have, and must be accepted with its limits as a package deal. We must avoid all attempts to deny or escape the limits of life — traditionally time, chance and death."[1044]

Another high-profile convert from belief, but to agnosticism rather than to atheism, was Charles Darwin, who explained life on earth as the result of evolution by natural selection. The story of Darwin's struggle to reconcile belief in God with what he saw in nature is well-known, but it is often blown out of proportion. As his biographer Randal Keynes points out, "by his own later admission, 'the religious sentiment' was never 'strongly developed' in him, and he laid no store by soul-searching or prayer; but he wanted to be clear about the articles of faith."[1045] Darwin was very strongly affected by the death of his young daughter Annie, and believed "it was easier to come to terms with pain and suffering if there was no question of a Divine purpose governing the life and death of individuals you cared for. ... [I cannot] overlook the difficulty from the immense amount of suffering through the world ... The safest conclusion seems to me that the whole subject is beyond the scope of man's intellect; but man can do his duty."[1046]

Atheists are always more than happy when church leaders and preachers lose their faith and turn to join the 'freethinkers'. Most published accounts come from the USA. Amongst the high-profile converts from believer to atheist was Charles Templeton, a former minister and close confidante of Billy Graham, who tells his story in *Farewell to God; my reasons for rejecting the Christian faith*.[1047] Richard Dawkins was pleased to welcome into the fold Don Barker with "the story of his gradual conversion from devout fundamentalist minister and zealous travelling preacher to the strong and confident atheist he is today. Significantly, Barker continued to go through the motions of preaching Christianity for a while after he had become an atheist, because it was the only career he knew and he felt locked into a web of social obligations."[1048] Barker himself writes, in *Godless: How an evangelical preacher became one of America's leading atheists*, that he did not lose his faith - he gave it up on purpose once he rejected "the very concept of faith as a valid tool of knowledge." He "made the leap, not to atheism, but to the commitment to follow reason and evidence wherever they might lead" and he realised that faith - "intellectual bankruptcy... the evidence of non-evidence" - was only ever going to be an obstacle to his search for truth.[1049]

CHAPTER 10

RE-FRAMING GOD

"The God question does not go away. No sooner have the intelligentsia
of one generation confined the Almighty to the history books
than popular opinion rises against them."

A N Wilson (2000)

God may not be as popular now as he once was, particularly in developed
western cultures, but he won't go away. This will doubtless remain
the case while big questions remain, which challenge and trouble every
generation, questions embodied in the enigmatic title of Paul Gauguin's
famous mural "Where do we come from? What are we? Where are we
going?"[1050] Despite the falling popularity of God, Karen Armstrong reminds
us that "we are talking far too much about God these days and what we say
is often facile. In our democratic society, we think that the concept of God
should be easy and that religion ought to be readily accessible to anybody."[1051]

God as an entity

As we have seen in earlier chapters, views about the existence and relevance
of God differ a great deal between believers and non-believers, and views
about the nature of God vary a great deal between believers.

To believers there is little doubt that God has made himself known to
humans (who he created in the first place) in various ways, in different
places, and at different points in time. Viewed this way God is not a
concept or an idea but an entity, and ideas about God evolved from human
experience of God. Viewed this way God is an inventor, the designer and
creator of the universe and everything in it, including humans. From this

perspective, as John Polkinghorne points out, "the rational transparency and beauty of the universe are surely too remarkable to be treated as just happy accidents. Belief in God can make all this intelligible, for it sees the deep order of the world – a world shot through with signs of mind, one might say – as being indeed a reflection of the truth that the mind of the Creator is revealed in this way. Science is then understood to be possible because the universe is a creation and we are creatures made in the image of the Creator."[1052]

To non-believers, God is nothing more than a concept or idea, dreamed up by humans (who were not created but evolved) to help them make sense of the world around them. New Atheist Daniel Dennett calls this "the intentional stance".[1053] By that he means that as humans we have a natural tendency to believe that other people and inanimate objects affect us both directly and indirectly, which creates a starting point for mystical and other religious beliefs. Karen Armstrong concludes that "it seems that creating gods is something that human beings have always done."[1054] As we saw in Chapter 4, Freud and Marx developed the so-called 'projection theory', according to which all religion is just wishful thinking. That is the essence of Richard Dawkins' argument in *The God Delusion*. Viewed this way God is an invention, made up by humans to help them cope with existential angst, the ultimate comfort blanket.

These two ways of seeing God and thinking about God are polar opposites so they can't both be right. Kathleen Jones points out that, "if God is not real, merely a projection of our own wishes, desires and prejudices, Richard Dawkins is clearly right: the human race has wasted an immense amount of time and effort over the centuries on what is no more than a mass delusion. If he is wrong (and I think he is) then God is the reality on which everything else in human life depends. And it matters."[1055]

Like many other people, I believe that God exists. But, more than that, I believe that God makes his existence known to us, not by pre-forming us with that knowledge already fixed or encoded in our brains, or by dropping heavy tablets of stone on us from above, but by giving us curious minds and allowing us to explore and discover effective ways of encountering and experiencing God in our embodied day-to-day existences. In short, God created us, and he wants us to know him and not just know *about* him. Viewed from this perspective, the idea of God can be seen as ultimately inspired by God but expressed and shaped by humans and thus open to adaptation and change in the light of experience and understanding. This very human but ultimately God-driven process of exploring, discovering, encountering and experiencing God allows the prospect of non-believers finding faith. That is the story of my journey into faith, as it has been for a great many people through the ages.

To the non-believer this must be a curious notion, rather like arguing that Pinocchio was made with the ability to understand the carpenter who built him, or that Othello was able to understand Shakespeare who wrote him. Changing the metaphor, John Polkinghorne vividly describes how "the creation of the God whose nature is love will not be a kind of cosmic puppet theatre in which the divine Puppet-Master pulls every string. The gift of love is always the gift of some due form of independence granted to the beloved. The creation has been endowed with great potentiality ... but the manner in which that potentiality is brought to birth in particular ways is through the shuffling explorations of the evolutionary process. The history of the universe is not the performance of a fixed score, but it is a grand improvisation in which the Creator and creatures cooperate in the unfolding development of the grand fugue of creation. God is not a mere spectator of this process ... but neither are creatures caught up willy-nilly in a process in which they have no active part to play."[1056]

God and us

I am convinced about the existence of God not purely from personal experience but from a wider consideration of how God and people (including non-believers) interact. I believe that God the inventor 'invented' humans as an act of love, so it is no surprise that he retains a desire to know us and continue loving us. He also created us with an inbuilt desire to know him.

God wants us

John Baillie points out that "not one of us has been left alone by God. Not one of us has been allowed to live a purely human life with complete peace of mind. ... try as we may, we never quite succeed in shutting God out. We never quite attain the self-containedness we so impiously desire. We can live in forgetfulness of him, but not with peace of mind."[1057] He continues that "not one of us has been left quite alone by God, that we have been sought out from the beginning, that from the beginning we have possessed more light than we have used …"[1058]

Keith Ward argues that "a believer in God sees all experience as an encounter, however indirectly, with the mind of the Creator. Belief makes an enormous difference to how life is seen. If you see in morality the inviting voice of a loving God, if you see in the beauties of nature the artistry of a creative spirit, if you see in science the wisdom of a cosmic intelligence, and if you sense in and through all the events of life a presence that leads you to ever greater life, joy, compassion and courage, then that will, or should, make a great practical difference to your life."[1059]

We want God

There is evidence that, since time immemorial, humans have had an interest in God or the gods. As John Baillie points out, "we know of no human society, however savage and backward, which does not already find itself confronted with the divine. It may be a matter of dispute whether all peoples are aware of deity as personal, or even as spiritual, being; but it is not disputed that all peoples have such an awareness of the divine as is sufficient to awaken in them what it is impossible to regard otherwise than as a typically religious response."[1060] Francis Collins notes that "while the search for the divine has been somewhat crowded out in modern times by our busy and overstimulated lives, it is still one of the most universal of human strivings."[1061]

This enduring interest partly reflects our human need not just for comfort but also for belonging. Alister McGrath believes that "we have been created to relate to God; if that relationship is absent, we experience a sense of longing. … the deep human longing has its origins in God, and can only find its true fulfilment in God. God is the name of the one we have been looking for all our lives, without knowing."[1062] C.S. Lewis wrote about the sense of intense longing which was sometimes triggered in his life by something as simple as a few lines of poetry, an experience that he described as "an unsatisfied desire which is itself more desirable than any other satisfaction."[1063]

Atheist John Humphreys pointed out that "there is [in people] a profound longing for something that will stimulate and satisfy them emotionally and spiritually. … atheists understand that longing perfectly well, but what puzzles them is why it cannot be satisfied by pottering about in the garden, a walk in the hills, watching a sunset, listening to a piece of great music. Yet that misses the point. Believers may very well find comfort and solace in all those things ... but where atheists are wrong is in failing to recognise and understand that most believers want something else as well."[1064]

This is precisely why Augustine believed that "our hearts are restless till they find their rest in you [God]", and why Pascal was convinced that "there is a God-shaped vacuum in the heart of every man, and only God can fill it."[1065] Anselm prayed "Lord, give me what you have made me want,"[1066] conscious that God had created in him the hunger for the faith that in turn he looked to God to provide. David Jenkins concluded that "God-consciousness or 'feeling for God' is, as a matter of fact, a universal feature of any consciousness that can properly be called human."[1067]

As well as a sense of belonging, people are driven by a desire to understand 'the big picture'. This human search for meaning and purpose is deep-rooted but profoundly important. What if the hokey-cokey really *is* what it's all about, as the song suggests? Does Alfie really know what it's all about, as another song asks? Is the number 42 really the answer to the question of the universe, as *The Hitchhiker's Guide to the Galaxy* would have us believe? In Douglas Adams' book, it takes the Deep Thought supercomputer more than seven million years to work it out; "I checked it thoroughly," says the computer, "and that quite definitely is the answer. I think the problem, to be quite honest with you, is that you've never actually known what the question is."[1068] In reality, of course, there is nothing magical or special about the number 42, which as Adams later confessed was "a completely ordinary number ... the sort of number that you could without fear introduce to your parents."[1069]

As Alister McGrath points out, "human beings long to make sense of things – to identify patterns in the rich fabric of nature, to offer explanations for what happens around them, and to reflect on the meaning of their lives, it is as if our intellectual antennae are tuned to discern clues to purpose and meaning around us, built into the structure of the world."[1070]

Writing from a secular perspective, Albert Einstein concluded that "the eternal mystery of the world is its comprehensibility."[1071] Writing from a religious perspective, William James concluded that "faith is faith in the existence of an unseen order of some kind in which the riddles of the natural order may be found and explained."[1072] James and others including McGrath and me are happy to accept that this 'unseen order' is God.

Why does God not make himself more obvious?

Why does God not make his existence, nature, and character blindingly obvious to everyone? Why is God so elusive? We looked at this a little in Chapter 7, but it makes sense to explore it in more detail here.

Tim Mawson is far from alone in voicing a frustration that, "if there's a God, then he could make his existence a lot more obvious to us than he has done. Indeed, if there's a God, then he could reveal himself to each of us in a direct and overwhelming way, convincing us beyond any shadow of a doubt that he exists."[1073] Even Richard Dawkins concedes that, "if he existed and chose to reveal it, God himself could clinch the argument, noisily and unequivocally, in his favour."[1074]

But God doesn't operate that way, and for good reason. God leaves us a choice, because he endowed us with free will and so any attention we decide to pay him is much more valuable than any attention given if we were automatically pre-programmed to and we had no option about it. God also leaves us with some work to do, like the best films and books that don't explain absolutely everything but give us clues to follow that we can fit together and work it out for ourselves.

English writer and Christian Sara Maitland reminds us that "Christianity has always known that you cannot prove the existence of God by any 'logical' method. This does not mean of course that you cannot think about God, speculate about God, say intelligent things about God, question the value of God, or even worship God. It just means that you cannot prove the existence of God. Indeed, many of the great Christian thinkers have gone further: they have argued that it is part of the essential nature of God, the love and immensity of the divine, that you cannot prove the existence of God."[1075]

As Australian Christian writer John Dickinson argues, "it just does not seem reasonable that the Almighty – if indeed the Almighty exists – would have left the world without a signpost to his presence, without some tangible moment on the world stage which turned the 'unknown God' into the known one."[1076] As well as through the Incarnation (God spending time on earth in the form of a human, Jesus), "many people have found strong clues for [God's] reality – divine fingerprints – in many places,"[1077] as Timothy Keller points out. These include the Big Bang, the Anthropic Principle, the regularity of nature, and the clue of beauty.

Elusiveness

David Watson points out that "in our natural self-centredness we tend to think that we are the centre of the universe, and that God (if he exists at all) is there simply to meet our needs. We regard him as a servant whom we call in from time to time to clear up the mess we are in – a mess often of our own doing."[1078] This partly explains why, when the chips are down, many people are inclined to ask 'Where is God when you need him?'

Watson explains how, "when God seems strangely silent and absent in spite of personal need, we wonder what he is doing, why he is withholding his presence from us."[1079] Like other believers, Watson does not interpret God's apparent silence in any given situation as evidence that God really is "withholding his presence from us", but he is voicing what many people tend to think at times like that. Recall from Chapter 9 Martin Buber's idea of an "eclipse of God" and Elie Wiesel's sense of God having "turned his face away".

Christian theologian Dietrich Bonhoeffer turns this idea on its head with his conclusion that "we are to find God in what we know, not in what we don't know; God wants us to realise his presence, not in unsolved problems but in those that are solved. That is true of the relationship between God and scientific knowledge, but it is also true of the wider human problems of death, suffering, and guilt."[1080]

David Jenkins urges caution in how we conceive of God, lest we fall into the trap of assuming that God behaves like we do or should behave that way. He reminds us that "God, being God, wholly dictates both the very existence of faith … and the shape and content of faith. It is clean contrary to the existence and being of the living and true God to whom the Bible bears witness to suppose that we can arrive at any conception of his existence, let alone his character, from any concepts of our own. We are men and not God and must never forget the infinite qualitative difference between God and man. Anything which fits into human moulds of thought or is derived from human thinking, and therefore moulded by human concepts, cannot possibly be God."[1081]

John Baillie picks up this point, reminding us that, "because we are so loath to find Him as He is, sometimes we cannot find Him at all. We have conceived our own idea of God, but it is an idea in the formation of which sloth and selfishness have played their part; and because there is no God corresponding to our idea, and because we are looking for none other, we fail to find the God who is really there."[1082]

The 'veiled presence of God'

God has chosen not to reveal himself as obviously as many people would like, but in rather more veiled ways. John Polkinghorne underlines the point that "God's existence is not self-evident in some totally unambiguous and undeniable way. The presence of God is veiled because, when you think about it, the naked presence of divinity would overwhelm finite creatures, depriving them of the possibility of truly being themselves and freely accepting God. ... out of love, God has self-limited the exercise of divine power to give creatures the space to be themselves and ... even to 'make themselves'. This does not mean that there are no signs of the will of the Creator or motivations to believe in God's existence but that we have to look a little below the surface of things to find them."[1083]

Polkinghorne goes on to remind us that, "moving away from science, there are further indications of the veiled presence of God if we are prepared to look for them. We have moral knowledge that assures us that love is better than hate, truth is better than a lie. Where does this come from? The religious person can understand our ethical intuitions to be intimations of God's good and perfect will. Similarly our aesthetic experience of encounter with deep beauty can be understood as a sharing in the Creator's joy in creation."[1084]

But as different people look behind 'the veil' they tend to see different things. Thomas Dixon points out that "many have continued to look beyond the seen to the unseen, hoping to succeed in the apparently impossible task of drawing back the veil of phenomena to discover how things really are. Among those who believe they have succeeded in seeing beyond the veil, there are conflicting accounts of what is to be found there – an impersonal cosmic machine, a chaos of matter in motion, a system governed by strict natural laws, or an omnipotent God acting in and through his creation. Which should we believe?"[1085]

Another way of describing God's elusiveness is in terms of mystery, neatly captured in the oft-used expression "God moves in mysterious ways, his wonders to perform." Krista Tippett reminds us that this mystery "eludes and evaporates beneath the demeaning glibness of debates and sound bites. Mystery eludes absolutes. It can hold truth, compassion, and open possibility in relationship. ... We could disagree passionately with each other and also better remember the limits of our own knowledge."[1086] John Haught picks up this theme of mystery, pointing out that "some scientific naturalists allow that the 'mystery' of the universe laid open by science is inspiration enough to arouse a religious kind of devotion. Many other scientists today also think of themselves as religious in this non-theistic sense. The mysterious silence of the cosmos is enough to fill their hearts, and it has the added advantage of being easy to reconcile with the lawful, impersonal universe of physics."[1087]

Despite God's apparent elusiveness, "the hidden glory of God is always there waiting to be revealed to those who seek it, to those who seek him," [1088] as English Christian writer David Adam rightly emphasises. In his autobiography Adam tells us that, as he grew up and progressed along his journey of seeking and discovering God, "I was slowly learning that Christianity was not a set of dogmas or about a 'happy land far, far away', but rather about a relationship with the living God here and now."[1089] Like many others before and after him, he realised that "God is not a theory about existence, but is ground of all being. ... Christianity is not about a set of beliefs; it is about our relationship of love with our God."[1090] He helpfully points out that "the mind may never fully grasp him [God] but we can hold him in our hearts."[1091]

Re-envisioning God

Whilst the modern materialist world-view remains the dominant world-view today, particularly in western society, many people find it lacking in various ways. For example, it makes no allowance for spiritual matters and regards the supernatural as an illusion. It looks down on believers as weak-minded and gullible, and privileges science as being the source of all genuine knowledge and scientists as purveyors of truth and ultimate meaning. Yet I would argue that this viewpoint, championed *par excellence* by Richard Dawkins, remains blind, deaf, and insensitive to many things that make good sense to believers.

Can the two world-views (the material and the spiritual) be reconciled, or must they remain forever separate? Must they stay in conflict with one another, like Stephen Jay Gould's Non-Overlapping Magisteria that we looked at in Chapter 6? Full reconciliation is probably too much to ask for or hope for, but there is no harm in seeking at least a partial reconciliation.

One approach, and the one favoured by Marcus Borg, has been to explore new ways of understanding God. I find Borg's argument persuasive and the conclusions it points to compelling. It is the path taken by those who, as Borg puts it, "seek to take seriously what the Christian tradition and other religious traditions say about God or the sacred, even as they take seriously what we have come to know in the modern period, but without absolutising it. They seek to integrate Christianity with modern and postmodern perceptions, producing a revisioning of Christianity."[1092]

To help us explore new ways of understanding God Borg identifies two what he calls 'root concepts' for thinking about God, which he calls supernatural theism and panentheism. He points out that both are found in the Bible and "are found throughout all periods of Christian history, though the first is more common. From roughly the fourth century - when Christianity became the dominant religion of Western culture - through the present, the monarchical [supernatural theism] model has dominated. But alongside it, as an alternative voice, the Spirit model [panentheism] has also persisted. ... They reflect two different voices within the Christian tradition."[1093]

Supernatural theism

Marcus Borg's first way of thinking about God, which he calls 'supernatural theism', is the traditional western way of viewing God and the way in which most people today think of God.[1094] This orthodox Christian image of God is also what modern atheists and sceptics reject, although both groups insist that they are rejecting the whole idea of God rather than a particular way of thinking about God. It is the concept of God that Borg himself struggled with in his twenties and thirties, as he tried to reconcile what he understood about God with what he understood about science.

Borg sketches out how his early view of God was shaped by his upbringing in a loving and supportive Christian family, as a result of which, as he puts it, "I thought I knew what the word *God* meant: a supernatural being 'out there' who created the world a long time ago and had occasionally intervened in the aeons since, especially in the events recorded in the Bible. God was not 'here' but 'somewhere else.' And someday, after death, we might be with God, provided that we had done or believed whatever was necessary to pass the final judgment."[1095]

As a child he believed this package of things about God without difficulty, but when he encountered science as a teenager he began to have doubts about it. Doubt turned to disbelief in his twenties. But, as he is at pains to make clear, "through this whole process, the same notion of God persisted. It was what I believed and then disbelieved."[1096]

Borg outlines the essence of this classical way of visualising God: "In harder and softer forms, it was doctrinal, moralistic, literalistic, exclusivistic, and oriented toward an afterlife. In this view, being Christian meant believing that a certain set of doctrinal claims were true, and it meant seeking to live in accord with Christianity's ethical teaching. It tended to take the Bible and doctrine literally, unless there were compelling reasons not to. It typically affirmed that Christianity was the only way to salvation. And it defined salvation as 'afterlife' - as going to heaven. Basically, then, Christianity was about believing in central Christian teachings *now* for the sake of heaven *later*. [his emphasis]"[1097]

In short, this traditional view is of a distant and judgmental God, separate from the world, who created the world way back in time, and who may occasionally intervene in it. Such a God cannot be known or experienced, but only believed in. It pictures God as 'somewhere else' but certainly not here, and salvation as 'sometime else' but certainly not now. It frames God as a God of requirements which have to be met now in order for us to enjoy an eternal reward later, after we die.[1098]

Borg also refers to this as the "Monarchical model" of God as king, law-giver, and judge. He argues that it leads to a "performance model" of the Christian life in which sin (disobedience to God) is the most important problem, which requires repentance and liberation before salvation is granted.[1099] He points out that, from this perspective, God can be confused with the superego, "the storehouse of *oughts* and *shoulds* within us, the cumulative product of messages about what we should do and how we ought to live. ... Life under the superego is a life of continually trying to measure up; it is life under the law."[1100] As he sees it, this image of God "makes it clear that God has requirements that must be met, either by obeying God's laws or by performing alternative service (typically involving belief in Jesus, sincere repentance, and perhaps penance.) ... Our eternal destiny depends on how well we 'perform', on whether we believe or do what is necessary in order to be saved."[1101]

From personal experience he highlights some real difficulties this traditional view of God gives rise to in the religious life. He argues that "it made believing in God difficult, as it has for many people. God became remote at best, unreal at worst ... [and] it also made the problem of evil acute. If one thinks of God as an all-powerful being who can intervene in the world at will (as this way of thinking about God most commonly does), then it follows that God could have intervened to stop the Holocaust and a whole host of other collective and personal disasters but chose not to. It is difficult to believe in such a God." It also "affected my sense of what the Christian life was about. Because I thought of God as remote, 'up in heaven,' and not here, I thought Christian faith was about believing in a distant God; indeed, this became the central meaning of faith." What's more, "it made prayer problematic. I could see no framework within which prayer made sense. It seemed like addressing a distant God who might not be there - like speaking into a universe that might be empty."[1102]

Panentheism

After graduating from university in the USA Borg studied for a doctorate at Oxford and then had a distinguished career as a professor of theology back in the US. Over time and through a great deal of study and reflection he came to see that the view of God he was exposed to as a child (the classical and still most common way of visualising God) was not the only way of visualising God that is consistent with personal experience and modern biblical scholarship. He would later write that "there are millions of people ... for whom this older understanding of God and Christianity does not work,"[1103] and admit that, "compared to that notion of God, the God I have come to know since is the God I never knew."[1104]

Borg called this alternative way of visualising God 'panentheism'. Panentheism sounds like pantheism - the belief that God and the universe are one and the same thing (as we saw in Chapter 3) - but is not the same thing at all. As Borg explains, "the Greek roots of the word point to its meaning: *pan* means 'everything,' *en* means 'in,' and *theos* means 'God.' Panentheism thus means 'everything is *in* God'. God is more than everything and so God is transcendent, yet everything is in God and so God is also immanent. For panentheism, God is 'right here,' even as God is also more than 'right here.' ... God is not to be identified with the sum total of things. Rather, God is more than everything, even as God is present everywhere. God is all around us and within us, and we are within God."[1105] From a panentheistic perspective "God is the encompassing Spirit; we (and everything that is) are in God. For this concept, God is not a supernatural being separate from the universe; rather, God (the sacred Spirit) is a non-material layer or level or dimension of reality all around us. God is more than the universe, yet the universe is in God. Thus, in a spatial sense, God is not 'somewhere else' but 'right here.'"[1106]

As Borg points out, "this way of thinking about God ... is not only faithful to the biblical and Christian tradition but also makes the most sense of our experience. ... [It is] found among many of the most important voices in the Christian theological tradition."[1107]

Borg calls panentheism the "Spirit model" of God. Unlike the performance-based Monarchical Model, this way of visualising God leads to a "relational model" of the Christian life "that stresses relationship, intimacy, and belonging."[1108] As he points out, visualising God as Spirit emphasises God's presence in and engagement with the world (God's immanence) and God's existence above and beyond the limits of material experience (God's transcendence).[1109] It also emphasises God's nearness and closeness, and gets away from "the exclusively male images of the monarchical model."[1110] Overall this perspective "suggests that the relationship to God is personal, even as God is more than a person. The sacred is not simply an inanimate mystery but a presence."[1111]

The Spirit model of God seems better able to 'explain' how many of us experience God than the more traditional Monarchical model. Borg writes that "there is much in our experience - of nature, human love, mystery, wonder, amazement - that conveys the reality of the sacred, a surpassingly great 'more' that we know in exceptional moments. Many of us experience life as permeated and surrounded by a gracious mystery, a surplus of being that transcends understanding, and when we come to know that mystery as God, our faith becomes full of meaning and vitality."[1112]

This way of looking at God, and thinking about and relating to God, has a number of implications for the Christian life. As Borg puts it, "Rather than God being a distant being with whom we might spend eternity, Spirit - the sacred - is right here. Rather than God being the lawgiver and judge whose requirements must be met and whose justice must be satisfied, God is the lover who yearns to be in relationship to us. Rather than sin and guilt being the central dynamic of the Christian life, the central dynamic becomes relationship - with God, the world, and each other. The Christian life is about turning towards and entering into relationship with the one who is already in relationship with us - with the one who gave us life, who has loved us from the beginning, and who loves us whether we know that or not, who journeys with us whether we know that or not. The Christian life thus has at its centre becoming conscious of that relationship."[1113]

Borg emphasises the transformational impact of panentheism, which "resolved the central religious and intellectual problem of the first three decades of my life. Indeed, becoming aware of panentheism made it possible for me to be a Christian again. The story of my own Christian and spiritual journey thus involves the movement from supernatural theism through doubt and disbelief to panentheism. The God I met as an adult is the God I never knew growing up in church."[1114] He goes further in arguing that, "for the most part, modern scepticism and atheism are a rejection of supernatural theism, but if God is not thought of as a supernatural being separate from the universe, then the persuasive force of much of modern atheism vanishes. The resolution of this intellectual difficulty about God is no small matter, for it means that the 'God Question' becomes an open rather than a closed one."[1115]

Conclusions

We have covered a lot of ground, explored many themes, and heard many voices in this book, as we have looked at the question of God from different perspectives. It was never my intention to persuade non-believers to change their mind and embrace the idea of God in a new and personal way, nor to encourage believers round to my way of thinking. I'd be happy if, through reading the book, the 'God Question' becomes an open rather than a closed one for more people.

For the avoidance of doubt, let me summarise my own position on 'the question of God'. I believe that God exists, and that God not only created the universe and everything in it but remains active and knowable - so this makes me a theist using the framework we looked at in Chapter 3. My Christian faith is rooted in developing a personal relationship with God but informed by Scripture, tradition and reason. I believe in revelation, and that I can and do have personal experiences of God (of the sort we looked at in Chapter 8). I also find it helpful to think of God in a panentheistic way, grateful for Marcus Borg's clarification of this model and its implications.

For the same reason, let me also make it clear that I believe that we humans are God's 'invention', in the sense that God created us. I also believe that God endowed us with the gift of natural curiosity and an inbuilt hunger to discover the reality of God in all that we see and experience in the world around us. Far from being invented by humans, I see God as the inventor of humans … along with everything else that is, was, and ever shall be.

I'm happy to leave the final word to Rowan Williams who was Archbishop of Canterbury between 2003 and 2012. He said in a sermon before he became archbishop: "If you want God, then you must be prepared to let go of all – absolutely all – substitute satisfactions, intellectual and emotional. You must recognise that God is so unlike whatever can be thought or pictured that, when you have got beyond the stage of self-indulgent religiosity, there will be nothing you can securely know or feel. You face a blank and any attempt to avoid that or shy away from it is a return to playing comfortable religious games … If you genuinely desire union with the unspeakable love of God, then you must be prepared to have your 'religious' view shattered. If you think devotional practices, theological insights, even charitable actions give you some sort of purchase on God, you are still playing games."[1116]

References

Adam, D. (2011) *The Wonder of the Beyond*. London: SPCK

Adams, D. (1995) *The Hitchhiker's Guide to the Galaxy*. London: Heinemann

Adler, M. (1980) *How to Think about God. A Guide for the 20th Century Pagan*. New York: Macmillan

Albrecht, A.L. and Heaton, T.B. (1984) Secularization, higher education, and religiosity. *Review of Religious Research* 26 (1): 43-58

Altizer, T.J.J. and Hamilton, W. (1968) *Radical Theology and the Death of God*. Harmondsworth: Penguin

Andrews, E. (2009) *Who Made God? Searching for a Theory of Everything*. Darlington: EP Books

Anon (1969) Modern Magi' put moon flight into scriptural perspective. *Christianity Today* 13 (8): 36-37

Arden, P. (2007) *God Explained in a Taxi Ride*. London: Penguin Books

Armstrong, K. (1993) *A History of God*. London: Heinemann

Armstrong, K. (2001) *The Battle for God: Fundamentalism in Judaism, Christianity and Islam*. London: HarperCollins

Armstrong, K. (2009) *The Case for God. What religion really means*. London: The Bodley Head

Atkins, P (1993) *Creation revisited*. New York: Freeman

Atran, S. (2004) *In gods we trust: the evolutionary landscape of religion*. New York: Oxford University Press

Attfield, R. (1978) Science and creation. *The Journal of Religion* 58 (1): 37-47

Baggini, I. (2003) *Atheism: a very short introduction.* Oxford: Oxford University Press

Baillie, J. (1939) *Our Knowledge of God.* Oxford: Oxford University Press

Baillie, J. (1962) *The Sense of the Presence of God.* London: Oxford University Press

Baly, D. (1976) *God and History in the Old Testament.* New York: Harper and Row

Barbour, I.G. (1974) *Myths, Models and Paradigms. A Comparative Study in Science and Religion.* San Francisco: Harper & Row

Barker, D. (2008) *Godless: How an evangelical preacher became one of America's leading atheists.* New York: Ulysses Press

Barrett, D. *et al* (2001) *World Christian Encyclopedia: A comparative survey of churches and religions - AD 30 to 2200.* Oxford: Oxford University Press

Barrett, J.L. (2004) *Why would anyone believe in God?* Walnut Creek California: AltaMira

Barrow, J.D. and Tipler, F.J. (1988) *The Anthropic Cosmological Principle.* New York: Oxford University Press

Behe, M.J. (1996) *Darwin's Black Box.* New York: Simon & Schuster

Berry, R.J. (2003) *God's Book of Works. The Nature and Theology of Nature.* London: Continuum

Berry, R.J. (editor) (2009a) *Real Scientists, Real Faith.* Oxford: Monarch Books

Berry, R.J. (2009b) I believe in God, maker of heaven and earth. Pp. 5-12 in Berry, R.J. (editor) (2009a) *Real Scientists, Real Faith.* Oxford: Monarch Books

Blackburn, S. (2010) Review of *Dishonest to God*: on keeping religion out of politics. *Times Higher Education* (4 November): pp.56-57

Blackmore, S. (1999) *The Meme Machine.* Oxford: Oxford University Press

Borg, M.J. (1995) *Meeting Jesus again for the first time: the historical Jesus and the heart of contemporary faith.* San Francisco: HarperCollins

Borg, M.J. (1998) *The God we never knew: Beyond dogmatic religion to a more authentic contemporary faith.* New York: HarperCollins

Bouquet, A.C. (1941) *Comparative religion. A short outline.* Harmondsworth: Penguin Books

Bowker, J. (1995) *Is God a virus? Genes, culture and religion*. London: The Society for Promoting Christian Knowledge

Bowman, D. (2007) Review of *The God Delusion* by Richard Dawkins. *The Midwest Quarterly* 48 (4): 609-611

Boyer, P. (2001) *Religion Explained: the human instincts that fashion gods, spirits and ancestors*. New York: William Heinemann

Brown, C.G. (2009) *The death of Christian Britain: understanding secularisation, 1800-2000*. London: Routledge

Brown, L. (1988) *The Psychology of Religion*. London: SPCK

Brueggemann, W. (1993) *Texts under negotiation: the Bible and postmodern interpretation*. Minneapolis: Fortress Press

Buber, M. (1958) *I and Thou*. Translated by R.G. Smith. Edinburgh: T & T Clark

Buckman, R. (2002) *Can we be good without God? Biology, behaviour, and the need to believe*. London: Prometheus

Carlyon, R. (1981) *A guide to the gods*. London: Heinemann

Carter, B. (1983) The anthropic principle and its implications for biological evolution. *Philosophical Transactions of the Royal Society of London A*, 310: 347-63

Chargaff, E. (1977) *Voices in the labyrinth: nature, man, and science*. New York: Seabury Press

Clarke, P.J. (2001) *Questions about God. A guide for students*. Cheltenham: Nelson Thornes

Collins, F. (2009) What do *you* believe, doctor? Pp.246-260 in Berry, R.J. (editor) (2009a) *Real Scientists, Real Faith*. Oxford: Monarch Books

Collins, F.S. (2006) *The language of God: a scientist presents evidence for belief*. New York: Basic Books

Collins, F.S. (2010) *Belief: Readings on the Reason for Faith*. New York: HarperOne

Corlett, J.A. (2009) Dawkins' god*less* delusion. *International Journal of the Philosophy of Religion* 65: 125-138

Cornwell, J. (2007) *Darwin's Angel: an angelic riposte to The God Delusion*. London: Profile Books

Cottingham, J. (2009) *Why Believe?* London: Continuum

Cupitt, D. (1998) *After God: the future of religion*. London: Phoenix

Curtis, S. (2006) Book review: Richard Dawkins, *The God Delusion*. *British Journal of General Practice* 56 (533): 980

Davies, P. (1983) *God and the New Physics*. London: Penguin

Davies, P. (1993) *The Mind of God*. London: Penguin

Davies, P. (2006) *The Goldilocks Enigma*. London: Allen Lane

Davis, J.H. and Poe, H.L. (2002) *Designer Universe. Intelligent Design and the Existence of God*. Nashville: Broadman and Holman Publishers

Dawkins, R. (1976) *The Selfish Gene*. Oxford: Oxford University Press

Dawkins, R. (1986) *The Blind Watchmaker*. London: Penguin

Dawkins, R. (1995) *River out of Eden*. London: Weidenfeld and Nicolson

Dawkins, R. (2003) *A Devil's Chaplain*. London: Weidenfeld and Nicolson

Dawkins, R. (2006) *Climbing Mount Improbable*. London: Penguin

Dawkins, R. (2006) *The God Delusion*. London: Houghton Mifflin

De Botton, A. (2012) *Religion for Atheists*. London: Hamish Hamilton

Dennett, D. (1995) *Darwin's dangerous idea*. New York: Simon and Schuster

Dennett, D.C. (1993) *Consciousness Explained*. London: Penguin Books

Dennett, D.C. (2006) *Breaking the Spell: religion as a natural phenomenon*. London: Penguin Books

Dickson, J. (2002) *If I were God, I'd make myself clearer. Searching for clarity in a world full of claims*. New Malden: The Good Book Company Ltd

Dixon, T. (2005) Religion and science. Pp.456-472 in Hinnells, J.R. (ed) *The Routledge Companion to the Study of Religion*. London: Routledge

Dixon, T. (2008) *Science and religion: a very short introduction*. Oxford: Oxford University Press

Downing, D. (2002) *The Most Reluctant Convert: C.S. Lewis's Journey to Faith*. London: Inter-Varsity Press

D'Souza, D. (2007) *What's so great about Christianity*. New York: Regnery Publishing

Dunne, M. (2006) How not to be an atheist. Review of *The God Delusion*. *Yearbook of the Irish Philosophical Society 2006*, pp.213-220

Durkheim, E. (1915) *The Elementary Forms of the Religious Life*. New York: Free Press

Durkheim, E. (1952) *Suicide. A study in sociology*. London: Routledge & Kegan Paul

Dyson, F. (1981) *Disturbing the universe*. New York: Basic Books

Eagleton, T. (2006) Lunging, flailing, mispunching. Review of *The God Delusion. The London Review of Books* 28 (20): 32-35

Eagleton, T. (2009) *Reason, Faith, and Revolution: reflections on the God Debate.* New Haven: Yale University Press

Ecklund, E.H. (2010) *A godless universe? What scientists really think.* Oxford: Oxford University Press

Einstein, A. (1954) *Ideas and opinions.* New York: Bonanza Books

Eliade, M. (1963) *Myth and reality.* New York: Harper and Row

Ellis, G. (2004) *Science in faith and hope.* London: Quaker Books

Elsdon, R. (1981) *Bent world: science, the Bible, and the environment.* Leicester: Inter-Varsity Press

Everitt, N. (2004) *The non-existence of God.* London: Routledge

Falsani, C. (2006) *The God Factor: inside the spiritual lives of public people.* New York: Sarah Crichton Books

Farrer, A. (2009) *A Science of God?* (first published in 1966 by Geoffrey Bles, London) London: Society for Promoting Christian Knowledge

Feynman, R. (1998) *The meaning of it all: thoughts of a citizen-scientist.* New York: Basic Books

Flew, A. (2007) *There is a God: how the world's most notorious atheist changed his mind.* New York: HarperCollins

Fowler, J. (1978) *Life Maps: Conversations on the Journey of Faith.* Waco, Texas: Word Books

Freud, S. (1927) *The Future of an Illusion.* London: Hogarth Press

Freud, S. (1938) *Totem and taboo: resemblances between the psychic lives of savages and neurotics.* Harmondsworth: Penguin

Gale, R. (1991) *On the nature and existence of God.* Cambridge: Cambridge University Press

Gaskin, J.C.A. (1989) *Varieties of unbelief: from Epicurus to Sartre.* New York: Macmillan

Geaney, D. (2007) Book review: *The God Delusion. Psychological Medicine* 37: 757-758

Glenn, J. (1962) Why I know there is a God. *The Reader's Digest* 81 (483): 37-39

Glock, C.Y. and Stark, R. (1965) *Religion and society in tension.* Chicago: Rand McNally

Gould, S.J. (1997) Non-overlapping magisteria. *Natural History* (March) 107: 16-22

Gould, S.J. (1999) *Rock of Ages: Science and Religion in the Fullness of Life.* New York: Ballantine

Grigg, R. (2008) *Beyond the God delusion: how radical theology harmonizes science and religion.* New York: Fortress Press

Groothuis, D. (2009) Who designed the designer? : a dialogue on Richard Dawkins's *The God Delusion. Think* 21 (8): 71-81

Gumbel, N. (2008) *Is God a Delusion? What is the Evidence?* London: Alpha International

Habermas, J. (1998) *On the pragmatics of communication.* Cambridge: MIT Press

Hackney, C.H. and Sanders, G.S. (2003) Religiosity and mental health: a meta-analysis of recent studies. *Journal for the Scientific Study of Religion* 42 (1): 43-44

Hardy, A. (1979) *The Spiritual Nature of Man. A Study of Contemporary Religious Experience.* Oxford: Clarendon Press

Harris, S. (2005) *The end of faith. Religion, terror, and the future of reason.* London: The Free Press

Harris, S. (2006) *Letter to a Christian nation.* New York: Knopf

Harrison, P. (2008) *Christianity and the rise of Western Science.* Farmington Paper SC18. Oxford: Farmington Institute of Christian Studies

Harvey, V.A. (1995) *Feuerbach and the interpretation of religion.* Cambridge: Cambridge University Press

Haught, J.F. (2008) *God and the New Atheism: a critical response to Dawkins, Harris and Hitchens.* Louisville: Westminster John Knox Press

Hawking, S. (1988) *A Brief History of Time.* London: Bantam

Hawking, S. and Mlodinow, L. (2010) *The Grand Design.* London: Bantam

Hecht, J.M. (2003) *Doubt: a history.* San Francisco: Harper

Hegel (1984) *Lectures on the philosophy of religion.* (edited by Peter C. Hodgson). Berkeley: University of California Press

Heidegger, M. (1976) The age of the world view. *Boundary* 2: 341-356

Henig, R.M. (2007) Darwin's God. *The New York Times Magazine, Section 6.* 4 March: 36-85

Herzfeld, N.(2007) "The end of faith"? Science and theology as process. *Dialog: A Journal of Theology* 46 (3): 288-293

Hick, J. (1995) *John Hick: an autobiography*. London: OneWorld Publications

Hill, S. (2010) *The No-Nonsense Guide to Religion*. Oxford: New Internationalist Publications

Hinde, R. (2009) *Why Gods persist*. New York: Routledge

Hinnells, J.R. (editor) (2005) *The Routledge companion to the study of religion*. London: Routledge

Hitchens, C. (2007) *God is not Great: How Religion Poisons Everything*. New York: Warner Twelve

Hume, D. (1777) *The natural history of religion*. [quotes from 2004 edition, Kessinger Publisher]

Humphreys, J. (2008) *In God We Doubt: confessions of a failed atheist*. London: Hodder & Stoughton

James, W. (1902) *The Varieties of Religious Experience*. New York: Longmans, Green and Co. [quotes from 1982 Penguin edition, edited by Martin E. Marty]

Jenkins, D. (1966) *Guide to the Debate about God*. London: Lutterworth Press

Jenkins, D. (1969) *Living with Questions. Investigations into the Theory and Practice of Belief in God*. London: SCM Press

Jenkins, T. (2009) Closer to Dan Brown than to Gregor Mendel: on Dawkins' *The God Delusion*. *Scottish Journal of Theology* 62 (3): 269-281

Jones, H. (2006) *The Thoughtful Guide to God*. Winchester: O Books

Jones, K. (2007) *Challenging Richard Dawkins*. Norwich: Canterbury Press

Keller, T. (2008) *The Reason for God. Belief in an Age of Scepticism*. London: Hodder & Stoughton

Keynes, R. (2009) *Creation: the true story of Charles Darwin*. London: John Murray Publishers

Klein, T. (2007) Adventures in alterity: Wittgenstein, aliens, Anselm and Aquinas. *New Blackfriars* 88 (1013): 73-86

Klostermaier, K.K. (2008) Reflections prompted by Richard Dawkins's *The God Delusion*. *Journal of Ecumenical Studies* 43 (4): 607-616

Knippenberg, H. (ed) (2005) *The changing religious landscape of Europe*. Amsterdam: Het Spinhuis Publishers

Kuhn, T. (1962) *The structure of scientific revolutions*. Chicago: University of Chicago Press [quotes from 1970 reprint]

Lane, N. (2010) *Life ascending: the ten great inventions of evolution*. London: Profile

Lash, N. (2007) Where does *The God Delusion* come from? *New Blackfriars* 88 (1017): 507-521

Ledwig, M. (2007) Book Review: Richard Dawkins, *The God Delusion*. *Religious Studies* 43: 368-372

Lewis, C.S. (1955) *Surprised by Joy*. London: Geoffrey Bles [quotations from 2002 edition, London: HarperCollins]

Lewis, C.S. (1961) *A Grief Observed*. London: Faber and Faber

Lewis, C.S. (1971) *God in the Dock*. Glasgow: Collins

Lewis-Williams, D. (2010) *Conceiving God: the cognitive origin and evolution of religion*. London: Thames & Hudson

Loftus, J.W. (2008) *Why I became an atheist: a former preacher rejects Christianity*. New York: Prometheus Books

Lundstrom, P. (2008) *God. The Short Version*. Oxford: Lion Books

Maitland, S. (2002) *A joyful theology. Creation, commitment, and an awesome God*. Minneapolis: Augsburg Books

Markusson, G.I. (2007) Book review: Richard Dawkins, *The God Delusion*. *Journal of Cognition and Culture* 7: 369-373

Martin, D. (1967) *A sociology of English religion*. London: SCM Press

Martin, D. (2008) Does the advance of science mean secularisation? *Scottish Journal of Theology* 61 (1): 1-51

Martin, M. (2003) *Atheism, morality and meaning*. London: Prometheus Books

Martin, T.M. (2009) Book review: Richard Dawkins, *The God Delusion*. *Dialog: Journal of Theology* 48 (2): 209-212

Mawson, T. (2005) *Belief in God. An Introduction to the Philosophy of Religion*. Oxford: Oxford University Press

Mayr, E. (1982) *The growth of biological thought: diversity, evolution, and inheritance*. London: Harvard University Press

McBain, J. (2007) Review: *The God Delusion* by Richard Dawkins. *The Midwest Quarterly* 48 (4): 611-615

McFague, S. (1987) *Models of God. Theology for an Ecological, Nuclear Age*. London: SCM Press

McGrath, A. (2004a) *The Science of God. An introduction to scientific theology*. London: T&T Clark International

McGrath, A. (2004b) *The Twilight of Atheism*. New York: Doubleday

McGrath, A. (2007) *Dawkins' God: genes, memes, and the meaning of life*. Oxford: Blackwell Publishing

McGrath, A. (2009) Science, faith and making sense of things. Pp.13-26 in Berry, R.J. (editor) (2009a) *Real Scientists, Real Faith*. Oxford: Monarch Books

McGrath, A. and McGrath, J.C. (2007) *The Dawkins delusion: atheist fundamentalism and the denial of the divine*. London: SPCK

Medd, J. (2010) What kind of atheist are you? *The Times*, 17 September: p.58

Mitchell, J. (1973) *The Justification of Religious Belief*. London: Macmillan

Montague, R. (2008) Dawkins' infinite regress. *Philosophy* 83: 113-115

Montefiore, H. (1985) *The Probability of God*. London: SCM Press

Naugle, D.K. (2002) *World-view: the history of a concept*. New York: Eerdmans

Newberg, A. and Waldman, M.R. (2007) *Born to believe. God, science and the origin of ordinary and extraordinary beliefs*. New York: Free Press

Newberg, A. and Waldman, M.R. (2009) *How God changes your brain*. New York: Ballantine Books

Newberg, A., D'Aquili, E. and Rause, V. (2001) *Why God won't go away*. New York: Ballantine Books

Nietzsche, F.W. (2009) *The gay science*. New York: Dover Publications

Novak, M. (2007) Lonely atheists of the global village. *National Review* 19 March: 43-54

Ogden, C. (2000) *God: a beginner's guide*. London: Hodder & Stoughton

Onfray, M. (2007) *In defence of atheism: the case against Christianity, Judaism and Islam*. London: Profile Books

Otto, R. (1923) *The idea of the holy*. Quotations from the 1958 edition, translated by J. Harvey. London: Oxford University Press

Park, C. (1980) *Ecology and environmental management*. London: Butterworths

Park, C. (2001) *The environment: principles and applications*. London: Routledge

Park, C. (2008) *Oxford dictionary of environment and conservation*. Oxford: Oxford University Press

Pascal, B. (1669) *Pensées*. (quote from 1958 edition) New York: E.P. Dutton & Co

Pearce, J. (1998) *Tolkien: man and myth*. London: HarperCollins

Persinger, M. (1987) *Neuropsychological bases of God beliefs*. New York: Praeger

Persinger, M.A. (2009) Are our brains structured to avoid refutations of belief in God? An experimental study. *Religion* 39: 34-42

Pessin, A. (2009) *The God Question*. Oxford: Oneworld Publications

Pierre, J.M. (2001) Faith or delusion? At the crossroads of religion and psychosis. *Journal of Psychiatric Practice* 7 (3): 163-172

Pinker, S. (1997) *How the mind works*. New York: Norton

Pinker, S. (2002) *The blank slate: the modern denial of human nature*. London: Penguin

Pirsig, R.M. (1974) *Zen and the art of motorcycle maintenance: an inquiry into values*. London: Corgi

Playfair, J. (1802) *Illustrations of the Huttonian Theory of the Earth*. Edinburgh: W. Creech

Polkinghorne, J. and Beale, N. (2009) *Questions of truth: fifty-one responses to questions about God, science, and belief*. Louisville, Kentucky: Westminster John Knox Press

Poole, M. (2007) *User's guide to science and belief*. Oxford: Lion Hudson

Poole, M. (2009) *The 'New' Atheism: ten arguments that don't hold water*. Oxford: Lion Books

Popper, K. (1959) *The logic of scientific discovery*. London: Hutchinson

Pratt, V. (1970) *Religion and secularisation*. London: MacMillan

Prozesky, M. (1992) *A new guide to the debate about god*. London: SCM Press

Rajeev, B. (2007) Book review – *The God Delusion*. *Current Science* 92 (8): 1166

Ravetz, J. (2006) *The no-nonsense guide to science*. Oxford: New Internationalist

Rees, M. (1997) *Before the beginning: our universe and others*. New York: Simon and Schuster

Rees, M. (1999) *Just six numbers*. London: Weidenfeld & Nicolson

Rees, M. (2001) *Our cosmic habitat*. London: Weidenfeld and Nicolson

Reisz, M. (2010) The dogma delusion. *Times Higher Education* 23 September: pp.38-43

Rincon, P. (2010) Large Hadron Collider to start hunt for 'God particle'. BBC News online. http://news.bbc.co.uk/1/hi/sci/tech/8582778.stm

Robertson, D. (2007) *The Dawkins letters: challenging atheist myths*. Fearn: Christian Focus Publications

Robinson, J.A.T. (1963) *Honest to God*. London: SCM Press

Ruse, M. (2007) Book review: Richard Dawkins, *The God Delusion. Isis* 98 (4): 814-816

Russell, B. (1957) *Why I am not a Christian*. New York: Simon & Schuster

Sacks, J. (2010) Even great science tells us nothing about God. *The Times*, 3 September: p.27

Sagan, C. (1980) *Cosmos*. New York: Random House

Sample, I. (2010) *Massive: the missing particle that sparked the greatest hunt in science*. New York: Basic Books

Schleiermacher, F. (1989) *The Christian faith*. Translated by H.R. MacKintosh and J.S. Stewart. Edinburgh: T & T Clark

Schroeder, G.L. (1997) *The Science of God. The convergence of scientific and biblical wisdom*. New York: Broadway Books

Segal, R.A. (2005) Theories of religion. Pp.355-378 in Hinnells, J.R. (ed) *The Routledge Companion to the Study of Religion*. London: Routledge

Shermer, M (2000) *How we believe. The search for God in an Age of Science*. New York: W.H. Freeman

Sire, J.W. (1997) *The universe next door: a basic world-view catalog*. 3rd edition. Downers Grove: Inter-Varsity Press

Slone, D.J. (2006) *Religion and cognition: a reader*. London: Equinox

Smart, N. (1969) *The religious experience of mankind*. Glasgow: Collins

Smith, G.H. (1989) *Atheism: the case against God*. Amherst: Prometheus Books

Smolin, L. (2006) *The trouble with physics: the rise of string theory, the fall of a science, and what comes next*. London: Houghton Mifflin Harcourt

Sobel, J.H. (2004) *Logic and theism: arguments for and against beliefs in God*. Cambridge: Cambridge University Press

Stark, R. (2001) *One true God: historical consequences of monotheism*. Princeton: Princeton University Press

Stark, R. and Bainbridge, W.S. (1996) *A theory of religion*. New Jersey: Rutgers University Press

Stark, R. and Finke, R. (2000) *Acts of faith: explaining the human side of religion*. Berkeley: University of California Press

Strobel, L. (2000) *The case for faith: a journalist investigates the toughest objections to Christianity.* New York: Zondervan

Strobel, L. (2004) *The case for a creator; a journalist investigates scientific evidence that points toward God.* Grand Rapids: Zondervan

Swinburne, R. (1979) *The existence of God.* Oxford: The Clarendon Press

Swinburne, R. (1996) *Is there a God?* Oxford: Oxford University Press

Templeton, C. (2000) *Farewell to God; my reasons for rejecting the Christian faith.* New York: McClelland & Stewart

Tillich, P. (1958) *Dynamics of faith.* New York: Harper & Row

Tippett, K. (2007) *Speaking of faith.* New York: Viking

Tippett, K. (2010) *Einstein's God: conversations about science and the human spirit.* London: Penguin Books

Vardy, P. (1999) *The puzzle of God.* London: HarperCollins

Vardy, P. and Arliss, J. (2003) *The thinker's guide to God.* Ropley, Hants: O Books

Varghese, R.A. (2007a) Preface to Anthony Flew *There is a God: how the world's most notorious atheist changed his mind.* New York: HarperCollins

Varghese, R.A. (2007b) Appendix A. The 'New Atheism: a critical appraisal of Dawkins, Dennett, Wolpert, Harris and Stenger. P.161-183 in Anthony Flew *There is a God: how the world's most notorious atheist changed his mind.* New York: HarperCollins

Vigué, J. (2002) *Great masters of Western art.* New York: Watson-Guptil Publications

Viney, D.W. (2007) Review: *The God Delusion* by Richard Dawkins. *The Midwest Quarterly* 48 (4): 602-605

Voas, D. and Ling, R. (2010) Religion in Britain and the United States. In Park, A., Curtice, J., Thomson, K., Phillips, M., Clery, E. and Butt, S. (editors) *British social attitudes 2010.* London: Sage

Vorda, A. (2007) Review: *The God Delusion* by Richard Dawkins. *The Midwest Quarterly* 48 (4): 605-609

Walsh, B.J. and Middleton, J.R. (1984) *The Transforming Vision: shaping a Christian world view.* Downers Grove: Inter-Varsity Press

Ward, K. (2003) *God: a guide for the perplexed.* Oxford: Oneworld Publications

Ward, K. (2008) *Why there almost certainly is a God: doubting Dawkins.* Oxford: Lion Books

Ward, K. (2009) *The God Conclusion. God and the Western philosophical tradition.* London: Darton, Longman and Todd

Watson, D. (1979) *Is anyone there?* London: Hodder & Stoughton

Watson, D. (1984) *Fear no evil: one man deals with terminal illness.* London: Hodder & Stoughton

Watson, J.D. (1999) *The double helix: a personal account of the discovery of the structure of DNA.* London: Penguin

Watson, L. (1973) *Supernature: a natural history of the supernatural.* London: Hodder and Stoughton

Weber, M. (1966) *The sociology of religion.* (First published in Germany in 1922). London: Methuen

Weinberg, S. (1988) *The first three minutes: a modern view of the origin of the universe.* New York: Basic Books

Weinberg, S. (1992) *Dreams of a final theory: the search for the fundamental laws of nature.* New York: Pantheon

Welsh, J.M. (2007) Book reviews: *The God Delusion* by Richard Dawkins, and *Letters to a Christian nation* by Sam Harris. *Journal of American Cultures* 30 (3): 370-372

White, M. (2009) Keeper of the sacred flame. *The Times T2,* 1 May 2009, p.18

Wiesel, E. (1981) *Night.* London: Penguin Books

Wilson, A.N. (2000) *God's funeral.* London: Abacus

Wilson, A.N. (2006) *Betjeman: a life.* New York: Farrar, Straus and Giroux

Wilson, A.N. (2009) Why I believe again. *New Statesman* (2 April 2009)

Wilson, B.R. (1966) *Religion in a secular society.* London: Penguin

Wilson, D.S. (2002) *Darwin's cathedral: evolution, religion, and the nature of society.* Chicago: Chicago University Press

Wilson, E.O. (1975) *Sociobiology: the new synthesis.* Cambridge: Harvard University Press

Wilson, E.O. (1978) *On human nature.* Cambridge: Harvard University Press

Winston, R. (2005) *The story of God: a personal journey into the world of science and religion.* London: Bantam

Wittgenstein, L. (1961) *Tractatus Logico-Philosophicus.* London: Routledge, Kegan Paul

Wolf, G. (2006) The Church of the Non-Believers. *Wired* 14/11

Wright, R. (2009) *The Evolution of God*. New York: Little, Brown and Company

Zeiler, M. (2007) On the reality of tooth fairies: a review of *The God Delusion*. *Journal of the Experimental Analysis of Behaviour* 88 (3): 435-443

Zuckerman, P. (2006) Atheism: contemporary rates and patterns. In M. Martin (ed) *The Cambridge companion to atheism*. Cambridge: Cambridge University Press

NOTES

Chapter 1. The God debate

[1] Wright (2009) p.444

[2] Jones (2007) p.133

[3] Charles Darwin quoted in Henig (2007)

[4] Carlyon (1981)

[5] Henig (2007)

[6] Wilson (1978) p.169

[7] Dawkins (2006) p.166

[8] Winston (2005) p.19

[9] http://en.wikipedia.org/wiki/ God_Only_Knows

[10] *The Times*, 8 April 2008, p.26

[11] Barack Obama, quoted in Falsani (2006) pp.46-47

[12] Quoted in *The Times*, 16 September 2010, p.6

[13] Pope Benedict quoted in *The Times*, 20 September 2010, p.8

[14] http://uk.answers.yahoo.com/ question/index?qid=2008112610 4228AAz95YE

[15] http://en.wikipedia.org/wiki/ José_Mourinho

[16] *The Times*, 22 February 2011, p.59

[17] http://en.wikipedia.org/wiki/ Eric_Clapton

[18] http://www.starpulse.com/forum/ index.php?topic=5002msg197130 ;topicseen

[19] http://www.ask.com

[20] http://www.bbc.co.uk/news/ technology-11368424

21 Armstrong (1993) p.8

22 http://oxforddictionaries.com/definition/God

23 http://www.merriam-webster.com/dictionary/god

24 Weinberg (1992)

25 Dawkins (2006) p.33

26 Adler (1980) p.64

27 Annie Lennox, quoted in Falsani (2006) p.157

28 Falsani (2006) p.160

29 http://en.wikipedia.org/wiki/Great_Spirit

30 Baley (1976) p.36

31 Genesis 1: 27

32 Wilson (2006) p.240

33 Eagleton (2009) p.51

34 Lewis (1955)

35 Humphreys (2008) p.5

36 http://en.wikipedia.org/wiki/One_Of_Us_(Joan_Osborne_song)

37 http://answers.yahoo.com/questionindex?qid=20061007130843AAgS4uW

38 Dawkins (2006)

39 Jenkins (1969) p.1

40 Dawkins (2006) p.23

41 Humphreys (2008) p.73

42 Ward (2008) pp.10-11

43 Dawkins (2003)

44 Wilson (2000) p.223

45 McGrath and McGrath (2007) pp.63-64

46 John Polkinghorne, in Polkinghorne and Beale (2009) p.31

47 Dunne (2006) p.214

48 McBain (2007) pp.614-615

49 Pessin (2009)

Chapter 2. Ways of seeing

50 Humphreys (2008) pp.5-6

51 Borg (1998) p.20

52 Pessin (2009) p.7

53 Armstrong (1993) pp.49-50

54 Ward (2003) p.115

55 Armstrong (1993) p.345

56 Ogden (2000) pp.49-50

57 McGrath (2004b) p.218

58 Borg (1998) p.6

59 Borg (1998) p.20

60 Borg (1998) p.21

61 Ward (2009) pp.144-146

62 Borg (1998) pp.6-7

63 http://en.wiktionary.org/wiki/naturalism

64 Haught (2008) pp.xiii-xiv

65 Armstrong (2009) pp.277-278

66 McGrath (2004b) pp.226-227

67 Sire (1997) pp.174-179

68 McGrath (2004b) pp.218-219

69 Armstrong (2009) p.297

[70] Watson (1973)

[71] Walsh and Middleton (1984)

[72] Elsdon (1981)

[73] Otto (1923)

[74] Borg (1995), p.14

[75] http://www.quotationspage.com/quote/401.html

[76] http://en.wikipedia.org/wiki/The_Hound_of_Heaven

Chapter 3. Religion and the idea of God

[77] http://www.oed.com/view/Entry/186904?redirectedFrom=spirituality#eid

[78] Hardy (1979) p.131

[79] http://www.oed.com/view/Entry/161944?redirectedFrom=religion#eid

[80] Mawson (2005) p.1

[81] Cornwell (2007) pp.108-109

[82] Dennett (2006) p.15

[83] Durkheim (1915)

[84] Smart (1969) pp.15-25

[85] Jones (2006) p.viii

[86] Emile Durkheim, quoted in Cornwell (2007) p.45

[87] Novak (2007) pp.44-45

[88] Cornwell (2007) p.50

[89] Borg (1998) pp.6-7

[90] Cornwell (2007) p.95

[91] Hill (2010) p.50

[92] Tippett (2007) pp.14-15

[93] Cornwell (2007) p.95

[94] Harris (2005) p.14

[95] Harris (2005) p.20

[96] Dawkins (2006) pp.345-346

[97] Dawkins (2006) p.321

[98] Dawkins (2006) p.324

[99] Harris (2005) p.29

[100] http://en.wikipedia.org/wiki/Mysticism

[101] James (1902) pp.380-381

[102] James (1902) pp.422-423

[103] http://wordnetweb.princeton.edu/perl/webwn?s=mysticism

[104] Durkheim (1915) p.47

[105] Cornwell (2007) pp.43-45

[106] Dennett (2006) p.7

[107] Barrett *et al* (2001)

[108] http://www.adherents.com/Religions_By_Adherents.html viewed 28 July 2010

[109] http://www.adherents.com/rel_USA.html viewed 28 July 2010

[110] http://www.statistics.gov.uk/cci/nugget.asp?id=293 viewed 28 July 2010

[111] Brown (1988) p.51

[112] Voas and Ling (2010)

[113] Lundstrom (2008)

[114] http://wordnetweb.princeton.edu/perl/webwn?s=pantheism

[115] http://en.wikipedia.org/wiki/Pantheism

[116] Dawkins (2006) pp.39-40

[117] Lundstrom (2008)

[118] Eagleton (2009) pp.40-41

[119] Sire (1997) p.144

[120] http://www.etymonline.com/index.php?search=polytheism&searchmode=none

[121] Lundstrom (2008)

[122] http://en.wikipedia.org/wiki/Hinduism

[123] http://www.etymonline.com/index.php?search=monotheism&searchmode=none

[124] Shermer (2000) p.10

[125] Mawson (2005) p.71

[126] http://www.thefreedictionary.com/deism

[127] Armstrong (2009) p.206

[128] Dawkins (2006) pp.39-40

[129] Mawson (2005) p.71

[130] Gasgin (1989) p.240

[131] Haught (2008) p.81

[132] Dawkins (2006) pp.39-40

[133] Einstein, quoted in Hitchens (2007) p.271

[134] Dawkins (2006) p.34

[135] Hawking (1988)

[136] Dawkins (2006) p.34

[137] Dawkins (2006) p.41

[138] Dawkins (2006) p.36

[139] Dawkins (2006) p.36

[140] Dawkins (2006) p.31

[141] Haught (2008) p.44

[142] Eagleton (2006)

[143] Cornwell (2007) p.49

[144] Ward (2008) p.65

[145] Robertson (2007) p.45

[146] Dawkins (2006) p.24

[147] Dawkins (2006) p.31

[148] Lash (2007) p.509

[149] Haught (2008) p.43

[150] Ward (2008) p.28

[151] Dawkins (2006) p.31

[152] Ward (2008) p.14

[153] Armstrong (2009)

[154] Armstrong (1993)

[155] Smart (1969)

[156] Winston (2005)

[157] Wright (2009)

[158] Dennett (2006) p.215

[159] Armstrong (1993) p.7

[160] Smart (1969) pp.54-60

[161] Smart (1969) pp.71-72

[162] Smart (1969) p.33

[163] Smart (1969) pp.71-72

[164] Smart (1969) pp.71-72

[165] Armstrong (2009) p.21

[166] Carlyon (1981)

[167] Smart (1969) p.73

[168] Cupitt (1997) p.31

[169] Armstrong (2009)

[170] Weber (1966) p.xxviii

[171] Dennett (2006) p.205

[172] Dennett (2006) p.205

[173] McGrath and McGrath (2007) p.31

[174] Jones (2007) pp.47-48

[175] Hill (2010) p.48

[176] Pearce (1998) p.58

[177] Shermer (2000) pp.xvi-xvii

[178] Shermer (2000) pp.148-170

[179] Tillich (1958) pp.48-49

[180] Borg (1998) p.101

[181] De Botton (2012)

[182] Pirsig (1974)

[183] Robert Pirsig, quoted by Dawkins (2006) p.28

[184] Dawkins (2006) p.208

[185] Ward (2008) p.133

[186] Dennett (2006) p.103

[187] Dawkins (2006) p.190

[188] Cupitt (1997) p.11

[189] Dawkins (2006) p.190

[190] Dennett (2006) p.103

[191] Tippett (2007) p.13

[192] Newberg, D'Aquili and Rause (2001) p.132

[193] Newberg, D'Aquili and Rause (2001) p.132

[194] Dennett (2006) p.103

[195] Dawkins (2006) p.190

[196] Tippett (2007) p.13

[197] James (1902) p.58

[198] Armstrong (2009) p.5

[199] Schleiermacher (1989)

[200] Otto (1959)

[201] Otto (1959)

[202] Buber (1958)

[203] Armstrong (2009) p.19

[204] Shermer (2000) p.143

[205] Watson (1984) p.111

[206] Haught (2008) p.65

[207] Dawkins (2006) p.241

[208] Haught (2008) p.66

[209] Dawkins (2006) p.267

[210] Haught (2008) p.72

[211] Poole (2009) p.11

[212] Dennett (2006) p.279

[213] Dawkins (2006) p.259

[214] Haught (2008) pp.68-69

[215] Dawkins (2006) p.245

[216] Haught (2008) pp.68-69

[217] Haught (2008) p.71

[218] Robertson (2007) pp.90-92

[219] McGrath and McGrath (2007) p.52

[220] Dawkins (2006) p.194

[221] Newberg, D'Aquili and Rause (2001) p.129

[222] Newberg, D'Aquili and Rause (2001) p.130

[223] Newberg, D'Aquili and Rause (2001) p.130

[224] http://www.thefreedictionary.com/secular

[225] Ogden (2000) p.65

[226] Tippett (2007) p.6

[227] Armstrong (2009) p.277

[228] Pratt (1970)

[229] Albrecht and Heaton (1984)

[230] Martin (2008) p.1

[231] Walsh and Middleton (1984) pp.131-146

[232] Walsh and Middleton (1984) pp.133-134

[233] http://www.thefreedictionary.com/economism

[234] Brown (2005) p.1

[235] Voas and Ling (2010)

[236] Wilson (1966)

[237] Martin (1967)

[238] http://en.wikipedia.org/wiki/Martin_Heidegger

[239] Heidegger (1976) p.342

Chapter 4. God in the dock

[240] Lewis (1971)

[241] Lewis (1971) p.100

[242] http://news.bbc.co.uk/1/hi/world/Americas/7673591.stm

[243] Tippett (2007) p.149

[244] Dawkins (2006) p.51

[245] Varghese (2007a) p.ix

[246] Blackburn (2010) p.56

[247] Varghese (2007a) pp.vii-viii

[248] Flew (2007)

[249] Flew (2007)

[250] Armstrong (1993) p.366

[251] Armstrong (1993) p.366

[252] Pessin (2009) p.131

[253] Armstrong (1993) p.366

[254] Hitchens (2007) p.96

[255] McGrath (2004b) p.25

[256] Armstrong (1993) p.413

[257] http://en.wikipedia.org/wiki/Arthur_Schopenhauer

[258] Armstrong (1993) p.414

[259] http://en.wikipedia.org/wiki/Ludwig_Feuerbach

[260] McGrath (2004b) pp.56-57

[261] McGrath (2004b) pp.56-57

[262] Ludwig Feuerbach quoted in Pessin (2009) p.182

[263] Prozesky (1992) p.57

[264] http://en.wikipedia.org/wiki/Friedrich_Nietzsche

[265] Nietzsche, quoted in Armstrong (1993) p.417

[266] Hitchens (2007) p.67

[267] McGrath (2004b) p.149

[268] Ward (2003) p.226

[269] Ogden (2000) p.62

[270] Pessin (2009) pp.195-96

[271] Freud (1938)

[272] Armstrong (1993) p.419

[273] Armstrong (1993) p.419

[274] Prozesky (1992) p.59

[275] Pessin (2009) p.209

[276] Clarke (2001) p.122

277 Clarke (2001) p.122

278 http://en.wikipedia.org/wiki/
Karl_Marx

279 Karl Marx, quoted in McGrath
(2004b) pp.65-66

280 Clarke (2001) p.115

281 Armstrong (1993) p.416

282 Clarke (2001) p.124

283 Clarke (2001) p.124

284 Ogden (2000) p.34

285 Ward (2003) pp.193-194

286 Ward (2003) p.191

287 Armstrong (1993) p.406

288 Altizer and Hamilton (1968)
p.40

289 Altizer and Hamilton (1968)
p.13

290 McGrath (2004b) p.144

291 Shermer (2000) p.17

292 Armstrong (2009) p.279

293 McGrath (2004b) p.160

294 Robinson (1963) p.15

295 Clarke (2001) p.159

296 Armstrong (2009) p.270

297 Robinson (1963) pp.17-18

298 McGrath (2004b) pp.158-159

299 Cupitt (1997) p.81

300 Cupitt (1997) p.82

301 Wilson (2000)

302 Armstrong (2009) p.246

303 McGrath (2004b) p.141

304 Hitchens (2007) p.10

305 Hitchens (2007) p.54

306 Dennett (2006) p.25

307 Henig (2007)

308 Dennett (2006) p.108

309 Atran (2004)

310 McGrath (2004b) p.77

311 McGrath (2004b) p.77

312 Andrews (2009) pp.17-18

313 Haught (2008) p.x

314 McGrath and McGrath (2007)
pp.29-30

315 McGrath and McGrath (2007)
p.31

316 Cornwell (2007) pp.23-24

317 Dawkins (2006) p.222

318 Dennett (2006) p.86

319 Dawkins (2006) p.219

320 Dawkins (2006) p.202

321 Dawkins (2006) p.188

322 Haught (2008) pp.57-58

323 Dawkins (1976) pp.212-213;
quoted in Dennett (2006) p.230

324 Dawkins (2006) p.176

325 Haught (2008) p.58

326 McGrath and McGrath (2007)
pp.39-40

327 McGrath and McGrath (2007)
pp.29-30

328 Robertson (2007) p.79

329 McGrath and McGrath (2007)
p.43

330 Robertson (2007) p.79

331 Shermer (2000) p.71

332 Cornwell (2007) p.130

333 Robertson (2007) p.79

334 McGrath and McGrath (2007) p.41

335 McGrath and McGrath (2007) p.41

336 McGrath and McGrath (2007) p.41

337 Jones (2007) p.17

338 Cornwell (2007) p.130

339 Cornwell (2007) p.138

340 Newberg, D'Aquili and Rause (2001) p.129

341 Eagleton (2009) p.88

342 McGrath (2007) p.121

343 McGrath and McGrath (2007) pp.29-30

344 McGrath (2007) p.121

345 Geaney (2007) p.757

346 http://www.goodreads.com/quotes/show/13977

347 Shermer (2000) p.xv

348 McGrath (2004b) p.190

Chapter 5. Doubt and denial

349 Humphreys (2008) p.67

350 Voas and Ling (2010)

351 Smith (1989) p.8

352 http://www.yougov.co.uk/extranets/ygarchives/content/

pdf/Humphrys%20Religion%20Questions.pdf

353 Humphreys (2008) p.127

354 Humphreys (2008) p.128

355 Winston (2005) p.21

356 Borg (1998) pp.6-7

357 Smith (1989) p.27

358 Tippett (2007) p.18

359 Adler (1980) p.6

360 Poole (2009) p.29

361 Tippett (2007) p.3

362 http://wordnetweb.princeton.edu/perl/webwn?s=agnosticism

363 http://en.wikipedia.org/wiki/Agnosticism

364 http://www.etymonline.com/index.php?term=agnostic

365 Smith (1989) p.10

366 http://en.wikipedia.org/wiki/List_of_agnostics

367 Humphreys (2008) p.40

368 Humphreys (2008)

369 Dawkins (2006) p.69

370 Dawkins (2006) p.70

371 Dawkins (2006) p.70

372 Lundstrom (2008) p.14

373 Baillie (1939) p.48

374 Smith (1989) p.7

375 McGrath (2004b) p.175

376 Hitchens (2007) p.253

377 Onfray (2007) p.17

378 Hitchens (2007) p.254

379 Baggani (2003) quoted in
Dawkins (2006) p.34

380 Smith (1989) p.26

381 Dawkins (2006) p.35

382 McGrath (2004b) p.47

383 McGrath (2004b) p.113

384 McGrath (2004b) p.116

385 Dawkins (2006) p.26

386 Dawkins (2006) p.27

387 Onfray (2007) p.67

388 Onfray (2007) p.70

389 Medd (2010) p.58

390 Hill (2010) p.51

391 http://www.wired.com/wired/
archive/14.11/atheism.html

392 Varghese (2007a) pp.xv-xvi

393 Haught (2008) p.1

394 Harris (2004)

395 Welsh (2007) p.371

396 Ruse (2007) p.814

397 Dennett (2006) p.17

398 Hitchens (2007)

399 Hitchens (2007) p.56

400 Humphreys (2008) p.13

401 Hitchens (2007) p.4

402 Dawkins (2003)

403 Dawkins (2006) p.1

404 Dawkins (2006) p.28

405 Martin (2009) p.209

406 Varghese (2007a) pp.xv-xvi

407 Dawkins (2006) p.351

408 Harris (2005) p.109

409 Harris (2005) p.123

410 Hitchens (2007) p.10

411 Varghese (2007a) p.xxiv

412 Dawkins (2006) p.227

413 Dawkins (2006) p.233

414 Haught (2008) p.3

415 Hitchens (2007) p.32

416 Haught (2008) p.16

417 Haught (2008) p.20

418 Haught (2008) p.20

419 Ruse (2007) p.815

420 Haught (2008) p.10

421 Armstrong (2009) p.8

422 Eagleton (2009) p.14

423 Humphreys (2008) p12

424 Ward (2008) pp.10-11

425 Humphreys (2008) p.220

426 Haught (2008) pp.xii-xiii

427 Armstrong (2009) p.293

Chapter 6. Science and the challenge to God

428 Tippett (2007) p.75

429 Attfield (1978) p.37

430 Eagleton (2009) pp.76-83

431 Hitchens (2007) p.64

432 Eagleton (2009) p.75

433 Winston (2005) p.375

434 McGrath (2004b) p.83

435 *The Times*, 17 December 2010,
p.29

[436] Dixon (2008) p.31

[437] Hitchens (2007) p.67

[438] Shermer (2000) pp.198-199

[439] Winston (2005) p.334

[440] Hitchens (2007) p.58

[441] Poole (1009) p.59

[442] Sobel (2004)

[443] Clarke (2001) p.61

[444] Clarke (2001) p.61

[445] Jones (2007) p.24

[446] Sample (2010)

[447] Jones (2007) pp.33-34

[448] Rincon (2010)

[449] Poole (2007) p.68

[450] Dawkins (2006) pp.169-170

[451] Rees (1999)

[452] Dawkins (2006) p.172

[453] Flew (2007) p.119

[454] Poole (2009) p.80

[455] Dawkins (2006) pp.163-164

[456] Dawkins (2006) p.164

[457] Flew (2007) p.115

[458] Dawkins (2006) pp.165-166

[459] Rees (2001)

[460] Ward (2008) p.61

[461] Dawkins (2006) pp.163-164

[462] Dawkins (2006) p.176

[463] Dixon (2008) p.52

[464] Dyson (1981) p.57

[465] Ward (2008) p.70

[466] McGrath and McGrath (2007) p.9

[467] Haught (2008) p.81

[468] Richard Dawkins, quoted in Cornwell (2007) p.63

[469] Hawking and Mlodinow (2010)

[470] Hawking (1988)

[471] Stephen Hawking quoted on http://www.bbc.co.uk/news/uk-11161493

[472] Richard Dawkins quoted in *The Times*, 3 September 2010, p.1

[473] Don Page, letter to *The Times*, 6 September 2010 p.20

[474] Genesis1: verse 1

[475] Genesis1: verse 31

[476] Park (2001) p.531

[477] Dixon (2008) p.69

[478] Armstrong (2009) p.237

[479] Armstrong (2009) p.237

[480] Clarke (2001) pp.54-55

[481] Dixon (2008) pp.73-76

[482] Jones (2007) p.11

[483] Dixon (2008) p.62

[484] Armstrong (2009) p.237

[485] Cornwell (2007) p.13

[486] Charles Darwin, quoted in Cornwell (2007) p.12

[487] Armstrong (2009) p.237

[488] Dixon (2008) p.59

[489] Dawkins (2006) p.127

[490] Cornwell (2007) p.11

[491] Haught (2008) p.x

[492] Ward (2009) p.133

[493] http://en.wikipedia.org/wiki/ Supernatural

[494] Dixon (2008) p.17

[495] Berry (2003) p.33

[496] Albert Einstein, quoted in Tippett (2010) p.22

[497] Tippett (2010) p.16

[498] Albert Einstein, quoted in Tippett (2010) p.23

[499] Hawking (1988)

[500] Dunne (2006) p.214

[501] Hitchens (2007) p.65

[502] Dawkins (2006) p.59

[503] Ward (2008) pp.83-84

[504] Varghese (2007a) p.xii

[505] Ellis (2004) p.30

[506] Sire (1997) p.181

[507] Brueggemann (1993) pp.8-9

[508] Kuhn (1962)

[509] Dixon (2008) p.35

[510] Ravetz (2006) p.130

[511] Eagleton (2009) p.132

[512] McGrath and McGrath (2007) p.15

[513] Poole (2007) p.91

[514] Ellis (2004) p.19

[515] Cornwell (2007) p.61

[516] Peter Medawar, quoted in McGrath (2009) p.17

[517] McGrath and McGrath (2007) p.17

[518] Cornwell (2007) p.86

[519] Dixon (2008) p.35

[520] Eagleton (2009) p.125

[521] Ravetz (2006) p.78

[522] Dixon (2008) pp.49-50

[523] Dixon (2008) p.35

[524] Dixon (2008) p.31

[525] Dixon (2008) p.35

[526] Dixon (2008) p.31

[527] Dawkins (2006) p.55

[528] Lash (2007) p.510

[529] Dunne (2006) p.218

[530] Haught (2008) pp.18-19

[531] Farrer (2009) p.14

[532] Schroeder (1997)

[533] McGrath (2004a)

[534] Reisz (2010) p.41

[535] Hitchens (2007) p.64

[536] McGrath and McGrath (2007) pp.23-24

[537] Dixon (2008) p.2

[538] Polkinghorn and Beale (2009) p.97

[539] Henry Drummond, quoted in Dixon (2008) p.45

[540] Armstrong (1993) p.355

[541] Dixon (2008) p.46

[542] Dixon (2008) p.46

[543] Leibniz, quoted in Dixon (2008) p.46

[544] Ward (2009) p.132

[545] Ward (2003) pp.2-3

[546] Poole (2007) p.35

547 Dawkins (2006) p.218

548 McGrath and McGrath (2007) pp.11-12

549 McGrath and McGrath (2007) p.10

550 John Polkinghorne, quoted in Tippett (2010) p.263

551 Park (1980) p.118

552 Hitchens (2007) pp.64-5

553 McGrath and McGrath (2007) Chapter 2

554 Smith (1989) p.213

555 Klostermaier (2008)

556 Haught (2008) p.83

557 Borg (1998) p.30

558 Jones (2007) p.45

559 Tippett (2007) p.75

560 Pope Benedict XVI, quoted in *Times Higher Education*, 23 September 2010 p.4

561 Gould (1997); http://www.stephenjaygould.org/library/gould_noma.html

562 Gould (1997); http://www.stephenjaygould.org/library/gould_noma.html

563 Gould (1999) quoted in Dawkins (2006) p.79

564 Dennett (2006) p.30

565 Dunne (2006) p.216

566 McGrath and McGrath (2007) pp.18-19

567 Collins (2006) p.6

568 Shermer (2000) p.123

569 Sacks (2010) p.27

570 Dixon (2008) p.3

571 Dawkins (2006) p.35

572 Dawkins (2006) pp.126-130

573 McGrath (2009) p.13

574 McGrath and McGrath (2007) p.21

575 Dixon (2008) p.3

576 Berry (2009)

577 Ecklund (2010)

578 John Polkinghorne, quoted in Tippett (2010) p.268

579 John Polkinghorne, quoted in Tippett (2010) p.258

580 McGrath (2009) pp.14-15

581 McGrath (2009) pp.20-21

Chapter 7. Arguments for God

582 Watson (1984) p.127

583 Jenkins (1966) p.8

584 Jenkins (1966) p.8

585 Harris (2005) pp.39-40

586 Harris (2005) p.204

587 Dennett (2006) p.246

588 Dennett (2006) p.27

589 Hegel (1984) p.258

590 Jenkins (1966) p.23

591 Swinburne (1979) p.9

592 Swinburne (1979) p.9

593 Collins (2010) p.44

594 Ward (2003) p.127

595 Pessin (2009) p.47

596 Ogden (2000) p.2

597 Clarke (2001) p.24

598 Armstrong (1993) pp.240-241

599 Vardy (1999) p.81

600 Dawkins (2006) pp.104-105

601 Dawkins (2006) p.107

602 Ward (2008) p.120

603 Ward (2008) p.122

604 Pessin (2009) p.117

605 Clarke (2001) p.30

606 Dawkins (2006) p.101

607 Poole (2007) p.50

608 Armstrong (2009) p.141

609 Shermer (2000) p.91

610 Thomas Aquinas, quoted in Clarke (2001) p.30

611 Pessin (2009) p.13

612 Ward (2008) p.105

613 Thomas Aquinas, quoted in Clarke (2001) p.30

614 Ward (2008) p.106

615 Wittgenstein (1961) p.44

616 Rees (2001)

617 Cornwell (2007) p.150

618 Shermer (2000) p.91

619 Thomas Aquinas, quoted in Clarke (2001) p.30

620 Cornwell (2007) p.153

621 Ward (2008) p.107

622 Cornwell (2007) p.152

623 Dixon (2008) p.51

624 Thomas Aquinas, quoted in Clarke (2001) p.31

625 Dawkins (2006) p.102

626 Ward (2008) p.115

627 Swinburne (1979) p.11

628 Ward (2008) p.117

629 Baillie (1939) p.126

630 Vardy (1999) p.106

631 Dawkins (2006) p.100

632 McGrath and McGrath (2007) p.7

633 Ward (2009) p.21

634 Dunne (2006) p.217

635 Armstrong (1993) p.245

636 McGrath and McGrath (2007) p.7

637 Robertson (2007) p.71

638 Shermer (2000) p.xvi

639 Clarke (2001) p.37

640 Armstrong (2009) p.220

641 Dawkins (1986)

642 Feynman (1998) p.43

643 Dixon (2008) pp.46-48

644 Charles Darwin, quoted in Keynes (2009) p.291

645 Dixon (2008) p.47

646 Flew (2007) p.103

647 Stephen Hawking quoted on http://www.bbc.co.uk/news/uk-11161493

648 Ward (2008) pp.35-36

649 John Henry Newman quoted in Ruse (2007) p.815

650 Ward (2008) p.104

651 Dawkins (2006) p.185

652 Dixon (2008) p.51

653 Stephen Hawking quoted in *The Times*, 3 September 2010, p.8

654 D'Souza (2007)

655 Clarke (2001) p.34

656 Dawkins (2006) p.24

657 Dawkins (2006) p.145

658 Dawkins (2006) p.103

659 Dawkins (2006) p.141

660 Curtis (2006) p.980

661 Dawkins (2006) p.147

662 Dawkins (2006) p.149

663 Dawkins (2006) p.148

664 Poole (2009) p.77

665 Dennett (2006) p.243

666 Dawkins (2006) pp.157-58

667 Ward (2008) pp.39-40

668 Dawkins (2006) pp.157-58

669 Ledwig (2007)

670 Dawkins (2006) p.151

671 Dawkins (2006) p.149

672 Dawkins (2006) p.109

673 Dawkins (2006) p.145

674 Ledwig (2007) p.118

675 Robertson (2007) pp.67-68

676 Atkins (1993)

677 Dawkins (2006) p.144

678 Ledwig (2007) p.118

679 Collins (2009) pp.251-252

680 Hardy (1979) p.10

681 Dawkins (2006) p.101

682 Dixon (2008) pp.51-52

683 Dixon (2008) pp.87-88

684 Winston (2005) pp.95-96

685 http://en.wikipedia.org/wiki/Scopes_Trial

686 Dixon (2008) p.90

687 Poole (2009) p.75

688 Dawkins (1995) pp.76-83

689 Poole (2009) p.75

690 Dixon (2008) p.82

691 Hitchens (2007) p.86

692 Dawkins (2006) p.138

693 Haught (2008) p.42

694 Cornwell (2007) pp.25-26

695 Cornwell (2007) p.98

696 McGrath and McGrath (2007) pp.11-12

697 Poole (2007) pp.113-114

698 Swinburne (1979) p.150

699 Swinburne (1979) p.198

700 Vardy (1999) pp.106-107

701 Swinburne (1979) p.150

702 Ward (2009) p.13

703 Armstrong (2009) pp.220-222

704 Dawkins (2006) p.111

705 Dawkins (2006) pp.86-87

706 Tippett (2007) p.201

707 http://www.mozartforum.com/Lore/article.php?id=101

708 Swinburne (1979) p.11

709 Shermer (2000) p.91

710 Clarke (2001) p.109

711 Clarke (2001) p.109

712 Vardy (1999) p.211

713 Vardy (1999) p.203

714 Dixon (1008) p.47

715 Dunne (2006) p.216

716 Dawkins (2006) p.117

717 Haught (2008) p.30

718 Haught (2008) p.35

719 Dawkins (2006) p.118

720 Dawkins (2006) p.117

721 Hitchens (2007) p.122

722 Lash (2007) p.513

723 Ward (2008) pp.64-65

724 Tippett (2007) p.57

725 Ellis (2004) p.37

726 Dennett (1993) p.21

727 Ward (2008) p.16

728 Dennett (1993) p.173

729 Dennett (1993) p.182

730 Dennett (1993) p.182

731 Dennett (1993) pp.199-208

732 Dawkins (2006) pp.24, 139-141, 161, 172

733 Ward (2008) p.96

734 Swinburne (1979) p.11

735 Swinburne (1979) pp.153-154

736 Harris (2005) p.209

737 Pessin (2009) p.171

738 Swinburne (1979) p.176

739 Clarke (2001) p.39

740 Jones (2007) p.59

741 Collins (2010) p.xiv

742 Ward (2003) p.90

743 Swinburne (1979) p.179

744 Dawkins (2006) p.137

745 Montefiore (1985) p.169

746 Dawkins (2006) p.137

747 Dawkins (2006) p.136

748 Andrews (2009) 23-24

749 Dawkins (2006) p.137

750 Dawkins (2006) p.114

751 Ward (2008) pp.99-100

752 Andrews (2009) 23-24

753 Dawkins (2006) p.54

754 Dawkins (2006) p.50

755 Dawkins (2006) p.48

756 Dawkins (2006) p.51

757 Dawkins (2006) p.73

758 Dawkins (2006) p.47

759 Corlett (2009) p.129

760 Swinburne (1979) pp.64-69

761 Dawkins (2006) p.133

762 Dawkins (2006) p.134

763 Collins (2010) p.58

764 Armstrong (1993) p.351

765 Clarke (2001) p.13

766 Pessin (2009) p.125

767 Pessin (2009) p.126

768 Dawkins (2006) p.130

769 Armstrong (1993) p.351

770 Mitchell (1973)

771 Clarke (2001) p.43

772 Prozesky (1992) p.17

773 Poole (2009) pp.33-35

Chapter 8. Personal experience of God

774 Swinburne (1979) p.244

775 Pessin (2009) pp.205-06

776 C.S. Lewis, quoted in Collins (2010) p.219

777 Haught (2008) p.81

778 Cottingham (2009) p.86

779 Clarke (2001) p.110

780 Cottingham (2009) p.92

781 Jones (2007) p.90

782 Dixon (2008) pp.56-57

783 Cottingham (2009) p.94

784 Cottingham (2009) p.98

785 Baillie (1939) p.37

786 Dixon (2008) p.22

787 Hitchens (2007) p.97

788 Hitchens (2007) p.107

789 Jenkins (1966) p.23

790 Sire (1997) pp.30-31

791 Armstrong (1993) p.448

792 Adler (1980) p.16

793 Vardy (1999) p.133

794 Vardy and Arliss (2003) p.71

795 http://en.wikipedia.org/wiki/Epiphany_(feeling)

796 Ward (2008) p.128

797 James (1902) p.16

798 Armstrong (2009) pp.258-259

799 Baillie (1939) p.17

800 Baillie (1939) p.20

801 Tippett (2007) p.115

802 Ward (2008) pp.127-128

803 Ward (2008) p.128

804 William James, quoted in Vardy and Arliss (2003) p.89

805 Smart (1969) p.28

806 Swinburne (1979) p.246

807 Clarke (2001) p.94

808 James (1902) p.6

809 Borg (1998) p.7

810 Borg (1998) p.4

811 Ward (2008) p.123

812 Robertson (2007) p.57

813 Armstrong (2009) pp.112-113

814 Harris (2005) p.41

815 Newberg, D'Aquili and Rause (2001) pp.146-147

816 James (1902) p.20

817 Dawkins (2006) pp.87-92

818 Clarke (2001) p.92

819 Swinburne (1979) pp.250-251

820 Clarke (2001) p.92

821 Clarke (2001) p.92

822 Borg (1998) p.41

823 Jenkins (1966) p.93

824 Clarke (2001) p.92

825 Armstrong (1993) p.453

826 Pessin (2009) pp.214-215

827 Pessin (2009) pp.214-215

828 Clarke (2001) p.8

829 Borg (1998) p.42

830 Ward (2003) p.33

831 James (1902) p.238

832 Borg (1998) pp.40-41

833 Borg (1998) pp.40-41

834 Borg (1998) p.38

835 Borg (1998) p.38

836 Ward (2008) pp.126-127

837 Borg (1998) p.41

838 http://en.wikipedia.org/wiki/
Mysticism

839 Borg (1998) p.37

840 James (1902) p.381

841 Shermer (2000) p.96

842 Borg (1998) p.37

843 Newberg, D'Aquili and Rause
(2001) pp.135-136

844 Borg (1998) p.40

845 James (1902) p.68

846 James (1902) p.70

847 Newberg, D'Aquili and Rause
(2001) p.148

848 Vardy and Arliss (2003) p.90

849 Clarke (2001) p.100

850 Vardy and Arliss (2003) p.90

851 Borg (1998) p.52

852 Borg (1998) pp.37-38

853 Borg (1998) p.45

854 Dawkins (2006) p.112

855 McGrath and McGrath (2007)
p.38

856 Hardy (1979)

857 Hardy (1979) pp.25-29

858 Dawkins (2006) pp.87-92

859 Newberg and Waldman (2009) p.4

860 Newberg, D'Aquili and Rause
(2001) p.129

861 McGrath and McGrath (2007)
p.38

862 Newberg, D'Aquili and Rause
(2001)

863 Newberg, D'Aquili and Rause
(2001) p.8

864 Newberg and Waldman (2009)
pp.6-7

865 Newberg and Waldman (2009)
p.60

866 Newberg, D'Aquili and Rause
(2001) p.143

867 Geaney (2007) p.757

868 Harris (2005) p.72

869 Pierre (2001)

870 Henig (2007)

871 Tippett (2007) p.95

Chapter 9. The nature of belief

872 http://www.thefreedictionary.
com/reality

873 Newberg, D'Aquili and Rause
(2001) p.36

874 Sire (1997) p.17

875 Walsh and Middleton (1984)
  pp.31-34

876 Dawkins (2006) p.133

877 Dawkins (2006) p.361

878 Klostermaier (2008)

879 Dixon (2008) p.19

880 Dixon (2008) p.21

881 Winston (2005) pp.18-19

882 Ward (2003) p.189

883 http://en.wikiquote.org/wiki/
  Yuri_Gagarin

884 Keller (2008) p.122

885 http://www.speroforum.com/
  site/article.asp?id=2867

886 Sire (1997) p.178

887 Eagleton (2009) p.115

888 Sire (1997) pp.53-54

889 Ravetz (2006) p.67

890 Lash (2007) p.507

891 Eagleton (2009) p.131

892 Hitchens (2007) p.70

893 Dennett (1995)

894 Dawkins (2006) p.99

895 Dawkins (2006) pp.157-58

896 Haught (2008) p.86

897 Haught (2008) p.89

898 Swinburne (1996)

899 McGrath and McGrath (2007)
  p.12

900 Sacks (2010) p.27

901 Haught (2008) p.45

902 Poole (2007) p.40

903 Vardy (1999) p.8

904 Vardy (1999) p.9

905 Ellis (2004) p.23

906 Cottingham (2009) pp.11-12

907 Curtis (2006) p.980

908 Walsh and Middleton (1984)
  p.169

909 Ledwig (2007)

910 Collins (2010) p.xv

911 Haught (2008) p.17

912 Clarke (2001) p.144

913 Dawkins (2006) p.135

914 Vardy (1999) p.132

915 Vardy (1999) p.50

916 Polkinghorne and Beale (2009)
  p.14

917 Newberg and Waldman (2007)
  p.25

918 http://www.thetallestman.com/

919 Eagleton (2009) pp.112-113

920 Smith (1989) pp.102-103

921 Newberg and Waldman (2007)
  p.21

922 Poole (2007) p.44

923 Newberg and Waldman (2007)
  pp.43-44

924 Newberg and Waldman (2007)
  p.5

925 Newberg and Waldman (2007)
  pp.21-22

926 Humphreys (2008) p.79

927 Newberg and Waldman (2007) p.25

928 Flew (2007) p.55

929 Haught (2008) p.31

930 Armstrong (2009) p.292

931 Haught (2008) p.45

932 Haught (2008) p.11

933 Haught (2008) p.30

934 Haught (2008) pp.38-39

935 Harris (2005) p.215

936 William James, quoted in McGrath (2009) p.22

937 Borg (1998) p.169

938 Clarke (2001) p.10

939 Douglas Adams, quoted in Humphreys (2008) p.89

940 Hebrews 11: 1

941 2 Corinthians 5: 7

942 2 Corinthians 4: 18

943 John 20: 29

944 1 Corinthians 13: 12

945 Dawkins (2006) p.199

946 Dawkins (1976)

947 Haught (2008) p.42

948 Haught (2008) p.13

949 Humphreys (2008) pp.338-340

950 Harris (2005) p.23

951 Clarke (2001) p.11

952 Poole (2007) p.52

953 Pessin (2009) p.191

954 Baillie (1962) p.126

955 Baillie (1962) p.259

956 Pessin (2009) p.30

957 Borg (1998) p.170-171

958 Armstrong (1993) p.1

959 Poole (2007) p.54

960 Newberg and Waldman (2009) p.20

961 Dawkins (2006) p.323

962 Dawkins (2006) p.199

963 Dawkins (2006) p.348

964 Polkinghorne and Beale (2009) p.27

965 Baillie (1939) p.113

966 Pearce (1998)

967 Tillich (1958) p.16

968 Tillich (1958) p.6

969 Tillich (1958) p.8

970 Eagleton (2009) p.37

971 James (1902) p.284

972 James (1902) p.285

973 James (1902) p.47

974 Poole (2009) p.17

975 Hitchens (2007) p.185

976 Dawkins (2006) p.380

977 Dawkins (2006) p.5

978 Hitchens (2007) p.5

979 Eagleton (2009) pp.109-110

980 Haught (2008) p.49

981 G.K. Chesterton, quoted in Collins (2010) p.281

982 Anselm, quoted in Armstrong (1993) p.240

983 Armstrong (1993) p.240

984 Haught (2008) p.5

985 Pascal (1669) *Pensées* number 278, p.79

986 Jenkins (1966) pp.108-109

987 Eagleton (2009) p.137

988 Clarke (2001) p.13

989 Martin Luther, quoted in Armstrong (1993) p.327

990 Armstrong (1993) p.411

991 Armstrong (1993) p.411

992 Ward (2003) p.19

993 Dennett (2006) p.241

994 Dawkins (2006) p.24

995 Dawkins (2006) pp.208-210

996 Dawkins (2006) p.209

997 Dawkins (2006) pp.209-210

998 Dawkins (2006) p.130

999 Humphreys (2008) p.196

1000 James (1902) p.202

1001 Montefiore (1985) p.3

1002 *The Times*, 21 October 2008, p.11

1003 McGrath and McGrath (2007) p.xii

1004 Jones (2007) p.42

1005 Armstrong (2009) p.5

1006 Armstrong (2009) p.10

1007 Baillie (1939) p.54

1008 Collins (2007) p.34

1009 Keller (2008) pp.xvi-xvii

1010 Collins (2007) p.34

1011 Newberg and Waldman (2009) p.164

1012 Elie Wiesel, quoted in Falsani (2006) p.255

1013 Elie Wiesel, quoted in Falsani (2006) p.256

1014 Tippett (2007) pp.102-103

1015 James (1902) p.65

1016 Fowler (1978)

1017 Prozesky (1992) p.10

1018 Cornwell (2007) p.139

1019 Cornwell (2007) p.95

1020 Newberg and Waldman (2009) p.246

1021 James (1902) p.189

1022 James (1902) p.209

1023 James (1902) pp.226-227

1024 2 Corinthians 5: 17

1025 James (1902) pp.247-248

1026 James (1902) p.254

1027 Leo Tolstoy, quoted in Baillie (1939) p.82

1028 Hick (1995) p.33

1029 C.S.Lewis quoted in Downing (2002)

1030 Pearce (1998) p.57

1031 Lewis (1955) p.266

1032 Lewis (2002) p.266

1033 Collins (2009)

1034 Collins (2009) p.249

1035 Collins (2009) p.250

1036 Collins (2007) p.225

1037 Flew (2009)

1038 Flew (2007) p.15

[1039] Flew (2007) p.91

[1040] Flew (2007) p.93

[1041] Flew (2007) p.155

[1042] James (1902) p.176

[1043] Dennett (2006) p.205

[1044] http://www.doncupitt.com/ doncupitt.html

[1045] Keynes (2009) p.43

[1046] Charles Darwin, quoted in Keynes (2009) pp.250-251

[1047] Templeton (2000)

[1048] Dawkins (2006) p.365

[1049] Barker (2008)

Chapter 10. Re-framing God

[1050] Vigué (2002) p.397

[1051] Armstrong (2009) p.1

[1052] Polkinghorne and Beale (2009) p.12

[1053] Dennett (2006)

[1054] Armstrong (1993) p.10

[1055] Jones (2007) p.xi

[1056] Polkinghorne and Beale (2009) p.15

[1057] Baillie (1939) p.3

[1058] Baillie (1939) p.17

[1059] Ward (2009) p.73

[1060] Baillie (1939) p.6

[1061] Collins (2007) p.35

[1062] McGrath (2004b) p.188

[1063] Lewis (1955) p.17

[1064] Humphreys (2008) p.341

[1065] Pascal and Augustine, quoted in Sire (1997) p.28

[1066] McGrath (2004b) p.188

[1067] Jenkins (1966) p.47

[1068] Adams (1995)

[1069] http://en.wikipedia.org/ wiki/Phrases_from_The_ Hitchhiker's_Guide_to_the_ Galaxy

[1070] McGrath (2009) p.22

[1071] Albert Einstein, quoted in McGrath (2009) p.22

[1072] William James, quoted in McGrath (2009) p.22

[1073] Mawson (2005) p.220

[1074] Dawkins (2006) p.73

[1075] Maitland (2002) p.12

[1076] Dickinson (2002) p.49

[1077] Keller (2008) p.127

[1078] Watson (1984) p.128

[1079] Watson (1984) p.49

[1080] Dietrich Bonhoeffer, quoted in Tippett (2007) pp.99-100

[1081] Jenkins (1966) p.75

[1082] Baillie (1939) pp.56-57

[1083] Polkinghorne and Beale (2009) pp.11-12

[1084] Polkinghorne and Beale (2009) p.14

[1085] Dixon (2008) p.36

[1086] Tippett (2007) p.232

[1087] Haught (2008) pp.80-81

[1088] Adam (2011) p.124

[1089] Adam (2011) p.31

[1090] Adam (2011) pp.39-40

[1091] Adam (2011) p.58

[1092] Borg (1998) pp.6-7

[1093] Borg (1998) p.61

[1094] Borg (1998) p.26

[1095] Borg (1998) p.1

[1096] Borg (1998) pp.1-2

[1097] Borg (1998) p.2

[1098] Borg (1998) p.19

[1099] Borg (1998) p.65

[1100] Borg (1998) p.66

[1101] Borg (1998) p.67

[1102] Borg (1998) pp.28-29

[1103] Borg (1998) p.2

[1104] Borg (1998) pp.1-2

[1105] Borg (1998) p.32

[1106] Borg (1998) p.12

[1107] Borg (1998) p.12

[1108] Borg (1998) p.71

[1109] Borg (1998) p.72

[1110] Borg (1998) p.76

[1111] Borg (1998) p.76

[1112] Borg (1998) p.5

[1113] Borg (1998) p.79

[1114] Borg (1998) p.12

[1115] Borg (1998) pp.33-34

[1116] Rowan Williams, quoted in Humphreys (2008) pp.77-78

Index

A Brief History of Time, 39, 95, 102
A Devil's Chaplain, 9, 81
A History of God, 54
Abraham, 5, 36, 44
act of faith, 45, 196, 205
Adam, David, 225
Adams, Douglas, 199, 221
Addison, Chris, 79
Adler, Mortimer, 6, 163
aesthetics, 106
After God, 62
Age of Faith, 87
Age of Reason, 16, 87
agnostic, 7, 36, 48, 61, 68, 73, 75, 76, 99, 108, 117, 153, 213
agnosticism, 30, 55, 75, 76, 210, 213, 215
Allah, 5, 36
Altizer, Thomas, 60
ancestor worship, 42, 43
Andrews, Edgar, 151, 152
animism, 35, 42
Anselm, 122, 123, 124, 205, 221

Anthropic Principle, 92, 223
anti-evolutionism. *See* Intelligent Design
anti-realist, 108, 189
Aphrodite, 43
appearance of design, 133
Aquinas, Thomas, 123, 124, 125, 126, 127, 128, 129, 132, 145, 206
argument
  a posteriori, 122
  a priori, 122
Argument from Admired Religious Scientists, 116
Argument from Beauty, 143
Argument from Consciousness, 148
Argument from Contingency, 126
Argument from Degree, 127
Argument from Design, 128, 129, 132, 134, 142, 145
Argument from Miracles, 145
Argument from Morality, 150
Argument from Probability, 151, 153
Argument from Providence, 143

Argument from Religious Experience, 158
Argument from Sacred Texts, 146
Argument from Scriptures. *See* Argument from Sacred Texts
Argument, Cumulative Case, 156
arguments based on design, 142
Aristotle, 15, 89, 125, 127
Arliss, Julie, 163
Armstrong, Karen, 1, 4, 19, 21, 26, 37, 41, 42, 43, 47, 48, 51, 54, 56, 59, 60, 61, 62, 85, 98, 99, 123, 125, 129, 130, 143, 155, 156, 164, 168, 196, 202, 205, 206, 207, 208, 217, 218
Arnold, Matthew, 62
Arouet, Francois-Marie. *See* Voltaire
atheism, 9, 30, 34, 37, 44, 55, 58, 74, 75, 76, 77, 78, 79, 80, 81, 82, 83, 84, 85, 87, 88, 117, 118, 154, 191, 196, 200, 214, 215, 216, 230
atheist, 5, 8, 10, 18, 23, 38, 44, 49, 55, 56, 60, 73, 75, 76, 77, 79, 81, 85, 93, 99, 104, 110, 113, 125, 154, 167, 197, 199, 200, 204, 210, 213, 216, 220
Atran, Scott, 64
Attenborough, Sir David, 76
Attfield, Robin, 87
Attlee, Clement, 76
Augustine, 15, 145, 201, 221
Auschwitz, 208
Autobiography, 99
Ayer, Sir Alfred (Freddie), 55
Bach, 144
Baha'i, 29
Baillie, John, 77, 128, 161, 201, 203, 208, 219, 220, 224
Baly, Denis, 6
Barker, Don, 216
Barrett, Justin, 64
Barth, Karl, 162, 165

basic beliefs, 196
Bayes theorem, 154
Beach Boys, 3
Beagle, HMS, 97
Beethoven, 144
belief
    and knowledge, 193
    nature of, 181
belief in belief in God, 44
belief-making process, 194
Benedict, Pope, 4, 114
Bent World, 23
Berry, Sam, 101, 117
Betjeman, John, 7
Bible, 17, 29, 30, 39, 54, 56, 62, 89, 90, 96, 98, 101, 139, 140, 142, 146, 147, 161, 162, 163, 164, 168, 170, 188, 199, 211, 223, 226, 227
Big Bang, 91, 92, 103, 112, 135, 207, 223
black hole, 90
Blackburn, Simon, 55
Blackmore, Susan, 66
Blair, Tony, 3
blind faith, 199
Boeing 747 Gambit. *See* Ultimate Boeing 747 Gambit
Bonhoeffer, Dietrich, 223
Bono, 4
book of nature, 101
book of scripture, 101
Borg, Marcus, 13, 16, 17, 18, 24, 30, 45, 74, 114, 158, 167, 170, 171, 172, 173, 175, 181, 198, 199, 202, 226, 227, 228, 229, 230, 231
Boyer, Pascal, 64
Boyle, Robert, 116, 131
Brahma, 36
Brahman, 168
brain science, 178
Breaking the Spell: religion as a natural phenomenon, 80

brights, 23, 77, 204
British Humanist Association, 207
Brown, Callum, 51
Brueggemann, Walter, 104
Buber, Martin, 48, 170, 171, 209,
    223
Buchenwald, 208
Buffett, Warren, 76
Bush, George W., 3
Campbell, Alistair, 3
Camus, Albert, 55, 84
Carlyle, Thomas, 62
Carlyon, Richard, 2, 43
Categorical Imperative. *See* Moral
    Imperative
category error, 109, 135, 136, 190
CERN. *See* Large Hadron Collider
Chambers, Ernie, 54
Chesterton, G.K., 205
Christianity, 5, 19, 21, 24, 26, 30,
    34, 36, 44, 52, 53, 57, 62, 63, 78,
    83, 84, 96, 99, 111, 118, 120, 138,
    142, 163, 164, 213, 216, 222, 225,
    226, 227, 228
Clapton, Eric, 4, 192
Clarke, Patrick, 91, 99, 123, 133,
    156, 167, 169, 170, 171, 174, 191,
    199
cognition, 195
coherence theory of truth, 189
Collins, Francis, 115, 117, 123, 138,
    150, 155, 159, 190, 208, 213, 214,
    220
Collins, Judy, 24
complexity, 69, 134, 136
*Conceiving God: the Cognitive Origin
    and Evolution of Religion*, 64
conscience, 28, 151, 169, 210
consciousness, 17, 31, 32, 35, 47, 84,
    95, 106, 114, 148, 149, 150, 152,
    168, 172, 173, 174, 182, 195
Consciousness Explained, 66, 148

consciousness-raising, 149
*Contribution to the critique of Hegel's
    Philosophy of Law*, 59
conversion, religious, 14, 171, 207,
    210, 211, 212
    definition of, 211
    results of, 211
Conway, Simon, 68
Copernicus, 87, 105
Corlett, John, 154
Cornwell, John, 27, 30, 32, 40, 68,
    69, 84, 99, 100, 106, 126, 127,
    142, 209
correspondence theory of truth, 189
Cosmological Argument, 125, 126
Cottingham, John, 160, 161, 190
counter conversion, religious, 215,
    216
Cox, Harvey, 50
Creation Science. *See* Intelligent
    Design
creation stories, 42
creationism, 139, 140, 141
    definition of, 139
creator God, 15, 37, 90, 136, 143,
    188
Crusades, 29, 82
cultural evolution, 69
Cupitt, Don, 44, 46, 62, 215
Dao, 168
Darwin, Charles, 2, 9, 62, 65, 76, 97,
    98, 99, 100, 131, 133, 134, 135,
    136, 139, 140, 142, 176, 187, 196,
    215
*Darwin's Angel: an angelic riposte to
    The God Delusion*, 84
Darwinian evolution. *See* evolution,
    theory of
Dawkins, Richard, 2, 5, 8, 9, 23, 26,
    30, 32, 35, 36, 37, 38, 39, 40, 41,
    46, 47, 48, 49, 50, 54, 63, 64, 65,
    66, 67, 68, 69, 70, 75, 76, 77, 78,

79, 80, 81, 82, 83, 84, 85, 91, 92, 93, 94, 95, 96, 99, 100, 102, 103, 107, 109, 110, 113, 114, 115, 116, 117, 121, 124, 125, 127, 128, 129, 130, 132, 134, 135, 136, 137, 138, 140, 141, 144, 146, 147, 149, 151, 152, 153, 154, 155, 156, 169, 175, 176, 177, 178, 181, 183, 187, 188, 190, 191, 196, 197, 199, 200, 202, 203, 204, 205, 206, 207, 208, 214, 216, 218, 222, 225

view of God, 39

de Botton, Alain, 46

Death of God, 55, 61, 80

Deep Thought, 221

deism, 18, 36, 37, 102, 146, 214
  definition, 36

Dennett, Daniel, 28, 33, 42, 44, 46, 47, 48, 63, 64, 65, 66, 77, 80, 115, 121, 135, 136, 148, 187, 204, 206, 215, 218

Denying God. *See* atheism

Descartes, Rene, 124

design by a designer. *See* intelligent design

design by natural causes, 133

deus emeritus, 37, 113

Diagnostic and Statistical Manual of Mental Disorders, 179

Dickens, Charles, 62

Dickinson, John, 222

Dirac, Paul, 131

divine fingerprints, 223

Divine Idea, 2, 71

Divine Knob-Twiddler, 93

divine revelation, 16, 37, 161, 166, 203

Dixon, Thomas, 89, 94, 98, 100, 101, 107, 108, 110, 111, 116, 117, 127, 131, 133, 138, 139, 146, 161, 184, 185, 224

doctrine, 28

Does God exist?. *See* the God Question

doubt, 74, 207, 208

doubting God. *See* agnosticism

Dover Area High School, 141

dragons, 113

dreams, 171, 173

Drummond, Henry, 111

D'Souza, Dinesh, 133

Dunne, Michael, 10, 109, 115, 129, 146

Durkheim, Emile, 28, 29, 32, 59

Dyson, Freeman, 94

Eagleton, Terry, 7, 35, 40, 69, 84, 85, 87, 105, 107, 186, 193, 203, 205, 206

eclipse of God, 209

Ecology and Environmental Management, 113

economism, 51

ecstasy, 43, 173, 177, 212

Edwards, Jonathan, 79

Einstein, Albert, 38, 39, 95, 101, 102, 108, 116, 131, 144, 196, 221

Eliade, Mircea, 173

Elliot, George, 62

Ellis, George, 104, 106, 148, 189

Elsdon, Ron, 23

emotions, 195

empiricism, 104

encounter with the divine, 170

Enlightenment, 15, 16, 19, 21, 23, 37, 55, 56, 72, 87, 102, 112, 143

ethics, 16, 22, 28, 48, 83, 104, 106, 115, 150

Ethics, 56

evidence and proof, 189

evil, 30, 31, 48, 49, 69, 150, 155, 160, 202, 212, 214, 228

evolution, theory of, 9, 23, 41, 49, 63, 65, 68, 69, 70, 75, 87, 88, 96, 98, 99, 100, 118, 133, 134, 135,

136, 137, 138, 139, 140, 141, 142, 146, 149, 187, 215, *See* natural selection
ex nihilo, 15, 90, 137
Existential Argument. *See* Argument from Religious Experience
experience of God, 31, 60, 167, 217
  direct, 32, 170
  indirect, 169
  natural or divine causes?, 179
  personal, 158, 159, 161, 168, 169, 176, 200, 214, 231
explanation, 186
extremism, 30, 79, 80, 82
fact, 116, 187, 201
  definition of, 184
faith
  and reason, 204
  as journey, 209
  blind. *See* blind faith
  in God, 197
  in science, 196
  language of, 45
  leap of. *See* leap of faith
  symbols of, 45
faith, religious
  definition of, 198
fallacy of the excluded middle, 75
Falsani, Cathleen, 6, 208
Falwell, Jerry, 83
Faraday, Michael, 116
Farewell to God; my reasons for rejecting the Christian faith, 216
Feuerbach, Ludwig Andreas von, 57, 59, 78
Feynman, Richard, 131
fides qua, 199
fides quae, 199
Fifth Way. *See* Argument from Design
finding faith. *See* conversion, religious

fine-tuning, 92, 93, 94, 131
First Cause, 99, 126
First Way. *See* Prime Mover
Five Ways, 123, 124, 125, 129
flagellum, 141
Flew, Anthony, 55, 93, 131, 214
fossil, 140
Fourth Way. *See* Argument from Degree
Fowler, James, 209
Frankl, Victor, 208
Freud, Sigmund, 58, 78, 179, 191, 218
Fry, Stephen, 79
fundamentalism, 29, 30, 79, 80, 82, 85, 164
Gagarin, Yuri, 185
Galilei, Galileo, 87, 89, 110, 116
Ganga, 43
Gauguin, Paul, 217
Geaney, David, 70, 179
Genesis, 96, 97, 139, 142
genetic evolution, 148
Gervais, Ricky, 79
god, 5
God
  a scientific question?, 109
  absent or present?, 7
  and evolution reconciled, 137
  arguments for, 120
  as a disembodied being, 6
  as a physical object, 6
  as a supernatural being, 5, 18
  as an entity, 217
  as invented, 18
  as knowable, 161
  as ultimate cause, 133
  belief in, 72
  bossy or loving?, 7
  death of. *See* Death of God
  definition, 5
  elusiveness, 71, 120, 160, 222

invention of, 56, 57, 63
male or female?, 7
Richard Dawkins' description, 39
root concepts, 226
the case against, 54
the coming of, 44
the idea of, 2, 10, 16, 26, 52, 73, 187
the Ultimate Boeing 747, 152
unknowable or knowable?, 7
views of, 6
God and the New Atheism: a critical response to Dawkins, 84
God debate, the, 1, 8, 32, 46, 48
God Delusion, The, 2, 8, 9, 10, 23, 26, 36, 39, 40, 49, 67, 78, 81, 82, 84, 85, 109, 116, 178, 180, 196, 200, 218
critiques of, 9
reasons for success, 9
God Helmet, 177
God Hypothesis, the, 40, 41, 152, 187, 200
God in the Dock, 53
God is not Great, 81
God of the Gaps, 68, 87, 111, 113, 138, 141, 142
God Question, the, 10, 24, 77, 183, 217, 230
God spot, 178
God's Funeral, 62
God-consciousness, 221
Godless: How an evangelical preacher became one of America's leading atheists, 216
God-shaped vacuum, 221
God-talk, 3
Goldilocks
Effect, 92
Zone, 93, 94, 131
Gould, Stephen Jay, 76, 114, 115, 226
Graham, Billy, 216
Grand Canyon, 140

Grand Theory of Everything, 95
Great Mystery, 6
Great Spirit, 6
Guide to the Debate about God, 54
Guide to the gods, 43
Gump, Forrest, 198
Habgood, John, 160
Hamilton, William, 60
Hamlet, 185
Hapi, 44
Hardy, Alister, 27, 138, 176
Hardy, Thomas, 62
Harris, Sam, 30, 31, 77, 80, 82, 84, 85, 121, 149, 168, 179, 197, 198, 201, 205
Haught, John, 19, 38, 40, 41, 48, 49, 64, 67, 83, 84, 85, 100, 109, 114, 141, 142, 146, 159, 187, 188, 196, 197, 200, 205, 225
Hawking, Stephen, 39, 95, 96, 102, 116, 132, 133
heaven, 8, 49, 115, 176, 227, 228
Hegel, Georg Wilhelm Friedrich, 56, 57, 121
Heidegger, Martin, 52, 55, 59, 60
Heisenberg, Werner, 108, 131
Heisenberg's uncertainty principle, 108
Henig, Robin, 180
Hick, John, 212
hierophanies, 173
Higgs Boson, 91, 95
High God, 42
Hill, Symon, 30, 45, 79
Hinde, Robert, 64
Hinduism, 34, 35
Hitchens, Christopher, 48, 56, 57, 63, 77, 80, 81, 82, 83, 84, 85, 86, 87, 90, 102, 107, 110, 112, 113, 141, 147, 161, 187, 204
Holocaust, 160, 208, 228
Honest to God, 61

Houghton, Sir John, 117
hound of heaven, 24
How Religion Poisons Everything, 81
Hoyle, Fred, 91, 152
Huitzilopochtli, 43
human genome, 112
Human Genome
  Project, 115
  Research Institute, 117, 213
human reason, 16, 19, 102, 206
humanism, 9, 16, 18, 87
Hume, David, 124, 130, 154
Humphreys in Search of God, 76
Humphreys, John, 7, 9, 12, 71, 72,
  76, 81, 85, 195, 200, 206, 220
Huxley, Thomas, 9, 75, 99
hypothesis testing, 103
IC. *See* irreducible complexity
ID. *See* Intelligent Design
I-It, 170
illusion of objectivity in science, 186
immanence, 229
In God We Doubt, 76
In Gods We Trust, 64
Inari, 43
Incarnation, 162, 222
ineffability, 31
infinite regress, 132, 135, 136, 138,
  151
  definition of, 132
Inquisition, 89
intelligent design, 130, 133, 134,
  136, 141
Intelligent Design, 40, 110, 140,
  141, 142
  Movement, 140
intentional stance, 44, 64, 218
International Space Station, 185
irreducible complexity, 134, 141
Is God dead?, 60, *See* Death of God
Islam, 5, 26, 34, 36, 44, 82, 83, 84,
  96, 120, 138, 139, 163

I-Thou, 27, 48, 170
James, William, 31, 32, 47, 159, 164,
  167, 169, 171, 173, 174, 176, 198,
  203, 207, 209, 211, 215, 221, 222
Jehovah, 5
Jenkins, David, 8, 54, 120, 121, 122,
  162, 205, 221, 223
Jesus, 8, 36, 44, 122, 147, 162, 164,
  169, 203, 212, 214, 222, 228
jihad, 29
Jones, Howard, 29, 69, 84, 99, 160
Jones, Kathleen, 2, 45, 91, 114, 150,
  207, 218
Judaism, 5, 36, 44, 56, 83, 84, 96,
  120, 138, 163
Jung, Carl Gustav, 58, 153, 154
Kant, Immanuel, 124, 150, 154
Keats, John, 78
Keller, Timothy, 208, 223
Kelvin, Lord, 116
Kepler, Johannes, 116
Keynes, Randal, 215
Kierkegaard, Søren, 24, 60, 201
King, Larry, 76
Klostermaier, Klaus, 114, 183
knowledge, 162, 185, 194
  criteria for, 193
  definition of, 184
  measurable, 186
  natural, 184
  ownership and reliability, 185
  revealed, 184
  sources of, 184
Koran, 29
Kuhn, Thomas, 105
Laplace, Pierre-Simon, 89
Large Hadron Collider, 92
Lash, Nicholas, 40, 109, 147, 186
laws of nature, 127, 131, 132, 145,
  214
leap of faith, 201
Ledwig, Marion, 136, 137, 190

legend, 42
Leibniz, G.W., 112
Lennox, Annie, 6
Lewis, C.S., 7, 12, 53, 185, 203, 212, 213, 220
Lewis-Williams, David, 64
liberalism, 21
life
  absurdity of, 60
  origin and nature, 96
life-force, 6, 43, 56
life-form, 91, 99, 136
Lightfoot, Dr John, 90
Limits of Science, 118
literalism, 29, 139, 140, 146, 209
Living with Questions, 8
logical positivism, 104
Lord of the Rings, 45
losing faith, 215
Lundstrom, Peter, 34, 35, 77
Luther, Martin, 90, 206
Lyell, Charles, 62
magisteria, 115
Maitland, Sara, 222
Maradona, Diego, 3
Martin, Thomas, 81
Marx, Karl, 59, 78, 218
Marxism, 21
materialism, 16, 17, 18, 86
  discontents, 17
Mawson, Tim, 27, 37, 38, 222
Maxwell, James Clerk, 116
McBain, James, 10
McGrath, Alister, 9, 16, 20, 21, 44, 49, 54, 56, 57, 61, 62, 63, 64, 65, 67, 68, 69, 70, 77, 78, 84, 88, 95, 106, 110, 113, 115, 117, 118, 129, 142, 175, 177, 181, 188, 207, 212, 220, 221, 222
Medawar, Peter, 106, 118
Medd, James, 79
meme, 65, 66, 67, 68, 69, 70, 81, 149

critique of, 67
religion, 68
memetic evolution, 149
memory, 184
Mere Christianity, 213
metanarrative, 21
metaphysics, 104, 106, 191
Michelangelo, 6
Middleton, Richard, 23, 51, 183, 190
Mind of God, 15, 39, 95, 101, 131
  knowing the, 101, 102, 188, 201
  the nature of, 103
miracles, 37, 38, 63, 78, 113, 115, 142, 145, 146, 155, 159, 160, 169
Mitchell, Basil, 156
Modern Period, 16
modernity, 16, 31, 51
Modernity. *See* Modern Period
Mohammed, 44
monarchical model of God, 227, 229, *See* supernatural theism
monotheism, 36, 44
  definition, 36
Montefiore, Hugh, 151, 181, 207
Moral Imperative, 150
morality, 17, 19, 22, 35, 45, 48, 49, 63, 83, 150, 162, 220
  atheist basis, 49
  source of, 48
Mourinho, José, 4
Mozart, 144
multiple universe. *See* multiverse
multiverse, 94, 96
  hypothesis, 94
mystery, 10, 24, 33, 41, 47, 74, 88, 102, 112, 126, 131, 142, 144, 148, 165, 168, 171, 197, 207, 221, 225, 229
mystical experiences, 172
  features of, 174
mystical state, 32

mysticism, 31, 32, 35, 169, 172, 173
myth, 23, 28, 42, 45, 62, 87
    as a stepping stone towards
        religion, 45
    definition of, 45
    importance of, 45
narrative, 104
native dualism, 206
native teleology, 206
natural laws, 17, 38, 145, 224
natural replicator, 66
natural selection, 65, 66, 67, 69, 93,
    98, 100, 134, 135, 137, 138, 149,
    176, 187, 215
natural theology, 122, 163
Natural Theology, 130
naturalism
    scientific, 19
near-death experiences, 171, 173
Necessary Being, 127
necessary existence, 123, 127
Neolithic period, 43
Neptune, 43
neurotheology, 177, 178
New Age, 6
    movement, 35
    spirituality, 6
New Atheism, 8, 9, 31, 73, 80, 81,
    82, 83, 84, 87, 196, 204
    core beliefs, 82
    critiques, 84
    definition of, 80
New Atheist, 19, 26, 28, 29, 30, 34,
    38, 46, 48, 53, 54, 55, 63, 65, 77,
    79, 82, 83, 84, 85, 110, 113, 141,
    147, 161, 168, 181, 186, 187, 197,
    198, 200, 204, 205, 207
New Design Argument, 136
New Guide to the Debate about God,
    54
New Testament, 40, 147, 212
Newberg, Andrew, 47, 69, 168, 173,

174, 177, 178, 182, 194, 195, 202,
    208, 211
Newman, Cardinal John Henry, 132
Newton, Isaac, 87, 90, 111, 112,
    116, 131
Nietzsche, Friedrich Wilhelm, 57,
    70, 84
Night, 208
Nirvana, 168
Noah's flood, 139, 140
Nobel Prize, 5, 131, 208
NOMA. *See* Non-Overlapping
    Magisteria
Non-Overlapping Magisteria, 115,
    226
Nothing, 59
number 42, 221
numinous, 48, 144, 169, 171, 173
    definition, 24
Obama, Barack, 3
Ockham's Razor, 186
Odin, 43
Ogden, Caroline, 16, 50, 59, 123
Old Testament, 26, 36, 39, 40, 102,
    162, 164
*On the Origin of Species by Means
    of Natural Selection or, The
    Preservation of Favoured Races in
    the Struggle for Life. See The Origin
    of Species*
One Mind, 173
One of Us, 7
Onfray, Michael, 79
Ontological Argument, 122, 123,
    124, 125, 127
Osborne, Joan, 7
Othello, 219
Otto, Rudolf, 24, 48, 169, 173
pagan religions, 35
Page, Don, 96
Paley, William, 98, 130
Paley's watch, 130

Paltrow, Gwyneth, 192
panentheism, 226, 228, 229, 230
pantheism, 228
  definition, 34
PAP. *See* Permanent Agnosticism in
  Principle
paradigm, 105, 139, 190
  definition of, 105
  shift, 105
partially-overlapping magisteria, 115
Pascal, Blaise, 74, 155
Pascal's wager, 155, 156
Pearce, Joseph, 203, 213
Pele, 44
Pentecostalism, 164
perception, 195
Perfection. *See* Argument from
  Degree
performance model. *See* monarchical
  model of God
Permanent Agnosticism in
  Principle, 76
Persinger, Michael, 177, 178
personal religious experience, 159,
  168, 175
Pessin, Andrew, 10, 15, 124, 125,
  150, 156, 170, 192, 201
phenotypic plasticity, 148
physicalism. *See* materialism
physics
  Einsteinian, 105
  Newtonian, 105, 108
Pierre, Joseph, 179
Pinocchio, 219
Pirsig, Robert, 46
Pitt, Brad, 76
Planck, Max, 131
Plato, 15, 143
Polkinghorne, John, 9, 111, 113,
  117, 118, 191, 202, 218, 219, 224
polytheism, 35, 43
  definition, 35

POMA. *See* partially-overlapping
  magisteria
Poole, Michael, 106
Poole, Robert, 75, 84, 92, 93, 112,
  125, 135, 140, 142, 157, 189, 194,
  201, 202
postmodern, 14, 20, 21, 22, 104, 226
postmodernism, 19
Potter, Harry, 9
Prance, Sir Ghillean, 117
prayer, 27, 30, 39, 157, 160, 165,
  168, 215, 228
Prime Mover, 125, 126, 132
primitive cultures, 14
primitive religions
  characteristics of, 42
Principles of Geology, 62
probability, 76, 94, 152, 153, 154,
  155, 156
profane, 28, 32
progressive adaptation. *See*
  evolution, theory of
projection, 59
projection theory of religion, 42,
  218
Prozesky, Martin, 54, 156
psychedelic drugs, 35
psychic phenomena, 35
Ptolemy, 89, 105
quantum
  entity, 108
  mechanics, 95
  physics, 131
  theory, 108
radical theology, 60
Ramsden, Leigh, 53
rational thinking, 18
rationality, 18, 19, 72, 78, 186, 196,
  204, 205
Ravetz, Jerry, 105, 107, 186
Real Scientists, Real Faith, 117
realist, 108, 189

reality
  definition of, 182
  explanation of, 20
  layers of, 13
  levels of, 121
  material, 13, 31, 77, 114, 174, 183,
    204
  nature of, 182
  personal interpretation, 20
  spiritual, 13, 14, 15, 18, 31, 173
reason, 122
*Reason, Faith, and Revolution:
  reflections on the God Debate*,
  84
re-envisioning God, 225
Rees, Martin, 93, 94, 126, 142
reformed epistemology, 163
Reisz, Matthew, 110
religion
  and health, 50
  and well-being, 50
  as a by-product of human
    evolution, 9
  as an accidental byproduct, 66
  common ingredients, 28
  definition, 27
  dimensions, 28
  functions and benefits, 46
  nature of, 28
  organised, 51
  origins and development, 41
  varieties of, 28
  views of God, 34
Religion Explained, 64
Religion for Atheists, 46
religions
  number of, 33
religious believers
  number of, 33
religious experience, 64, 144, 157,
  166, 167, 168, 176, 177
  characteristics, 167

  definition of, 167
  scientific study of, 175, 176
religious instinct, 2, 12, 64
religious observance, 51
revelation, 37, 38, 122, 144, 146,
  147, 149, 159, 161, 162, 163, 164,
  165, 166, 168, 171, 183, 184, 199,
  203, 231
ritual, 28, 32
River out of Eden, 141
Robertson, David, 40, 49, 68, 84,
  129, 137, 167
Robertson, Pat, 83
Robinson, John, 61, 62
Romantic Movement, 78, 143
root concepts for thinking about
  God, 226
Ruse, Michael, 84
Ruskin, John, 62
Russell, Bertrand, 55, 76, 126
Sacks, Lord, 116, 188
sacred, 28, 32, 45, 229
sacred mystery
  experience of, 24
sacred texts, 44, 133, 139, 140, 146,
  147, 162, 163, 197
Sartre, Jean-Paul, 55, 60, 84
satisficing behaviour, 188
scepticism. *See* agnosticism
Schleiermacher, Friedrich, 47, 169,
  206
Schopenhauer, Arthur, 56
Schrödinger, Erwin, 131
Schroeder, Gerald, 110
science, 68, 113
  and rationality, 72, 86
  history of, 89, 107, 188
  limitations, 105
  nature of, 103
  the challenge to God, 86
science and religion, 6, 86, 88, 89,
  114, 116

competition and conflict, 100
conciliation, 110
conflict, 110
reconciliation, 113
views of reality, 183
science of the gaps. *See* meme
scientific method, 103, 109
scientism, 51, 104, 187, 197
Scopes trial, 140, 141
Scopes, John, 140
scripture
    authority of, 147
search for meaning, 46
Second Way. *See* First Cause
secular, 32, 50
secular culture, 31, 46
secular ideology, 16
secularisation, 18, 34, 50, 51, 52, 53, 73, 80
secularism, 9, 50, 51, 55, 70, 87
    definition, 50
selfish gene, 150
sense of absolute dependence, 48
sense of mystery, 47
sense of the divine, 169, 170
Shakespeare, William, 185, 219
shaman, 42
Shelley, Percy Bysshe, 78
Shermer, Michael, 36, 45, 48, 61, 68, 70, 116, 120, 126, 129, 173
Shiva, 36
Sire, James, 21, 101, 104, 162, 182, 185
skyhook, 187
Smart, Ninian, 28, 41, 42, 167
Smith, George, 72, 74, 75, 77, 193
social consensus, 195
Songs of Praise, 52
soul, 19, 42, 43, 57, 78, 100, 114, 200, 208, 215
Spanish Inquisition, 82

Spinoza, Baruch, 56
Spirit, 56, 144, 164, 168, 177, 226, 229, 230
Spirit model of God. *See* panentheism
spiritual journey, 211
spirituality
    definition, 27
    personal, 22
spirituality and religion, 26
    differences, 27
spontaneous creation, 133
Starbuck, Professor, 211
Steady State theory, 91
supernatural, 16, 35, 169, 183, 226, 230
supernatural theism, 226
Supernature, 23
Supreme Being, 6
Surprised by Joy, 213
Swinburne, Richard, 122, 123, 143, 145, 149, 150, 151, 158, 167, 169, 187, 188
Taliban, 85
TAP. *See* Temporary Agnosticism in Practice
technicism, 51
Teleological Argument, 125, 128
Templeton, Charles, 216
Temporary Agnosticism in Practice, 76
testimony, 184
The 'New' Atheism: ten arguments that don't hold water?, 84
The Blind Watchmaker, 130
The Case for God, 41, 54
The Dawkins delusion: atheist fundamentalism and the denial of the divine, 54, 84
The Dawkins letters: challenging atheist myths, 84
The Descent of Man, 2, 98

The Elementary Forms of the Religious Life, 59
The End of Faith: Religion, terror and the future of reason, 80
The Essence of Christianity, 57
The Evolution of God., 41
The Future of an Illusion, 58
The Gay Science, 57
The Grand Design, 95, 96, 102, 133
The History of God, 41
The Hitchhiker's Guide to the Galaxy, 199, 221
The Idea of the Holy, 169
The Meme Machine, 66
The Origin of Species, 62, 97, 99
The Phenomenology of Mind, 56
The Principles of Natural Philosophy, 111
The Religious Experience of Mankind, 41
The Science of God. An introduction to scientific theology, 110
The Science of God. The convergence of scientific and biblical wisdom, 110
The Selfish Gene, 66, 176, 200
The Spiritual Nature of Man, 176
The Story of God, 41
The Structure of Scientific Revolutions, 105
The Transforming Vision, 23
The Twilight of Atheism, 54
The Varieties of Religious Experience, 31, 166, 176
The World as Will and Idea, 56
theism, 36, 37, 38, 75, 77, 102, 146, 153, 154, 191, 196, 226, 230
definition, 37
supernatural, 226
theological literacy, 85
theology, 28, 37, 40, 60, 61, 62, 65, 85, 99, 109, 114, 141, 146, 159, 197, 198, 205, 228
theophanies, 173

theory testing, 103
There is a God: how the world's most notorious atheist changed his mind, 55
There is a God: how the world's most notorious atheist changed his mind, 214
Third Way. *See* Argument from Contingency
Thomson, William. *See* Lord Kelvin
Thought for the Day, 52
Thunder Bird, 43
Thus Spake Zarathustra, 57
Tillich, Paul, 45, 61, 170, 203, 208
Time magazine, 60
Tippett, Krista, 30, 47, 74, 75, 86, 101, 114, 144, 147, 165, 180, 209, 225
Tolkien, J.R.R., 45, 203, 213
Tolstoy, Leo, 212
totemism, 42
transcendence, 229
trust and commitment, 202
truth
absolute, 20
and viewpoint, 191
criterion, 186
definition of, 188
personal interpretation, 20
truth claims
competing, 100
evaluation of, 188
TV evangelists, 84
Twain, Mark, 76
Ultimate Boeing 747 Gambit, 134, 151, 152
ultimate meaning and purpose, 4
Uncaused Cause Argument. *See* First Cause
unitary state, 173
universe, 35, 48, 96, 102, 105, 132, 139, 140, 221

age of, 90, 139
  nature and age, 89
  origins, 88, 90
Unmoved Mover, 15
  Argument. *See* Prime Mover
Unwin, Stephen, 154
Ussher, James, 90
Vardy, Peter, 123, 128, 143, 145,
  163, 189, 191
Varghese, Roy, 80, 81, 83, 104
veiled presence of God, 224
virus of the mind, 66, 68, 69, *See*
  meme
Vishnu/Krishna, 36
visions, 43, 165, 168, 170, 171, 173,
  177
Voltaire, 56
Walsh, Brian, 23, 51, 183, 190
Ward, Keith, 15, 17, 40, 41, 46, 60,
  84, 85, 94, 101, 103, 112, 123,
  124, 125, 126, 127, 128, 129, 132,
  136, 143, 147, 148, 149, 150, 152,
  164, 165, 166, 167, 171, 172, 185,
  220
Watson, David, 48, 120, 223
Watson, Lyall, 23
ways of knowing, 16
ways of seeing, 12
Weber, Max, 44
Weinberg, Steven, 5, 95
Welsh, James, 80
What I Believe, 212
Why Gods Persist, 64
*Why there almost certainly is a God:
  doubting Dawkins*, 84
Why would Anyone Believe in God?,
  64
Wiesel, Elie, 208, 223
Wilberforce, Samuel, 99
will to believe, 207
Williams, Jeff, 185
Williams, Rowan, 231

Wilson, A.N., 9, 62
Wilson, Brian, 3
Wilson, E.O., 2, 217
Winston, Robert, 2, 41, 71, 73, 88,
  90, 140, 185
Wired, 80
Wittgenstein, Ludwig, 126
Wordsworth, William, 78, 144
World Christian Encyclopedia, 33
world-view, 23, 41, 72, 115, 182
  definition, 13
  dominant, 14, 105, 225
  modern, 15
  postmodern, 19
  pre-modern, 14
Wright, Robert, 1, 41
Yahweh, 5, 36
Young Earth Creationism. *See*
  Intelligent Design
*Zen and the Art of Motorcycle
  Maintenance*, 46